PRACTICAL PRICING FOR RESULTS

IAN RUSKIN-BROWN

Viva Books

New Delhi | Mumbai | Chennai | Kolkata | Bengaluru | Hyderabad | Kochi | Guwahati

First Indian Edition 2012

VIVA BOOKS PRIVATE LIMITED

- 4737/23 Ansari Road, Daryaganj, New Delhi 110 002
  E-mail: vivadelhi@vivagroupindia.net, Tel. 42242200
- 76, Service Industries, Shirvane, Sector 1, Nerul, Navi Mumbai 400 706
  E-mail: vivamumbai@vivagroupindia.net, Tel. 27721273, 27721274
- Jamals Fazal Chambers, 26 Greams Road, Chennai 600 006
  E-mail: vivachennai@vivagroupindia.net, Tel. 28290304, 28294241
- B-103, Jindal Towers, 21/1A/3 Darga Road, Kolkata 700 017
  E-mail: vivakolkata@vivagroupindia.net, Tel. 22836381, 22816713
- 7, Sovereign Park Apartments, 56-58, K. R. Road, Basavanagudi, Bengaluru 560 004
  E-mail: vivabangalore@vivagroupindia.net, Tel. 26607409, 26607410
- 101-102 Mughal Marc Apartments, 3-4-637 to 641, Narayanguda, Hyderabad 500 029
  E-mail: vivahyderabad@vivagroupindia.net, Tel. 27564481, 27564482
- Beevi Towers, First Floor, SRM Road, Kaloor, Kochi 682 018, Kerala
  E-mail: vivakochi@vivagroupindia.net, Tel: 0484-2403055, 2403056
- 232, GNB Road, Beside UCO Bank, Silpukhuri, Guwahati 781 003
  E-mail: vivaguwahati@vivagroupindia.net, Tel: 0361-2666386

www.vivagroupindia.com

Published by arrangement with
Thorogood Publishers Limited
10-12 Rivington Street
London EC2A 3DU,
UK

ISBN: 978-81-309-0854-0

Published by Vinod Vasishtha for Viva Books Private Limited, 4737/23, Ansari Road, Daryaganj, New Delhi-110 002. Printed and bound by Raj Press, R-3, Inderpuri, New Delhi - 110 012.

THE AUTHOR

Ian Ruskin Brown is both an academic, a practising and incurable businessman, consultant and trainer.

Over the last 36 years Ian has gained a wide range and depth of experience in marketing and in management.

He is a full member of the Chartered Institute of Marketing, the Business Graduates Association of MBA's, a fellow of the Institute of Sales and Marketing Management, a full member and Diplomate of the Market Research Society, and is a member of the British Institute of Management. He saw active service as an officer and sometime helicopter pilot in HM Royal Marines Commandos, before becoming a practising, if slightly unconvinced civilian in late 1966.

Ian's business career has a strong bias towards marketing management in the operational field and planning functions – working for such firms as: Lyons & Co., Reed Paper Group, Trebor Sharpes, Esso Petroleum and Goodyear Tyre & Rubber, to name but a few.

Following a major motor accident in 1973, his career has oriented toward the academic and consultancy, working as a Senior Lecturer at the SWRMC (*now the University of the South West*) and with visiting lectureships at the universities of Bath, Bristol, Oran (Algeria) and the NIHE Limerick (Eire). Ian was a long time member (13 years) of the Faculty of the Chartered Institute of Marketing's (CIM), training arm.

For several years Ian was the initial speaker on the FCO Management Training Programme for those who are due to take posts as UK Commercial Attachés in UK embassies overseas.

Until recently he was a member of the IBM International Business School, faculties of ST micro-electronics based in Aix-en-Provence. Currently he is a member of Faculties of Management Centre Europe (MCE) in Brussels, Singapore Institute of Management (International) and PKMH of Malaysia. He recently worked worldwide for Nokia Networks, and is currently working for Texas Instruments, Securitas, Amadeus, Alfa Laval and ChevronTexaco

Oil. For these and several other bodies, Ian runs open and 'client specific' courses.

Before taking up founding directorships in several very successful companies, MSS Market Research Ltd and Mercator Ltd (MR Software), Ian worked as an independent, freelance consultant, being involved in consumer, industrial, Government policy and tourism projects, often acting in the dual capacity of consultant/project leader.

In early 1983, Ian set up his own independent marketing consultancy, now operating as *Ruskin Brown Associates*, for training in marketing and sales skills, and for the provision of both consultancy and market research services.

These activities continually bring him into contact with a wide range of marketing situations at home and abroad. All of which experience has gone into his two previous books entitled *Mastering Marketing*, 2nd edition and *Marketing your Service Business* both published by Thorogood Publishing.

What qualifies the author?

The 13 years that Ian ran his marketing research business, and the concurrent training he conducted at the Chartered Institute of Marketing brought him into contact with a large number and a wide range of sales and marketing personnel and SME managers throughout the developed world. This experience, particularly when presenting research or financial data, revealed that far too many non-accountant decision makers in business were, by and large, lacking 'pricing savvy'.

As a result of this insight he:

- Teamed up with such people as Roy Hill MBE, Richard Collier, et al.
- Read widely the works of such luminaries as Thomas Nagle, Reed Holden, John Harris, John Winkler et al. (See Recommended reading list, Appendix 3.)
- Designed, launched and successfully ran the training course 'Marketing Pricing' at the CIM from 1992 to 1998, and from 1997 to 2001 via Frost & Sullivan.

- Designed and now runs a similar course at Management Centre Europe (*the Brussels arm of the American Marketing Association*).
- Currently Ian is a member of the Mid-East Faculty of International Industrial Research (IIRme.) which is the largest conference provider in the world. Via them he trains throughout the Mid-East. Specializing in pricing, the marketing businesses in the service sector, marketing research, and professional interpersonal skills.

Privately and via the above, over the subsequent years Ian has also delivered pricing training with such firms as Caltex (now ChevronTexaco), EuroRail, CMC of Dubai, PKMH of Kuala Lumpur, Philips International and Singapore Institute of Management International (SIMI). He has run successful pricing training and consultancy projects in the USA, throughout Europe, South Africa, Malaysia, China and the Mid-East.

PROLOGUE

The recorded history of the world is the history of Trade, and the history of Trade is the history of Price!

It is said that the earliest occurrence of writing as we know it today[i], was the Cuneiform Script that originated in Mesopotamia (mainly modern Iraq). This was done on clay tablets of which many exist to this day, and it seems that these piles of clay tablets are not recording the passage or enforcement of laws, or the immortalization of folk tales, songs nor romantic poetry, they are but instruments of commercial business, books of accounts, records of purchases and sales, invoices and the like[ii]. Price features largely in all these records. The main if not their only method of setting price in ancient Mesopotamia was 'cost plus' of which we will have more to say in Chapters 3 and 4.

The conduct of trade (mercantilism) was a major engine for the 'cradle of western civilization' the Mid-East and the Mediterranean. The mainstays were the staples of wine, sandalwood, grain, olive oil etc. from producer to consumer countries. In almost every case the principle was to acquire the produce where it was in plentiful supply and moving it to where it was in short supply and thus commanded a higher price. Specifically in the Eastern Mediterranean there was also some nascent marketing, such as the production and trade in more high value products such as paper from Biblos[iii] and the 'royal purple' dye[iv] from Crete that gave the ancient nobility their distinctive robes. Both of these 'products' had the advantage of low volume and high market value.

Countries and peoples have gone to war to protect their trade or take it from others. A major ulterior motive of the Crusades is said to be the control of the end of the 'silk road' which was bringing not only silk to the Mid-East and Europe but also spices, dyes, gunpowder technology and China pottery (*nearly all of which was also comparatively low volume but high value*).

These quasi monopoly/oligopoly sources of supply commanded such high prices for their goods that there was a strong motivation for their customer markets to find alternative routes to the producers. The Arabs / Ceylonese and their innovation of the 'Lateen Sail' were the first to break the monopoly of the silk road, AND in addition they brought to the west the spices from what we now call Indonesia. In their turn the Portuguese and the Spanish tried, each in their own way, to bypass the Moors to get to the 'Indies' direct.

Eventually the Dutch and the British got there and promptly fought a 40 year-long war trying to gain control of the Moluccas, the then only known source of nutmeg, which, at the time commanded a price in Europe of circa seven times its own weight in gold.

It was around this time that the Dutch became, if not the largest, then perhaps the smartest international trading nation in Europe. If any people should know about the law of supply and demand they should. And yet even some of the most experienced and wise of them got it wrong from time to time – once catastrophically.

During the 16th century, when Spain was fighting to keep the Low Countries inside the Spanish empire, the grand old Duke of Palma laid siege to Antwerp, not because he wanted to but because Philip told him to. Up to that time the Duke had never lost a battle in his long and venerable career as a soldier but he could not see how he could successfully lay siege to a city nearly completely surrounded by water.

He need not have worried, the City Fathers of Antwerp gave him an almost bloodless victory, not because they wanted to, but because they had forgotten some of the basics of trade upon which their very city was built.

As the city was being invested, the City Fathers were concerned that none should profit from the siege and that the rich would not exploit the poor so they set limits on the price of food.

Result: because the food producers in the adjacent countryside, and the merchants in the local towns saw no profit in taking the risk of being caught and punished by the Duke's besieging men, and that they could sell their produce elsewhere, they stopped supplying Antwerp at all.

The good citizens of the city saw no reason to conserve consumption when the produce was at the normal price, so, 100 days after the siege started the food stocks in Antwerp ran out and the city was forced to surrender within the following week[v].

Ironic really, that a city that had grown rich through the efforts of men to whom the law of supply and demand was second nature either forgot such basics or believed that they could buck the market: No one bucks the market – like a ship on a tide race you either go with it, or you get swamped by it.

It was ever so, even to this day. Those who can, next time they visit London, should go and visit Greenwich and see the 'Cutty Sark' a tea clipper that was the fastest commercial sailing ship of her day. It took only around 100 days for her to sail from the tea merchants of China to the London markets, where, because she was first into port, her owners were able to command the highest price for her cargo of tea.

At the time of writing, reflect how the growth of industry in mainland China is sucking in oil like there is no tomorrow – consider the price of oil as a consequence and how this will impact the world's economy. Fascinating!

Everything we do in business comes down to price. Commerce is basically about buying, adding some value and then selling. The difference between the prices we pay to our suppliers[vi] and the price we are able to get from our customers determines whether we thrive, just survive or die – it is as simple as that. And yet the discipline of pricing is a much-neglected area of study both in business at large and in Business Schools in particular. Those who do profess to teach it tend to surround the subject with 'mumbo jumbo'. Senior managers tend to keep all strategic pricing decisions to themselves as well as the control of the firm's day-to-day operation of its pricing policy (*if they have any such*).

Managers often have little understanding of the dynamics of price, and consequently approach Pricing in the most simplistic way (*see Chapter 3*). They often know little of how to manage Price in their firm themselves, and (*often quite rightly*) are frightened of the damage that their sales force can do to the firm's profitability via promiscuous discounting.

This is one of the best bad news/good news stories, you, dear reader, may ever come across. Those who do understand the dynamics of pricing and how to make and manage the best prices for their products in their markets will only have to do it conscientiously to succeed, they will have little real competition.

This book addresses the need to know how to buy well, and to sell well pricewise and thus make the best return on the investments that you have made in the operations and marketing of your business.

Because the small to medium enterprise (SME) is close to the author's heart – he having run one for some 15 years, this book is especially dedicated to managers of these smaller firms. With the tools you will find herein, and the lower intensity of politics in the SME compared with the large global firms of today, you will be the one best able to adopt these lessons and flourish. The super tankers like large conglomerates are another and very different game where few people have any chance to take the initiative – but if this applies to you, still read the book, it will come in useful when you start your own business sometime in the future.

References

i As opposed to the ideograms of the Egyptian Hieroglyphs or Chinese characters.

ii *'The Science of Secrecy'* by Simon Sing – and the *'Alphabet'* by David Sacks.

iii From whence we get so many words related to books and writing.

iv Dibromoindigo, or Tyrian Purple, an industry promoted by the Phoenicians in Crete, where the locals produced this dye from the local but rare sea molluscs, which was then traded by the Phoenicians throughout the then known world.

v As quoted by John Winkler (*Pricing for Results*) from *'The Unseen World and Other Essays'* by John Fisk.

vi Not just supplies of raw materials, but rent, wages, power, transport et al.

CONTENTS

INTRODUCTION

In 1978 the author started his own business in Bristol, England, a marketing research and consultancy firm 'MSS Marketing Research Ltd' – initially in partnership with others, then later in 1983 he branched-out on his own with 'Marketing Decisions International Ltd' also in Bristol, which in various forms has survived until the time of writing.

In relation to this book, two things came from those ventures:

Firstly there was the experience of having to price his own business. Located in Bristol, Ian's firm had to compete against London based firms with their higher costs. The temptation was to price so as to be substantially cheaper than the competition. However, therein lay the trap. To one type of client the fact that the business was not located in London tended to indicate that it was of a lower standard to those that were, and a lower price was often seen to confirm that prejudice. Whereas to other clients the firm's location and thus perceived lower cost base, translated into potentially lower prices, which to these clients was a major expectation and attractant. Thus Ian had to learn the skill of dual or multiple pricing early on.

Secondly much of the marketing research that his firm conducted was directly or indirectly about the client's customers and their sensitivity to pricing. Additionally there was often the need to communicate to the client the levels of statistical reliability, confidence intervals etc. of the data obtained by the research. The frustrating thing was that so few of the client's personnel, especially in the marketing and sales departments, could completely understand much of this. If they had covered any of this in college, it had been forgotten – outside managing their departmental budgets etc, they had become, to all intents and purposes, innumerate.

An awful lot of people in management will steer away from pricing decisions and financial management accounts out of a fear that they will not be able to handle the calculations involved.

Too many entrepreneurs, salespeople or their managers cannot argue their corner with their accountants, they:

- don't know how to calculate the volumes required to make a discount worthwhile,
- fail to understand the strategies or tactics of pricing,
- would not know where to start to set a price for their goods and/or services in one market compared with another.

Too many people at the heart of business would not be able to assess the probability of a price war, and the direction from which it may come. Thus they are unable to prevent them, and when a price war breaks out they don't have a clue how to defend themselves.

And be assured that with the economic rise of Asia and Mainland China the rest of the world must expect aggressive price competition, even price wars, as a real probability.

This book addresses the above and more.

The book lays out, in a logical and sequential way, the process of deriving a pricing strategy for the firm's goods and/or services, whilst monitoring the profit implications of any pricing decisions made.

It outlines:

- The basic financial tools such as the P&L account – overhead attribution etc.,
- How best to understand the buyer in B2C and B2B markets,
- The tactical skills and processes needed to implement and defend these strategies,
- The basics of price negotiation.

Style

The first chapter of this book outlines the whole process of setting, implementing and defending your price.

The following chapters examine each of these steps in detail.

The book uses current real-life, yet timeless examples throughout. They illustrate and exemplify the concepts discussed – in practice.

Exercises abound throughout this book. At minimum each chapter concludes with an exercise to enable the reader to apply that chapter's contents to their own business.

Each exercise will be worked through, with the answers, and maybe a short discussion in the appendix.

Appendices

The appendices include the following:

- Answers to each exercise together with an explanation and, where required, a short discussion;
- A list, plus explanations, of the most significant formulae involved in the calculation parts of the pricing decision;
- A reading list for those who wish to take their study further.

To keep up to date with this discipline please refer to the Author's website: **www.ruskin-brownassociates.com**

ONE

AN OVERVIEW OF THE PRICING PROCESS

AN OVERVIEW OF THE PRICING PROCESS

"Even a journey of a thousand miles begins with but one step, and the best 'first step' is to get a map of where you intend to go!"

Anon

Synopsis

This chapter provides both those directions and that map.

In giving the reader a concise outline of the pricing process, it puts into perspective the sequence and order in which successful pricing is conducted by the masters of the 'discipline'.[i]

The chapter takes this process step-by-step and concludes with a 'flow diagram' to put this process into a visual perspective.

If you are an accountant, or similar by training, you could well skip this chapter, though you may well find some interesting fresh perspectives herein.

Preparing the ground

As in much of life 'attitude is everything!' It's all in the mind. If you think things can be done, chances are you will accomplish them. If however, we believe there are insurmountable obstacles in our way, as hard as we may think we try, we will never excel.

So it is important to approach pricing with a positive attitude. Whatever the size of our business – whatever our market shares, to succeed we must take the initiative. Lets look at the first initiative that should be taken.

Who takes the overall responsibility for price in our firm?

Get the command structure firmly and authoritatively established. Who is in charge of deciding the firm's policies and strategies with respect to price? Where does the buck stop? *Who has the ultimate responsibility/accountability and authority?*

The answer to this must be quite clear to all involved in setting and implementing the firm's pricing policy and practise.

Because price has a major influence on the health of the organization's income, pricing policy is critical to the survival and success of any business. So much so that, in the author's view, the overall responsibility should reside with someone close to and reporting to the CEO, if not the CEO themselves (*some people term this position the 'Pricing Tsar'*).

This 'Tsar' person should be the head of a group of advisors selected on the basis of their profit responsibility to the firm. Such people in a large organization will be found in the positions of Senior Brand Managers (*strategic and operational pricing*), Marketing Managers (*price positioning in the firm's markets*), Sales Managers (*tactical pricing and price negotiations*), the CFO or at least someone close to him or her (*the overall financial structure of the firm*).

In the smaller firm, i.e. the so-called SME[1], several of these roles could well be wrapped-up in one person. Whatever, the 'Pricing Tsar' and their team set as policy they will thus establish the guidelines within which the rest of the team will have to work.

The job of the 'Tsar' is to oversee and ensure the following process, re. pricing within the firm, and its proper execution by those in the front line:

Magnitude of Responsibility	Event Sequence	Actions/Events to optimally implement Pricing Strategies
5	1	Get top management's full commitment in advance!
4	2	Set up monitoring mechanisms
3	3	Identify and allocate resources
2	4	Assign specific, individual responsibilities – and with each –
1	5	Identify specific action steps and timeframes

Within the above team, there has to be a realistic appraisal of the role of pricing in their business. Pricing is much more than the firm being 'competitive', whatever that may mean!

Pricing also has a dynamic role to play for the firm and its goods and/or services in the marketplace. Just taking one aspect in general – for customers, price is said to be their largest single indicator of 'product' quality!

So right at the start of this book, lets bring your views on price to the forefront in our first exercise:

Exercise 1.1: The Secrets of the Right Price

Below there are eleven statements that represent some very common attitudes/views on Pricing.

This exercise was one beloved of the author's original pricing mentor, Roy Hill[ii]. Work through these statements and see whether you agree, disagree or would argue somewhere in the middle, or otherwise qualify your answer. Then turn to the appendix where you will find our views.

These eleven points typify common opinions in business with respect to price.

1. The lowest price wins the order:
2. Buyers are rational when buying:
3. Customers know what the price should be:
4. Quality determines price:
5. Match the competition price to succeed:
6. In a recession the low priced product sells best:
7. Start with a low price to win the first order – increase the price on repeats:
8. Price is a policy – costs are a fact:
9. There is a set of rules, which provides the best pricing strategy:
10. Only large companies can control prices:
11. Manufacturers control the price consumer customers pay:

WHAT DO YOU THINK??

(When you have crystallized your opinions on the above turn to Appendix 1, Exercise 1.1.)

What is the firm's cost structure and policy, re. overhead allocation?

This, and the next issue, **'the firm's marketplace'**, are inextricably linked, they are interdependent, but for clarity must be dealt with separately – at least at the start. Whatever the costing mechanism employed by the firm, such as 'mark-up', 'marginal pricing', 'activity based costing' et al. the plain fact of the matter is that overall, income must exceed expenditure or the firm will fail.

> *"Annual income £20, annual expenditure £19.98.5, result happiness,*
>
> *Annual income £20, annual expenditure £20.02.5, result misery"*
>
> **Mr. Micawber in David Copperfield**
> *With apologies to Charles Dickens for going decimal.*

As we will see later in this book the issue is certainly not straightforward. In addition to the interminable discussions within the firm as to what method should be used, almost inevitably, internal politics will have a role to play.

Classically the person dealing with pricing decisions (*lets henceforth refer to this person as the* **'Pricer'**) will be dealing with two distinctive types of costs:

- **'Fixed costs'**, alternatively referred to as 'overheads'. In simple terms these are said not to change with alterations in price – though as we will see it's not quite as simple as that – and –
- **'Variable costs'** which vary directly with the volumes sold, often, though not always directly (*i.e. the more product you sell, the more the overall variable costs will be*).

Fixed costs/overheads

Some of these costs, with which the 'pricer' is concerned, are directly related to the product (*i.e. the goods and/or services*) being traded.

They fall into three categories:

Firstly what are known as the **'direct fixed costs'**. These are truly fixed, i.e. within limits, no matter what the volume of business they will stay the same. Examples here would be:

- The rent,
- Rates,
- Interest on capital, the wages of the workforce employed directly on the production or handling of the product.

The list goes on.

The **second** category is known as '**semi fixed costs**'. These costs will change in discrete steps in relation to changes in the business.

Examples are:

- An extra sales person (*wages, car administration et al*) to cope with increased sales,
- Warehouse space to store the extra stocks required,
- An extra shift in the factory so as to produce the extra volumes sold,
- Product advertising (*which may be purchased on a campaign-by-campaign basis*).

Again, the list goes on.

Thirdly will be **indirect costs** 'allocated' to the pricer by **head-office** so as to share out the costs of running the overall business.

The elements that build this cost may be such as:

- The maintenance and rents of the head-office building,
- The wages and salaries for the accounts department,
- The total costs of corporate research and development,
- Corporate advertising,
- The CEO's limousine,
- The costs of servicing corporate borrowing, etc.

The pricer is usually in a good position to do something about the former two types of fixed costs, and very little about the latter. Yet to the unwary it is this last category that, if unchallenged, can (*appear to*) destroy their business. For this category of costs the 'challenge' must be '***On what basis have these costs been allocated***?' and should these more properly have been taken as the head-office's responsibility so that headquarters must live within the means of the total 'contribution[iii]' made within the firm.

Unresolved, this is a festering thorn that can *(and does)* so often infect the morale of management within the firm. The larger the firm, the greater the chances that 'internal politics' will be a powerful influence on how overhead costs are attributed to the Pricer's product or division. But neither are smaller firms immune to this phenomenon.

Variable costs

These are the costs that are directly connected to the 'product', i.e. the items of the goods and/or the 'moments of truth' of the services that are being supplied to the firm's customers.

They could be things that are directly consumed by the 'production' of the good or service traded. For example, raw materials, components of the product, ink used in printing, the installation of units, and if the system is sophisticated enough, even the electricity consumed per item and/or the service giver's time, sometimes *(assuming that they are hired only when customers are served – e.g. freelance trainers)* etc.

But even these costs may not have a direct and straight-line relationship with volume.

It is not unknown for these costs to be influenced by internal politics/policies (*e.g. issues such that effect 'transfer pricing' within the business – see following*) which must be monitored with care.

Take the first issue, the relationship with 'variable costs' and volume.

A common phenomenon is that any increases in the sales volume of a good will improve the buying power of that vendor. Such that when they source the consumables/components etc. which constitute their 'variable costs', the extra volume of such purchases should translate into better buying power and thus into lower 'variable costs'. The above assumes a 'commodity market' (*see the following and Chapter 3*).

However, if there is a constraint on the supply of the required consumables and/or components that make up the 'variable costs' of the firm, this can translate into either the need for extra activity by 'procurement' so as to find alternative sources of supply and/or the need to out-bid other firms requiring these same consumables or goods – which can now translate into higher 'variable costs' for the firm.

Thus, the unit cost of a 'variable cost' can itself vary up or down depending on the volumes traded and the types of markets from which these consumables or components are sourced.

It does not end there!

For large global firms that source much of what they need from within their own firm, there is the spectre of 'transfer pricing' to be addressed.

This is not the platform on which to examine this activity in depth, however, suffice to say that the pricer, in a large global firm who encounters this phenomenon, must indeed keep their wits about them. Internal politics via aggressive 'transfer pricing' can play an adverse role in the apparent profitability, or lack of it, for departments within the firm.

We discuss the profit and loss accounts/calculations (so called P&L) in Chapter 2. For now it is sufficient to stress that the management of the firm's various P&L's will depend critically on the pricer having the above situation, re fixed and variable costs, constantly under surveillance and at their fingertips.

The firm's marketplace

Whoever is making the pricing decision in the firm, they must also be well informed about what is going-on in their marketplace.

The 'ten-point must-know list'

Such background information must encompass answers to questions such as:

1. 'How large is the market?'
2. How competitive is it?
3. What is the current 'market price'?
4. What is the firm's market position/market share?
5. Where are our products on the curves of:
    a. 'Supply and demand',
    b. Product 'life cycle' and perhaps the –
    c. 'Technology adoption curve'?
6. What are the price elasticity's of our products in these markets?
7. What are the types and extent of the elasticity's of price for our product/s?
8. Is the market structured or unstructured?[iv]

9. Is this a market in which our product/s are already established or is it a market we will have to enter anew? – and if so:

10. What will be our penetration strategy?

The list can extend further – but you get the drift of where this is going – **The more you know, the greater the chances that the pricing decisions will succeed.**

Before moving on, a few words about some of the items in the above list.

Most strategies fail because there is not the necessary level of 'tactical ability' to deliver them in the field (see Chapter 6). Therefore a major concern for the pricer is to ensure that, at 'the sharp end' (*i.e. within the sales force, at the point where customers encounter the prices the Pricer has helped to set*), there is an optimum level of:

- Familiarity with the firm's P&L structure, and an awareness of the dangers of discounting,
- Following-on from this:
  - The skill to calculate the impact of any contemplated volume/price deals on the firm's bottom line and when considering giving a discount the firm's representatives know:
  - How to calculate the volumes necessary *just to stand-still* in terms of net profit.
- Tactical skills and negotiating ability.

Additionally, the pricer should militate for the optimum type of compensation package for these frontline people. One that is not rewarded by bonuses on the volumes sold but on the profits they earn for the business. The author, having been a salesman, a sales manager and a sales director, as well as a CEO in his time, well appreciates the difficulty of the latter and the ease of the former approach. But the pricer should also know, and be able to prove the damage to profits that can be done by the former vs. the latter types of incentive scheme.

According to the Strategic Pricing Group (SPG)[v]:

> "The root causes of increasing price-centred negotiations with customers lie both in the way salespeople are paid and sales managers operate. If these two elements fail to promote the proper behaviour or provide effective selling tools, salespeople will quickly revert to the use

of price. The problem is not with the salespeople, it rests with the poor support behind them and their managers."

> *"Volume is Vanity! Profit is Sanity!*
> *But only CASH is Reality!!"* **Anon**

Any salesperson with a volume-based quota or bonus system and with some level of control over the final price, will have a natural incentive to use a lower price so as to 'close the deal'. Customers know and take advantage of this sales behaviour, they would be fools not to. A salesperson who can close a deal at a 10% discount is going to do it every time. The salesperson still gets 90% of their bonus. The problem is that the company often loses 100% or more of their profit on that sale (*see Chapter 6*). This problem can still exist even in bonus schemes that are based partially on profit or gross margin.

Sales targets

Another cause of poor price negotiation practice (*as apposed to the skills outlined in Chapter 8*) are 'quarterly sales targets'. While the need for sales targets is obvious, the question often not considered is: 'What is the cost to our profits of hitting these sales volumes?' Managers who push salespeople to meet periodic sales targets often either force the salesperson to use price to close the deal or, in the case of large accounts, the manager may actually take over the task of closing, and may often use price discounting as the primary tactic. These behaviours totally undermine any systematic approach to the firm's pricing.

Worse yet, these behaviours are often self-reinforcing. They send signals to both sides of the negotiation to continue down the price spiral. Customers often learn to hold orders until the end of a 'sales period' and salespeople soon come to believe that skilful price strategies and tactics are a waste of time and in no way reflect the real behaviours of their sales managers. The end result is a 'cycle of desperation' in which managers drive prices lower and lower to meet their quarterly targets and increasingly sacrifice operating margin to accomplish their volume goals. The author firmly believes that the use of price to close deals should be the exception, not the rule.

The pricer

Perhaps such a situation as above may require that the front-line people should have better sales training specifically on pricing tactics (Chapter 6) and on negotiating skills (Chapter 8), and/or the firm may consider hiring a better quality of representative. One thing is sure, the world is getting so competitive that the 'tactical' ability to implement good pricing strategies is key to the survival of any firm (*except those that generate income from a Monopoly or Oligopoly marketplace*). **Today, that means nearly all of us!**

We are now going to take as given the overall leadership of the Pricing Tsar: Instead, from this point onward we will concentrate on taking the perspective of the person who actually sets the core price for the products. For the larger SME this could indeed be the Tsar, in a modest sized firm however, this could be the product manager, sales manager, or the entrepreneur/owner of the business. Whoever – the question now is what does this pricer person have to know and do to be a success at the game?

The Pricer must ensure that they are kept in the picture with respect to the '**10 point must-know list**' issues of the marketplace as set out above. The market, left to itself, will tend to 'commoditize' products – as we shall see in Chapter 2, this state of play is unacceptable to most market players, and this tendency must be vigorously resisted at all times.

In addition, the state of the market with respect to the stage of its life cycle, and (*if applicable*) the stage of the product on its 'technology adoption curve' must also be known and understood.

With this information and given the Pricer's understanding of the issues, internal and external, they should choose which internally based process for setting price they should employ as a starting point. Although it should never be employed on its own, there is nothing wrong with starting the price setting process for a given business, by using a 'cost plus' approach. As we shall see, it has served business well for more than six thousand years already, so it must have something going for it. In the final analysis any failure to cover costs spells catastrophe. Indeed, for the very small firm with a limited range of products and processes there is no real benefit in being more sophisticated at this initial stage.

However, for the larger, and/or perhaps more sophisticated firm, especially if it is in aggressively competitive markets, say in the 'service sector', a pricer may choose to employ the 'activity based costing' system (*explained at the end of Chapter 3*).

Only the very able pricer or the gambler should countenance employing marginal pricing – it is a seductive idea, which like the call of the siren has led many businesses to their doom.

The break-even point

To do this realistically, a firm's pricer, and their field sales team, will need to be able to calculate break-even numerically; graphic methods are only for illustrating the concept. There is no substitute for numerical calculation – it is more precise AND the process will yield more information and more insights, in addition to the break-even point alone.

Sales teams should also be encouraged to adopt this skill and be able to check the workings for themselves. For this the firm will need the courage to share (*some of*) this data with (*some of*) their sales force. The data thus shared must be the truth (*whatever the salespeople are told, it must be realized that if they are indifferently motivated, one way or another, they will pass this information on to their customers, and from there you can bet on the data reaching the competition. So, although whatever you tell the sales teams must be the truth, remember, you don't have to tell them ALL of the TRUTH!!*). We encounter this issue of calculating BE in Chapter 3, and especially in Exercise 3.4.

Items 1, 2 and 3 in the 10 point must-know-list of issues shown above, are the next consideration for the Pricer. How do you meet the market price and be profitable if your business model is no better than the competition's and therefore your costs are no better than par? (*E.g. the 'South Western Airline' business model*[vi] *is successful BECAUSE it reduces the costs of running such an airline to a shadow of the costs incurred* ***by their competition, i.e. the mainstream international carriers***). If, as may be the case in most circumstances, we seem to be at the point where we cannot squeeze any more costs out of our business, and even if we can it will take time to apply or to work through the system; our attention should focus on our marketplace, and the prices of our competition. To beat the competition will require pricing that will provide a profitable 'competitive edge'. Hence a 'price positioning', plus a sound pricing strategy must be created that will be attractive to our customers whilst still being profitable to our business.

So, on to the next part of the jigsaw, the pricing process: Getting to grips with our target customers!

Assuming a free and open market, no given package of price and value will appeal to all customers simultaneously. So our pricing must be aimed at specific sectors of the market.

If we are in business-to-business markets (B2B) there are often occasions where we can tailor our offering and our pricing uniquely for a specific customer. If however, we are closer to the consumer, even though we may have to go via distributors, retailers et. al. (i.e. B2C), it would not normally be possible to deal with each individually.

In this situation we must cluster our customer types so that each customer has many relevant similarities with others in the cluster, and in respect to these factors are dissimilar to other customers not in that cluster. This is known as 'Segmentation',[vii] (*we discuss this early in Chapter 4*). Thus, optimally, each pricing strategy should be focused on a specific customer segment.

Price positions

The way we address that 'target' segment is often referred to as our price position. So what is our current perceived price position in our market?

Are our prices high, medium or low when compared to those firms competing for the same segment? Everything is 'relative' and in this case our prices are relative not only to the competition, but also to the value we provide for the prices we charge.

For each of our price points, we must be seen by our customers either to provide value commensurate with our price, or more value, or less value. The answers to these issues are plotted on what is known as the price position matrix (Chapter 4), which is a three cell by three cell matrix of price versus value (*as perceived by the customer*!). Later this concept is refined into a matrix of six-by-six-cells and is referred to as the 'Price/Value Landscape Grid' introduced in Chapter 4 and which is employed in the process of 'value-based-pricing' as set-out in Chapter 5.

These grids form an essential foundation to any pricing strategy. Once they are in place they should be kept-up-to-date via a sound customer/market information system (C/MIS)[viii]

Now we can start to compile a pricing strategy. The essential first stage of any strategy formulation is to ensure that we are clear about the aims and objectives to be achieved and that these are concise (*'too many and you don't have any'*), unambiguous, clear and SMART[2].

There are some twelve basic pricing strategies with which the Author has become familiar over the years, most others he has encountered are either variations on one of these themes, or are tactics rather than strategies. For example, so called 'value based pricing' is actually a collection of different approaches to adding value to the deal and thus supporting the price charged (*one variant being 'partnership pricing', as explained in Chapter 4*).

As we will see there are distinctive pricing strategies for entering a market, for leaving a market, for keeping the competition out of our market, for launching new products at the start of their product life cycles (PLC) and when well into their PLC, for trying to stop price wars and ones for fighting one if you can't prevent the war happening.

Value based pricing

Chapter 5 takes one particular strategy value based pricing and examines it in depth, because it is such a powerful tool for winning new business and for creating barriers to competitor entry in to our markets. The chapter explores how it works, the process of compiling/tailoring the specific value based price, how to use it and when to use it.

The starting point is customer value: Customers and consumers use goods and services to achieve something of value in their lives and/or businesses.

For business to business, the four levers of financial improvement (Chapter 2) lie at the heart of any value proposition, either singly or in some combination. The firm is either reducing its overall costs (*and our price IS a cost to them*), trying to sell more volume, obtain a good price **from its customers**, and/or optimize its investment – none of which are mutually exclusive.

For consumers, the levers of value lie in some permutation or combination of the five elements of Maslow's hierarchy of needs[ix].

By focusing on what that business value is, and how it may differ from competitor to competitor, businesses are able to accomplish a number of important things.

First, the firms are able to understand how to respond to different competitive situations with customers.

Second, the firms are better able to recommend assemblies of product 'features and benefits' which, when translated into customer 'value' either match or beat the competitor's product's performance and/or their price. This approach forces customers to make choices based on either price or value. Research confirms that, despite what they might say in the middle of a negotiation, most customers prefer value over low prices (*most customers, not ALL, see the three types mentioned and described in Chapter 4*).

Third, the firm obtains insights into new product and service features for which customers may be willing to pay more. This should translate into competitive advantage for the business.

The skill is in attaching a monetary value to our customer's decision to use our products versus those offered by a competitor. This monetary value should be based on specific results for the type of customer (*or segment*) being considered. Attractive products in B2B markets are those that produce either lower operating costs, increases in capacity, free up working capital, create more sales or enable our customer to charge higher prices to their customers (or any permutation or combination thereof).

Credible supporting documentation can make these values tangible to both the salesperson and their customers. Such documents help our salespeople to ask questions that are relevant to their customers and to elicit favourable responses from them. Such material should help identify how the customer will improve their business' performance as a result of adopting the right good or service from our business. These tools can be complex, web-based analytical programs or simple spreadsheets formatted to accept customer inputs and provide timely calculations of value and return on investment.

Not all customers behave the same way: There are considerable differences between customers in how they choose to approach their relationship with their suppliers. Not all customers want to, or will, be loyal. Nor will all customers be willing to pay vendors for the value they supply. Instead, their preference, stated and actual, is often to put high-value suppliers through the same tough bargaining process as they do for low-value suppliers. They do this in the hope that the high-value vendors will be intimidated into providing their higher value products but at the lower price. This sort of environment should encourage our salespeople to gain the skills to diagnose these customer behaviours and develop the appropriate approach for each.

Generally, customers employ one of three likely purchasing agendas when dealing with B2B suppliers:

- **Price buyers** drive to obtain products and services at the lowest possible prices. This includes qualifying many vendors to ensure an aggressive price battle for their business.
- **Value buyers** are willing to trade off different vendors based on the value they bring to the table and are willing to pay more for higher value offerings.
- **Relationship buyers** rely on vendors to help them understand and apply the offering and are willing to pay higher prices for those skills and expertise (*see Figure 4.5 et. seq.*).

When planning for the account the wise sales person should identify the likely behaviour of their 'target customer' and address this with an appropriate package of offerings. They should also adopt some well thought-out negotiating tactics to minimize the damage of 'price buyers'. Or perhaps worse, those 'value buyers' who have learned that they can get lower prices for higher value products by masquerading as a 'price buyer'. The really effective sales person knows that any single approach will not work for all their customers.

The skill is in creating approaches to negotiation that expose 'procurement's' true agenda, whilst having a proposition ready that will minimize the damage that the totally price oriented buyer can do.

It is perfectly acceptable to sell low price, low-value products if they fill our capacity with a useful contribution to our bottom line. The firm's pricing skill must ensure that their product range includes those products where the specific 'features, advantages and benefits' on offer are organized in a portfolio of low-value, medium-value, and high-value so as to match the typical agendas of each of the three different sorts of customers they can have. This, whilst simultaneously keeping in place the firm's approach to profitability.

A key to this process is to present what our firm offers with the appropriate 'fences' in-place to ensure that low-price oriented customers are prevented from getting access to high-value goods and/or services.

Sales planning for price

So, following on from the above: **sales planning and preparation are critical for successful pricing.**

Pricing is implemented in the offices of purchasing agents around the globe. A well-prepared sales force understands that advanced analysis and planning is essential so as to shift the discussion from price to value. **And that not all customers are willing to make that shift.** To be successful, salespeople need to prepare for all negotiations at three levels:

1. **Strategic**: Allocate resources where they can return the highest value to the organization
   - What is the relevant background data about the account?
   - How do our products create value relative to competitive offerings?
   - Who are the key members of the buying centre, what role do they play, and how much power do they have in the process?
2. **Negotiating approach**: by analyzing the research, how should the sales representative meet account objectives and develop plans for the following:
   - What is the customer's likely buying behaviour?
   - Given this behaviour, how best should our key executives be employed in the account?
   - What 'product packages' should our people plan for a given customer?
3. **Negotiation preparation:**
   - Following the analysis above, how should the team position and package the proposal?
   - What do we expect the customer's response to that proposal to be? This may be a guess, but it provides understanding of what product package is best and what approach may work
   - Given that response, what should our back-up approach be?

Conclusion

It's clear that improved sales planning and execution leads to more revenue, profits and customer loyalty. This planning must link the right value package to the right customers and do so in a way that suits their business needs and buying behaviours.

Effective value-based programs protect the firm's value packages and sell value to the customer, which only happens if firms have low-value 'fighter-brands' (*see Fighting a price war,* Chapter 7) with which to engage the low-priced competition.

In addition, our sales teams should have the necessary training and tools to support their understanding of the firm's market position and the value of these offers, plus when and how to use each different element. In addition, salespeople should be helped to develop the sophisticated skills necessary to understand the customer's business and their customer's value chains including how these operate. They should know how their products apply to those operations and how they provide a differential value advantage over the competition.

***'Selling is not telling!'* it is asking questions in the customer's language and listening to their response.** Only then can our representatives craft a specific product and sales solution to assure success with the account.

Managers who support the above process by developing comprehensive programs of value creation and 'value matching' will be successful. These programs should aim to help our salespeople to 'stick to their guns' when they are in complex and difficult negotiations. This is not easy, but it is the only way to gain the initiative in the value exchange process with our customers.

Tactical pricing

In all value exchanges, there are tensions as to who is getting the better part of the deal.

Both sides will try their uppermost to ensure that they are not the ones that 'end-up with the shorter stick!' Thus there is a need for those in the front-line to be tactically competent, and be able to negotiate the best 'win/win' deals. (*Tactics are dealt with in Chapter 6, and Negotiation in Chapter 8.*)

Tactically the salespeople in the firing line must not only be conversant with the dangers of discounting, e.g. that say a 10% discount **can** wipe-out the firm's net profit if not compensated for via larger volumes purchased by the customer in return for the discount given; but how much for how big a discount, that's the question. In Chapter 6 we provide not only the background to this dilemma but also three ways to calculate this situation, especially useful when 'under fire'.

In addition, Chapter 6 addresses such issues as:

- General discount policy and practice
- Pricing in a declining market (*what will be the long term implication on the business of any change in price*?)
- Pricing at the different stages of the product life cycle (PLC)
- Pricing a new product in a totally new PLC, things to do, and not to do
- Pricing when launching a new product into an already established market and PLC which requires a wholly different set of tactics which we discuss
- Bundling vs. Breaking (*to add value or not*?) during the various stages of the PLC.

Chapter 6 also examines the central rules in 'tough times' which centre around the need to preserve our gross profit and doing so via adopting 'business process outsourcing' as a part of our firm's business model. This enables the business to change many of its fixed costs into variable costs, and thus, in the process changing the nature of the breaking-even for our business.

In this theme the chapter goes-on to examine the dangers of 'marginal pricing' – which are many, apart from the frequent issue of not reaching overall break-even during the financial year, and thus putting the business in jeopardy. In this discussion we also examine the rules of marginal pricing which are for ***"the adherence of fools, but the guidance of the wise"***. That is to say if you have to employ marginal pricing – this is the way to do it. Towards the end of that chapter we also examine the various considerations for responding to the invitation to tender. We say that if this invitation is the first you have heard of the project, in all probability you are only making-up the numbers (i.e. the 'required 3 tenders' etc.). During the discussion of this topic we examine briefly a method for estimating the probabilities of winning the tender against known and studied opponents. We then proceed to an examination of how best to present your tender both in document form and personally, if you have the chance to do so.

The remaining Chapter 6 contains a set of stratagems and paradigms (*i.e. 'rules of thumb'*) for putting up the price of our products, how best to do it for the general market plus how to preserve our key relationships with major accounts. This discussion also includes ways to put up price – without appearing to – some ways of which are not available to all businesses, but when they are available to us they will make all the difference.

Price wars

In Chapter 7 we examine price wars – things to avoid like the plague. If our business is a large player in its markets then the best way to deal with this situation is to do our damnedest to ensure that they don't break-out if we can possible help it.

This chapter uses the price war between three broadsheet newspapers in the UK, in the mid 1980's, to provide an example of how they can happen and how they rarely achieve the objectives set by the belligerents.

The first part of this chapter examines the prophylactic regime we need to employ to prevent price wars ever breaking out in the first place. One major issue stemming from the fact that most price wars are caused by our customers, rather than by our competitors, is that we must learn to recognize when the client is lying. They admit to telling some ten to twelve lies in the normal course of business anyway – and these are detailed in that chapter.

We also examine the market conditions which can create the potential for commercial conflict, and set-out a series of symptoms for which we must keep 'a weather eye open'. It is also important to understand the necessary conditions for a belligerent to be so inclined, and we set-out these situations to act by way of being 'trip-wires' for our surveillance of the marketplace, which when 'tripped' should alert us to the potentially dangerous situation in our marketplace.

The regime for analysis to identify where the threat is most likely to originate is:

Firstly, to identify those with the muscle and motive. To a large extent this will depend on the firm's size. At one end of the size spectrum, the market leaders have much to lose by going to war, whilst the smaller niche players have little muscle and few resources with which to benefit. It is the middle sized players that can harbour the threat – the chapter uses a graphic (Figure 7.2) to illustrate that it is the market 'Princes' that are the ones to watch, not the small fry.

Secondly, the pricer must evaluate the opposition's potential strengths and weaknesses (Figure 7.3). Do these mid sized competitors have the lean and hungry look about them, or are they content to stay where they are? What sort of culture do they have, are they effectiveness focused or are they focused on efficiency?

Thirdly, as we see (in Figure 7.4) how do the opposition manage their business at this moment? Are they acting realistically, with clear strategies and objectives that seem logical and well thought-out and executed, or do they have more resources than they currently need? Are their objectives ambitious? Do we find that they are unpredictable and also copying our products, market moves and finally your prices? If the latter, as Machiavelli would say, *'keep them closer to you than your dearest friends'* in order to avoid the surprise attack.

And if you have to fight, then do so without mercy. Chapter 7 concludes with a distillation of the rules for fighting any war. The only difference is that in a price war, at least in the west, no blood is spilt, but nonetheless people can still lose everything they have built-up over the years. There are some 4,000 years of recorded conflict available, all over the world, so Chapter 7 draws on the various sources for its shibboleths, from Sun Tsu, through Alexander, Hannibal, Caesar, and Napoleon to Clausewitz.

Finally this chapter introduces the stratagems of the fighter brand and the diverter which are commercial applications often used successfully by the virtuoso pricer.

Negotiation

If our business is retail, then, unless we are in the Mid to Far East, we will not have to bargain or negotiate the price with our customers directly. However, for the rest of us, who are either in the business to business value chains, or are close to the business to consumer outlets, then everything is negotiable.

Negotiation is not bargaining. Bargaining is just one stage in the negotiation process.

In Chapter 8 we take an overview of negotiation and the processes associated with it.

The negotiation sequence is to:

- **Prepare one's ground:** preparation in negotiation, as in much else in life is the mark of the true professional. And in the negotiation meeting the aim is to:
- **Discuss** with the other side the situations, re their objectives and room for manoeuvre, then
- **Propose** a deal, as the starting point of the
- **Bargaining** process: and when the two sides are approaching a consensus – the aim is to
- **Agree:** and don't forget to spell everything out. Agree what you have agreed and do so in writing.

Finally, when the process is concluded, never let the other side know what they could have obtained. The best negotiations are when both sides feel they have accomplished all that they can, and that both sides were fair and worth doing business with in future.

Negotiation is not an easy skill to acquire – it requires practice and experience to do well.

The reward for being an accomplished negotiator is that it is applicable to many other pursuits in business and in one's personal life. But in business it is a critical part of getting the right price, making a reasonable return on the investment, and so living to do it all again another day.

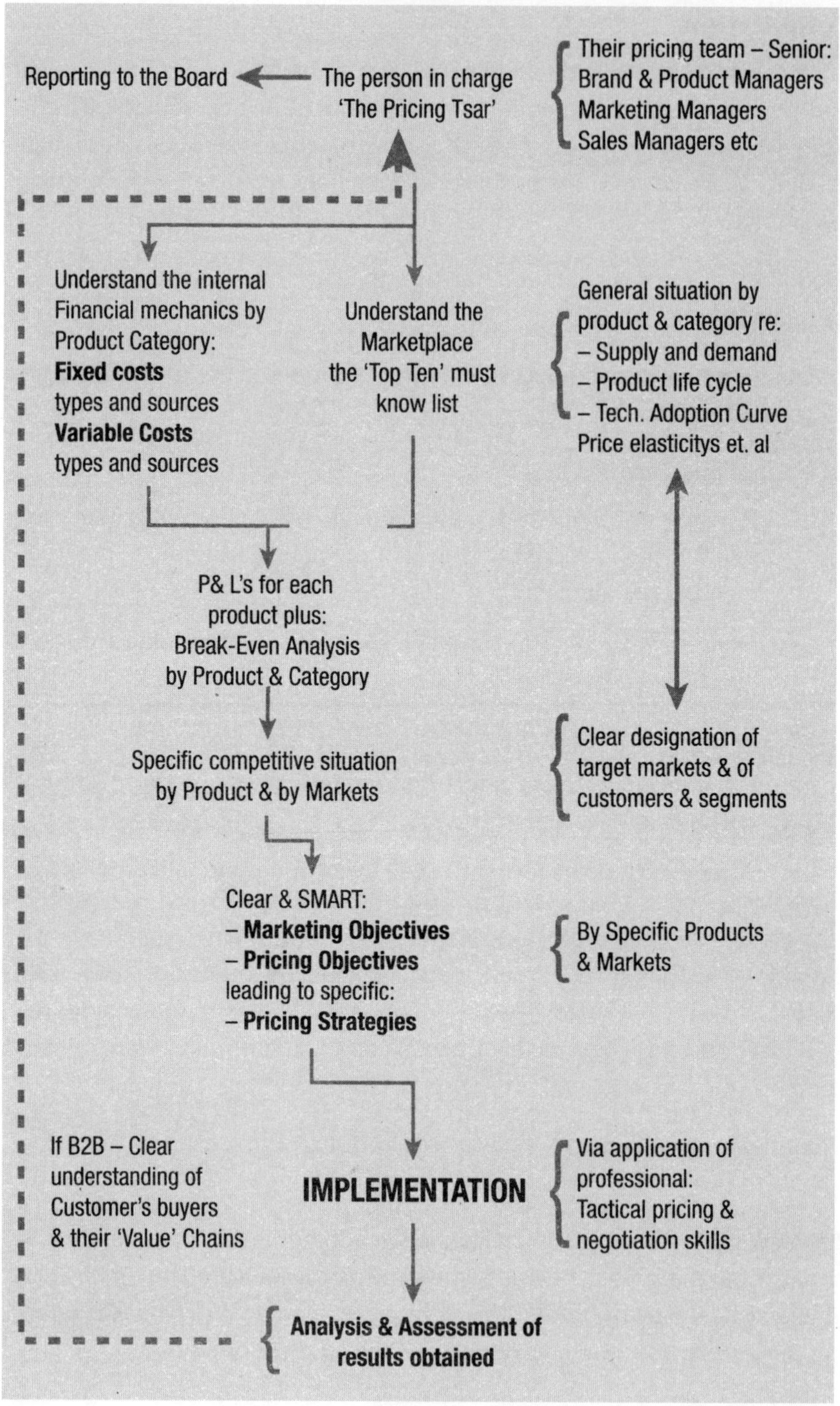

FLOW CHART OF THE PRACTICAL PRICING PROCESS

References

1 Small to Medium Enterprise.

2 Specific, Measurable, Actionable (and/or) Agreed, Realistic, Time-Bound (i.e. deadlines).

i According to Yehudi Menuhin a discipline is said to be the combination of an 'Art' and a 'Technology/Science'. In Pricing this is the Technology of cost control and internal financial management combined with the art of foreseeing sales volumes and profits arising from the options faced by the firm.

ii This exercise was one beloved of the Author's original Pricing Mentor, Roy Hill and has been used with his permission, by this Author, on every pricing course/consultancy since we worked together at the Chartered Institute of Marketing back in the early 1990's.

iii Another word for gross profit as we will see, which has its uses in the internal battles over price within the larger firm.

iv An unstructured market is said to be one where it takes more than 20% of the firms in the market, to account for 80% of that markets business i.e. it is very competitive. A structured market is the opposite.

v Adapted from a paper presented by Reed K. Holden of the SPG in 2003.

vi The main business model used by the low-cost carriers througout the world such as easyJet, Ryanair, AirAsia et.al.

vii See also *'Mastering Marketing'* (2nd edition, 2006), and *'Marketing your Service Business'* (2006) both by this Author and this Publisher.

viii Again see C/MIS in *'Mastering Marketing'* (2nd edition, 2006), by this Author and this Publisher.

ix For an excellent paper on this topic visit the Author's website **www.ruskin-brownassociates.com** and download the PDF of this concept which you will find there.

TWO

THE FOUNDATIONS OF THE PRICING DECISION

THE FOUNDATIONS OF THE PRICING DECISION

Synopsis

This chapter sets out the issues that constitute the very foundations of making any pricing decision, i.e the two critical essentials:

- Knowing your firm's P & L Ratios for each product line,
- Being continually aware of the state of the main market forces at work in your marketplace.

The first part examines the major ways in which a company can improve its financial performance and how these ways break down into various strategic imperitives. Toward the end of this chapter we will see how these strategies relate to the stages of the product life cycle (PLC). It will conclude with a brief examination of the Technology Adoption Curve (TAC) and its implications for pricing.

The chapter discusses which of the effectiveness vs. efficiency strategies have the greatest potency when it comes to making a contribution to financial performance. From this emerges the identification of effectiveness versus efficiency, and then, via an examination of the basics of the Profit and Loss account (P & L), it will demonstrate that revenue generation is an order of magnitude more powerful than cost cutting, i.e. effectiveness is more potent than efficiency at making contributions to the company's bottom line.

The latter half of this chapter examines the major market forces that constrain our ability to set prices. It starts with how the law of supply and demand determines which of three main business orientations may be imposed on an organization, depending on where the firm's markets are in that cycle. It goes on briefly to show how firms may break out of these constraints on its ability to set prices, via adopting a marketing orientation. It proceeds to examine the influence of the PLC and TAC on pricing decisions.

The chapter concludes by a brief examination of the technology adoption curve and how, for those in highly innovative markets, such as Information Technology (IT), the urge MUST be resisted to use low prices to penetrate this type of new market.

Exercise 2.1

Imagine that you have just received a fax/email inviting you to participate as a speaker in a conference on the other side of the world. You are asked to take one hour to present the context of your business expertise (in respect of the conference topic), and respond to questions for some 15 to 30 minutes following. Say you are free during these dates, with enough time either side to fly there and back. The organizers will pay all your reasonable expenses and accommodation.

Question: What fee (in $US) will you charge, and why?

[Consider this for a few moments and when you have arrived at a conclusion, turn to page 65 at the end of this chapter to check your thinking].

Introduction

There are essentially four ways in which an organization can improve its financial performance. Neither of these ways are mutually exclusive, any one or combination of the four can be employed at any one time. They are in no particular order of importance:

- Increasing sales volume
- Optimizing price
- Cutting costs
- Optimizing investment

Combining price and sales volume produces increased revenue. The last option, optimizing investment, assumes that overall revenue and profit are not affected, or at the very least remain static. Although the first three are normally considered to be within the remit of an organization's management, and the last (*i.e.investment*) the remit of the Board alone, it is interesting to note that although most management have little, if any, direct control over the levels of investment in their own organization, it is often the case that, via what they sell (*particularly in business to business situations*) the sales and marketing teams can have a significant impact on the customers' levels of investment.

Although these four ways of improving financial performance can be taken in any permutation or combination, the marketer must understand how these impact on the strategy of the company. They must know in what circumstances any particular combination is best employed, and which of these strategies have the most potent impact on the bottom line.

Strategic focus

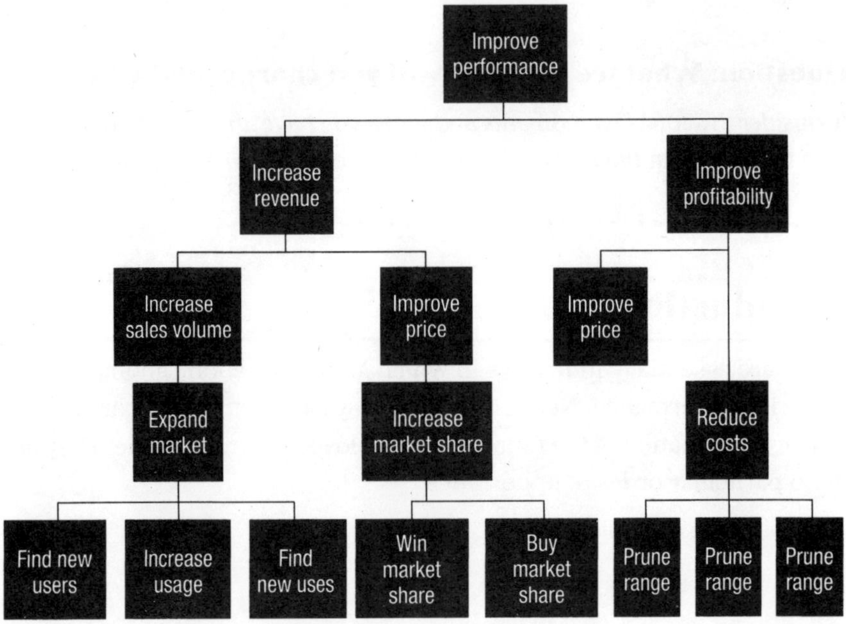

FIGURE 2.1: AN ORGANOGRAM CREATED FROM THE COMPANY'S THREE OPTIONS

Addressing the three options which are within the remit of a company's management we obtain the cascade (or organogram) as shown in Figure 2.1.

We can see from this, that in order to increase sales volume we may need either to expand our market and/or increase our share of that marketplace.

Expanding a market can mean creating new users, or alternatively increasing the rates at which a company's goods or service are used. It could also involve promoting new uses entirely. For example, the mobile telephone industry, how much of the emphasis during the first few years was to broaden the range of users of mobiles? Firstly, to executive level business people, then management and then into the general population. Within the general population the adult usage was broadened, from adult males, through to adult females and then into teenagers in the family, arguably, now mobile telephoney's main market by volume.

Increasing the 'take-up' and usage rate of the mobile telephone was initially all down to price, brought about by lowering the cost of handsets, the subscriptions, the cost of the call and eventually, by enabling people to pre-pay for their calls. Examples of conventional uses for a mobile telephone are as:

- a safety device for a woman alone at night
- a means for parents to stay in touch with children
- a tool for business travellers when abroad, to be able to make contact with the home country.

All of which are valuable uses and justify the extra cost of a call via the mobile versus the land line.

Relative potency

The strategies outlined in Figure 2.1 are often more appropriate in one set of circumstances than others. In addition to this they have different levels of power to make a contribution to the bottom line of the company. We illustrate this in Figure 2.2 below.

	A
Volume Required Price per Hour Revenue Labour @ $7.50 Plus Materials @ $7.50	4 hrs $25.00 $100.00 $60.00
Gross Profit = $	$40.00
Overhead per day	$30.00
Net Profit on the deal	$10.00
% profit ±	–

FIGURE 2.2: RELATIVE POTENCY

In Figure 2.2, we've taken a hypothetical circumstance of a business in the service sector selling its service by the hour. For example, a small word processing or desk top publishing bureau. In column A a rather simple profit and loss situation is outlined. Following it through:

- the company is charging its service at $25.00 per hour
- it is the first offer of business for today, and it is for four hours work.

Thereby potentially generating a revenue of $100.00.

The cost of sales is made up of $7.50 per hour of labour and $7.50 per hour of consumable materials (*such as toner, paper, electricity*), i.e. a total of $15 per hour. Thus for all of four hours, the variable costs amount to $60 which gives a gross profit of $40.00 to the company.

Say the company had approached its overhead attribution on a daily basis and that its gross overhead, rent, rates, fixed labour costs came to some $6,000.00 a year. There are some 200 working days in any one year, which equates to $30.00 per day. So, deducting this from gross profit we see that, in column 'A' everything else being equal, an order for four hours worth of work will produce a net profit of $10.00 for the day (***if no other business is done that day***).

Quick exercise

What would be the effect on the bottom line of reducing the cost of materials by say 1%?

For the moment, don't look at the table illustration 2.3 below: before reading on – see if you can mentally calculate the outcome on the bottom line of this table.

In column B of Figure 2.3 below, see the effect of applying the strategies outlined to the right of the organogram (Figure 2.1.) A reduction of 1% will have the effect of reducing the cost of sales by 30 cents in total. Thus, if we don't erode that saving, we put 30 cents directly on the bottom line, making the net profit $10.30. In other words, for a reduction of 1% on material, we have improved net profitability by 3%. Quite a potent trick and one that is the pride of the 'procurement' profession. It certainly tends to impress other people in the organization who are often mystified by the way that a 1% reduction in cost can multiply to a 3% or more increase in net profit.

	A	B Effect of 1% reduction in cost of Materials	C Effect of 1% improvement all round	D Where the improvement came from
Volume Required	4 hrs	4 hrs		
Price per Hour	$25.00	$25.00		
Revenue	$100.00	$100.00		
Labour @ $7.50 Plus Materials @ $7.50	$60.00	$59.70		
Gross Profit = $	$40.00	$40.30		
Overhead per day	$30.00	$30.00		
Net Profit on the deal	$10.00	$10.30		
% profit ±	–	+3%		

FIGURE 2.3: RELATIVE POTENCY

This magic, however, has its limitations. Firstly, there is a limit to the extent by which management can cut costs before damaging the ability of the business to compete in the marketplace (*certainly in the long-term and frequently in the short-term as well*). Secondly, this approach tends to blind people in the organization to the potency of increasing sales (*they see reduced costs as a certainty but increasing sales, at best, as only an aspiration*).

Exercise 2.2

Calculate the bottom line outcome if the business was to be able to make a 1% improvement to all the factors in its business P&L:

See if you can do this mentally, the best performing commodities traders, race-course bookies etc. never use a calculator when they are in the thick of the deal – it's too slow.

NB. *If you want to get an edge in pricing, re-learn those mental arithmetic skills instilled in you when you were at school.*

When you have the solution check it out with our calculations. You will find the answer to this and the other exercises in Appendix 1.

Continuing the improvement

It is important to note that of the total improvement of 23.16%, $2.01 has been derived from an increase in sales revenue (*i.e. volume multiplied by price*) and only $0.906 has been derived from a reduction in costs. In other words, the strategies on the left hand side of Figure 2.1 are more potent in terms of their ability to contribute to the bottom line than are the right hand strategies. Thus, for a fairly simple profit and loss account, with the ratios as shown in column A, the left hand strategies are more than twice as potent as the rest put together. This is the difference between the contribution potential to the bottom line of effectiveness versus efficiency strategies.

The above effect is only a 2:1 ratio, i.e. a 1% beneficial change to each of the revenue producing factors results in an improvement of more than twice any contribution that would be produced by a 1% reduction to the total costs of that organization. But the above is just an exercise, the real life facts are startling.

The results of two respected studies make the point:

A study published in the *Harvard Business Review* in 1992 and a Compustat study in the mid 1990's, showed the following effects on the bottom line of a 1% improvement as being:

Compustat Study c.3000 firms

Factor inproved by 1%	Contribution to the bottom line
Price	12.3%
Variable Cost	8.7%
Volume	3.6%
Fixed Costs	2.6%

Harvard Business Review 1992, 2000 firms in USA

Factor inproved by 1%	Contribution to the bottom line
Price	11.1%
Variable Cost	7.8%
Volume	3.3%
Fixed Costs	2.3%

FIGURE 2.4: TABLE OF BOTTOM LINE CONTRIBUTIONS FROM A 1% IMPROVEMENT

CONSIDER:

At the basic level, any changes to the various costs incurred by a firm only add-up, thus in the Compustat Study a 1% change in both types of cost only produced a c.11.3% extra contribution to the bottom line, in the Harvard study it was 10.1%

WHEREAS:

Any changes in prices charged are multiplied by the changes achieved in volumes. Thus in the Compustat study the bottom line contribution of these two was 44.28% and in the Harvard study was 33.63%. This is a ratio, Revenue to Cost of from c.4:1 for Compustat and c.3.3:1 for Harvard.

Thus, even in the real world, effectiveness strategies are more powerful than efficiency strategies. All firms are different, but it is not inconcievable that most firms, market forces permitting, can achieve a 3:1 ratio and maybe more given the right pricing and sales skills.

The effectiveness efficiency grid

In Figure 2.5 below, the effectiveness efficiency grid is shown as a 2 x 2 matrix. Effectiveness is doing the right things, addressing those issues that are important to the success of the organization. This would be, for example, obtaining the best possible price, which means selling to the most lucrative customers, and also perhaps the customers with the greatest ability to buy volume, the highest usage rates and so forth. Efficiency is all about keeping costs down, getting more bang for the buck; reducing wastage. In other words, efficiency is about doing things well or as we say in the diagram, doing things right.

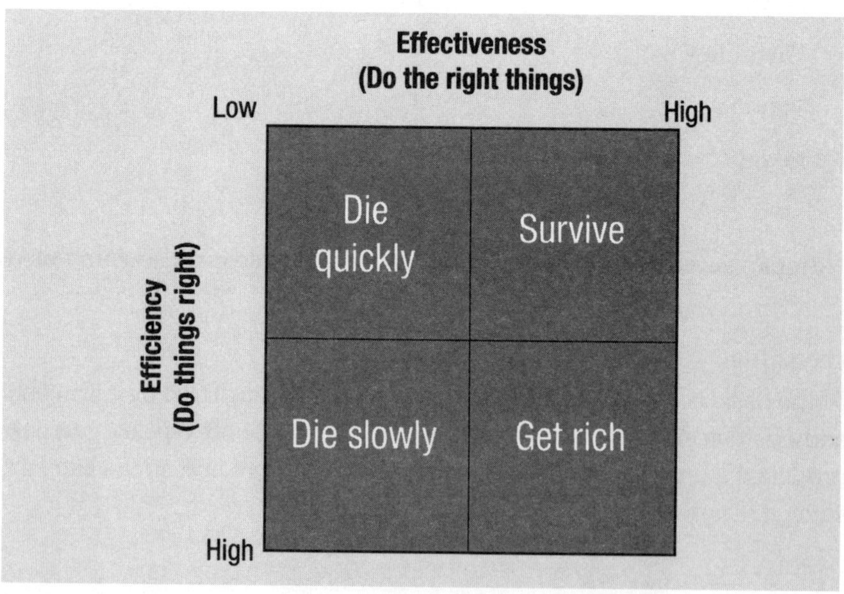

FIGURE 2.5: EFFECTIVENESS VS. EFFICIENCY GRID

We can see from Figure 2.5 that an organization which is not doing the right things is low in effectiveness, and if it's not 'doing it right' it's low in efficiency as well. This will predicate a fairly quick demise for such an organization. An example could be that the company is producing a first class product but is trying to sell it to the wrong customers, at the wrong price, and it is fairly poor at controlling its costs. In all but the most exceptional circumstances, such as if the firm were a monopoly, it would die fairly quickly.

The reflex of the financial controllers of most companies is often to ensure that costs are kept to the minimum, in other words, efficiency is a matter of priority. However, we see in the bottom left quadrant of the diagram that this approach, if taken alone, predicates a slow death. The company still hasn't got the right customers who are capable of buying the right volumes at the best possible prices, and the subsequent death will be slow, inevitable and painful. The top right of the matrix suggests that it is possible for an inefficient business to survive – indeed there is much evidence that says that an unprofitable company can survive (*in the short-term at least*). It does this best by focusing its efforts on customers who buy volume and who pay on time. These confer the benefit of positive cash flow, and if a company can pay its bills it will not be made bankrupt, i.e. it will survive (*maintaining positive cash flow is an effectiveness strategy*).

Of course, the ideal for any firm is to be high in effectiveness, in other words going for the best possible customers (*those prepared to pay the highest price and/or consume the largest volumes AND pay on time*), as well as being very efficient about doing this. In these circumstances the organization will become rich. Any approach to business that helps to generate and/or to increase sales revenue for a company, is 'effective'. There are two basic approaches to business which are 'effective' by nature, they are:

- a sales philosophy and
- a marketing philosophy (*see 'Mastering Marketing' by this author*).

However, as attractive as the left hand sides of the strategy shown in Figure 2.1 may appear to be, it is not always possible to adopt them. Market conditions may well predicate that the right hand strategies (efficiency) are more appropriate at the time. The market conditions which may inhibit or permit a company's freedom of manoeuvre are very much tied in with the law of supply and demand which is the topic we address next.

Market forces

Introduction

Marketing, as a method of generating sales revenue, is not the 'be-all and end-all' of running a business. There are at least two other business philosophies which are capable of producing lots of profitable revenue under the right circumstances (*refer to Mastering Marketing*).

The first of these is to be a 'monopoly', or at least an 'oligopoly' – which produces **'hard' markets** (*sometimes known as 'sellers' markets*).

In a monopoly market (*i.e. a 'hard' market*) the supplier is 'the only game in town', the customer has no other source of supply and must therefore pay the price demanded, or go without.

Where a few suppliers exist and there are many customers, the situation is hardly any better, this we call an oligopoly. An example of these types of business situations are to be found in the UK and EU telecoms industries.

T-mobile and Vodafone are (*at the time of writing*) the main carriers in the UK. Each other EU country having rarely more than two other carriers additional to the former state monopoly.

(*Throughout the world this is changing as more and more governments open up their mobile/wireless telephony to more and more competition, via the issuing of licences to companies other than their indigenous state telecoms.*) Another example is the UK utilities industries where previously the ordinary person could only take their water, gas or electrical power from the one and only pertinent local supplier.

'Hard markets' provide a vendor with the greatest freedom to manoeuvre. However, the monopoly (*or oligopoly*) company in the 'market' will most often pursue profit maximization via the adoption of one (*or a combination*) of two available strategies, which in no particular order are:

- 'screwing down' costs as far as possible, and
- 'jacking-up' prices as much as possible (*i.e. an efficiency strategy, re. the right hand in 2.3*).

NB. *Freedom to manoeuvre in the first stratagem may be constrained by legislative imperatives, possibly including quality specifications.*

On the second issue, monopolies/oligopolies will restrict their capacity so that 'supply' is always less than underlying demand. That way, price can be used as a tool to manage real demand (*i.e. a 'want' with the money to pay for it*). Price is raised to the point where demand falls off to meet the capacity available. There is frequently, little sense for a monopolist to invest in new plant and equipment so as to increase capacity. Such investment only makes sense if it leads to substantial reductions in the cost of production.

These companies have little if any intrinsic need for marketing, they have no competitors, and if the customer does not like what is being offered at the price demanded, there will be plenty more customers who may not be so inhibited.

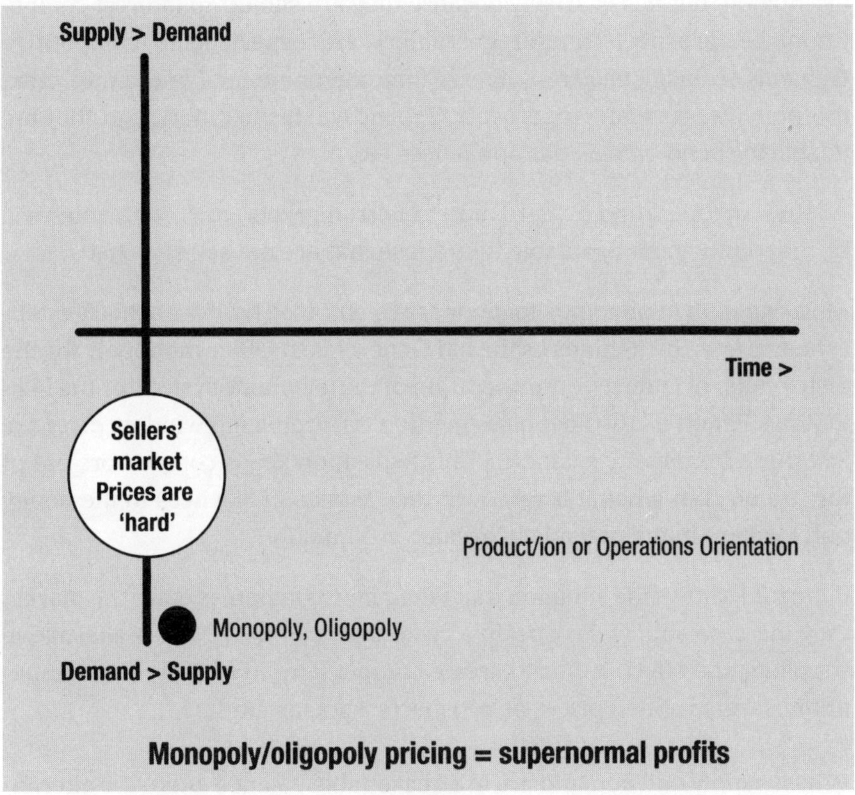

FIGURE 2.6: LAW OF SUPPLY AND DEMAND, PART 1

Figure 2.6 shows this situation. Below the horizontal central axis, markets are under supplied, they are therefore sellers markets and there is no pressure on prices.

Such companies are said to operate in 'hard markets', that is to say prices are hardened, because customers can do very little by way of getting a price concession.

What small amount of marketing may be exercised by oligopolies or monopolies is usually aimed at increasing traffic, particularly at slack times so as to increase the utilization of capacity.

An example of this would be a 'Telecoms Operator' promoting very cheap (late evening or very early morning) calls to friends and relations in Australia. The call traffic so generated will use exchange capacity that would otherwise be lying idle at that time of day in the UK.

Occasionally some oligopoly/monopoly companies may adopt a marketing orientation, but this is usually because they are subject to indirect competition, i.e. prospects and/or customers are experiencing competitive demands on their limited resources of time and/or money. For example, what the *'potential'* customer (*or prospect*[i]) spends on his/her mortgage, they are unable to spend on new gas appliances etc.

As they are operating in 'hard' and 'sellers' markets, such companies will be inherently more profitable than those that are not so privileged.

Most oligopoly/monopoly situations are re-enforced by, if not actually established, in law. Such things as the old General Post Office monopoly for the distribution of letters, or the operation of the telephone system, or the Pilkington's Patent on the float glass method for producing window glass are just three from many examples. This legislation keeps competitors out of the 'frame', but when it is removed they swarm in like bees to the honey pot, to share in the potentially greater profitability.

Figure 2.7 shows the situation that when new companies enter the market they increase supply. Prospective customers can now canvas alternative suppliers, the effect is thus to create competition. Eventually this competition starts to soften prices as prospects 'shop around'.

Whilst supply and demand are in a reasonable balance, there are alternatives to competing on price, the most popular of which is for the company to 'promote' its wares more effectively than the competition.

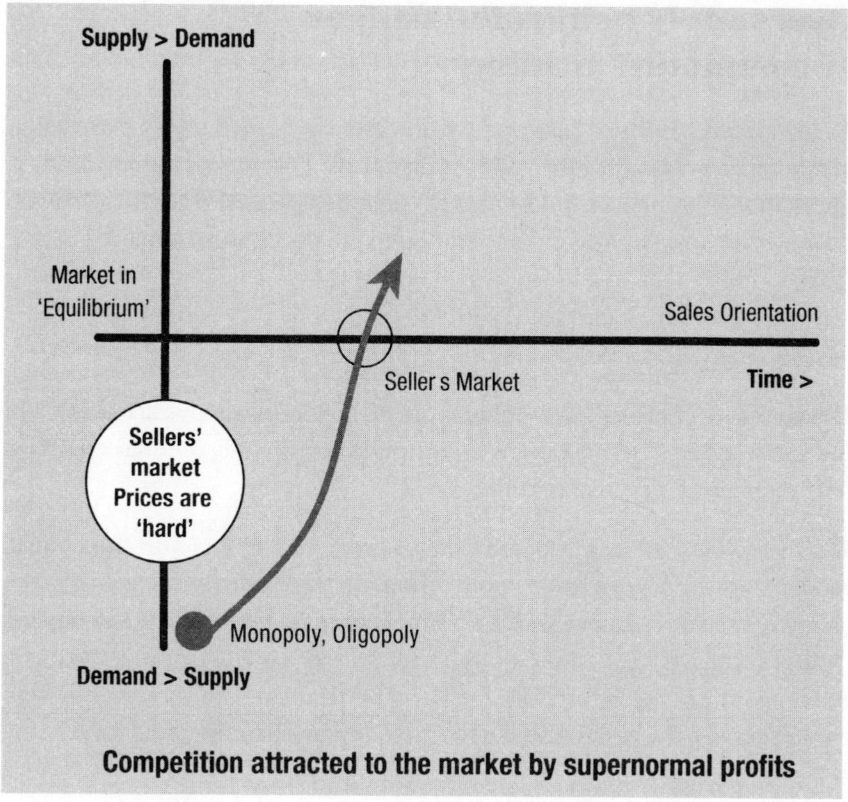

FIGURE 2.7: LAW OF SUPPLY AND DEMAND, PART 2

The main aim for such promotion (*i.e. advertising, PR etc.*) at this stage in the game is to persuade the prospect or customer to buy from the promoter in preference to anyone else. When this is the case, we refer to the company as being **'sales oriented'**.

The job of promotion is to move the customer along the buying processes toward the promoter, rather than the competition.

An example is the proposition from the 'Lever Corporation' in last century, that 'Cleanliness is next to Godliness'. This persuaded the working class chapel-goers of the North West of England to wash a little more often, especially on Sundays. As a result, a tremendous amount of Sunlight soap was sold. However, anyone could have claimed as much, and indeed the sales of soap so stimulated were not confined to 'Sunlight', but increased the whole market.

Oversupply brings the danger of commodity trading

As illustrated in Figure 2.8, because markets are essentially an expression of human behaviour, like the various 'Gold Rush' episodes of the last century, the numbers of people (*and through them businesses*) drawn to a given commercial opportunity are not limited to the purchasing capacity of that market. Almost always more supply enters the newly identified opportunity than the market can bear, with the result that very soon the market is oversupplied with a vengeance and customers are spoilt for choice.

This excess of choice allows the customer to become an active arbiter within the marketplace. The customer shops around and directly or indirectly plays one supplier off against another.

Thus suppliers will need to compete in order to survive, and the natural tendency is for severe price competition to take place (*because it is quick and easy to so do*) as more and more suppliers chase fewer and fewer buyers. Unless suppliers take a hold on the situation, price will become the focus of competition, the buyers are out for a better deal, and they will tend to try to simplify the task of buying so as to obtain the best price for:

- **a given** (common?) **specification, and**
- **a given** (common?) **availability.**

Specification and availability are made common in order for the buyer to be able to compare like with like.

This is a so called 'buyers market', in which prices are said to be 'soft' because, with comparative ease, the buyer drives down price with little if any regard for the suppliers' welfare.

These conditions are known as COMMODITY TRADING. Unless companies adopt deliberate positive strategies to counteract these natural forces, all markets will tend to go in this direction.

The consequences of this are shown in Figures 2.8 and 2.9. **The weakest companies will collapse as downward pressure on prices erodes profit margins.** This is one of the basic business cycles, it is as old as commerce and was noted by Adam Smith in his *Wealth of Nations*. The periodicity of the cycle depends upon the individual characteristics of the industry in question.

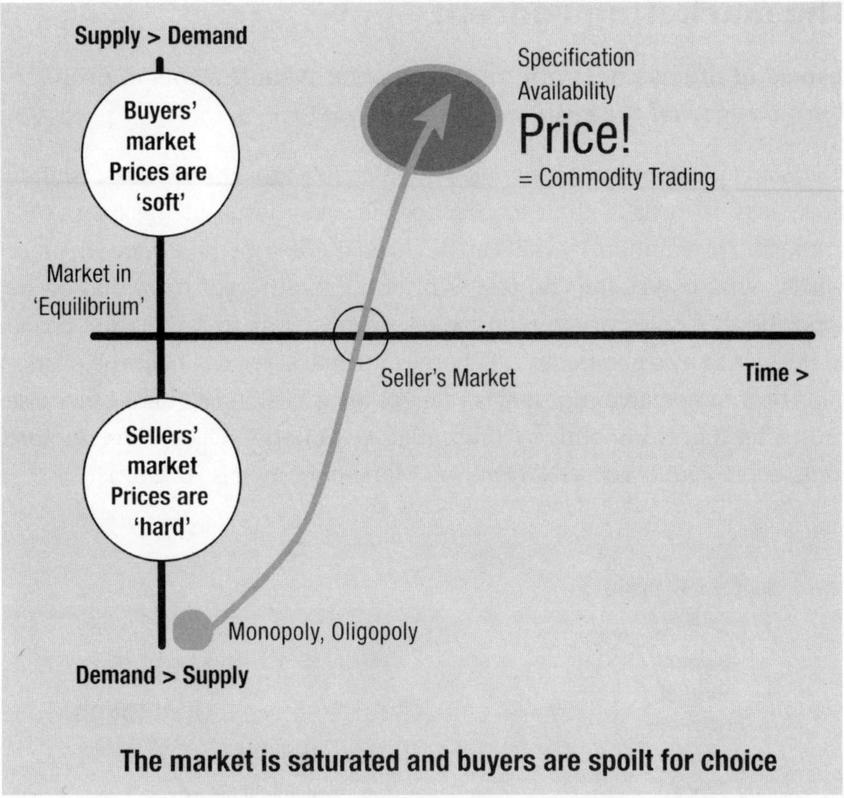

FIGURE 2.8: LAW OF SUPPLY AND DEMAND, PART 3

Surviving oversupply

There are basically only two ways to survive 'commodity trading':

The first and most favoured is 'aglomeration', which is where companies come together, usually by acquisition, so that existing fat and/or muscle is used to obtain more fat and muscle. So that the acquiring company ends up with more power and endurance than the competition. This process creates so called conglomerates. Some of the world's major commercial empires are thus formed. The second stratagem, and the only one open to the smaller company when entering 'soft markets', is to focus the business on the needs of the customer, by asking:

> ***"What do our (potential) customers want, and are willing to pay for at a price that allows us to supply at a profit?"***

This is commonly known as a MARKETING ORIENTATION.

The marketing concept

Instead of the business offering the market what it wants to produce, it produces what the customer wants to buy!

This is an apparently simple concept, which like most good ideas, is often more easy to preach than to practice. The key issue at the heart of a 'marketing orientation' is what can be called the 'competitive edge', in other words, what makes the company's offering so different from that of the opposition? A sales orientation makes propositions to the market based on the company's perspective. Whereas the marketer will base the proposition on a competitive edge that is valuable to the customer. This is otherwise known as the 'Competitive Differential Advantage' (CDA). (*For a more complete introduction see 'Mastering Marketing' by this Author.*)

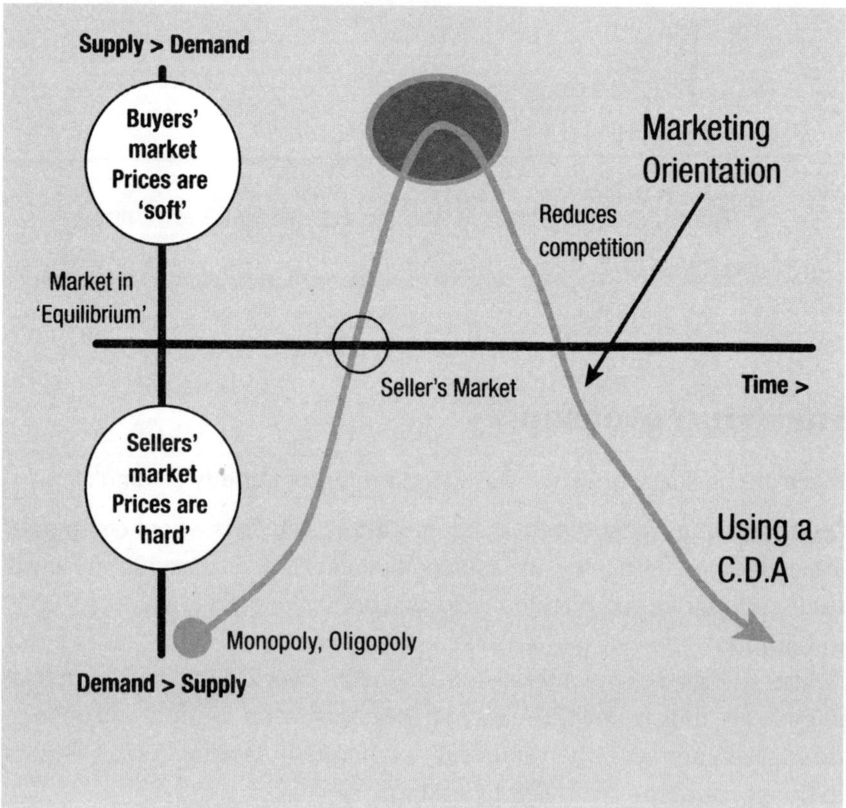

FIGURE 2.9: LAW OF SUPPLY AND DEMAND, PART 4

This approach involves tailoring the offering to the needs of the prospective customer. It is primarily aimed at defending price by creating a differential which is not only attractive to the customer, but also inhibits the potential customer's ability to compare like with like when shopping around. It works well when the prospect believes that the value of the perceived differential is worth the extra price and/or effort in order to acquire what is on offer.

The critical issue for marketing orientation is to know what the prospect/customer wants, and what price they are willing to pay for it.

The three questions below must be addressed, they are NOT mutually exclusive:

- "How do we produce/operate more efficiently?"
- "How do we persuade people to buy from us?"
- "What do people want, that they are willing to pay for?"

In order to be successful, the marketer will see these central questions as being critically interdependent, in that no matter how good the competitive differential, if customers are not made aware of:

- its existence,
- how and where it can be obtained, and
- for how much money (*raising this awareness being in the realm of sales activity*)

they will not be able to buy, and no matter how good the sales, if the costs of production and /or operation are not under control, the company can, and often will, bleed to death.

So far this argument has established that, for optimum pricing, a company should adopt the business orientation appropriate for the stage of the 'supply and demand' cycle pertaining at that time.

If 'supply and demand' were the only consideration, companies without the necessary muscle to dominate their market should be flexible enough to stay in step with, though perhaps slightly ahead of, their market's supply and demand cycle. However, there are forces in addition to supply and demand which ensure that nowadays, most companies have little option other than to adopt a marketing orientation.

Introducing the product life cycle [PLC]

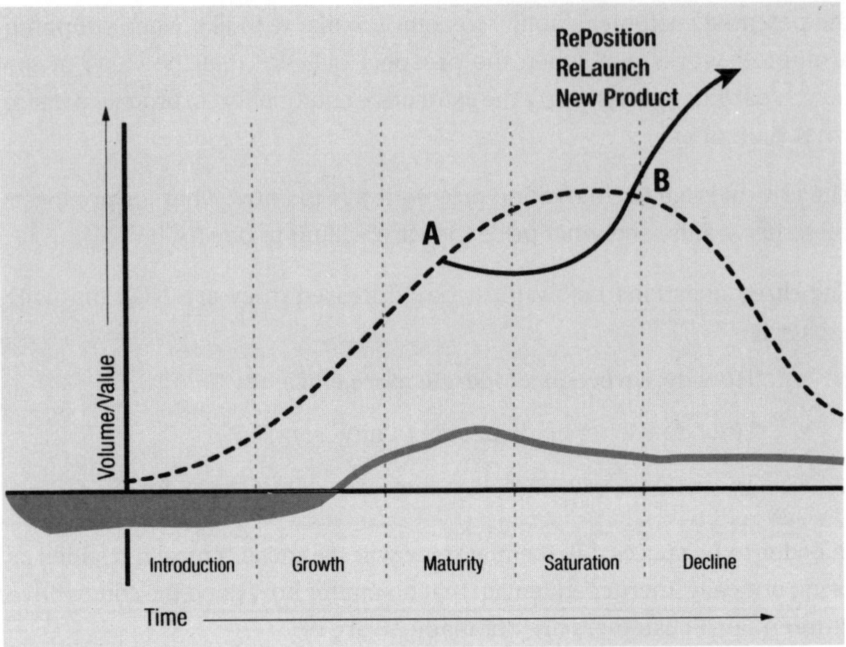

FIGURE 2.10: A STYLIZED 'PLC'

The product life cycle (PLC) is a very useful framework for thinking about the development of a company's products in its markets. We will examine the basics of the concept and the implications of the PLC on which pricing strategies are open in relation to where the product is in its life cycle.

The PLC stages

There are said to be some six distinct stages of a product life cycle. The reader will see each stage named, in chronological order in Figure 2.12.

What is happening during each stage and what are the price implications during it?

First we have to understand what type of innovation is in progress – is it:

- 'Continuous?'
- 'Discontinuous?'
- 'Dynamic discontinuous?'

To illustrate:

Continuous innovation (CI) is where the product is updated, often regularly (e.g. automobiles), more often than not in terms of style and colour rather than substance. It's the same product, often under the same generic name (e.g. the various 'Marques' of the Volkswagen Golf). It is more to do with shape, style and fashion and essentially does not change the way the product is used.

'Discontinuous' innovation (DI) is where the product has been changed in a way that improves the 'objective benefits' which may in turn mean that the product is used differently as a result (sometimes trivially – sometimes profoundly) so that, say, in the case of the Volkswagen Golf, the introduction of a 'turbo-diesel' engine enables more miles per gallon with no loss of performance compared with that of a petrol engine. This could result in either cost savings in the regular family use of the car, or even (additionally) the vehicle being used on motor rallies.

Dynamic discontinuous innovation (DDI) is where the new product causes a change in people's fundamental behaviour – two illustrations will suffice:

The 'Contraceptive Pill' resulted in not only more convenient families in terms of the number and timing of the children conceived, whilst at the same time freeing women to have careers of a character and timing of their own choosing.

The Jet Aero Engine applied to long-haul civil aviation, made tropical and/or winter sports vacations affordable for almost everyone in the developed world.

Gestation (Figure 2.10)

This stage is the period between 'conception' and 'launch', during which the 'new product' is being developed and its business future is being planned. At this stage it is all investment so we see that the revenue line is below the horizontal axis. This condition applies well into the next stage (*introduction*) and often into the third stage (*growth*). New products require a lot of support and it is by no means certain that they will be successful. On average some 15 new ideas have to be launched in an industry before one of them is successful.

Introduction

At this stage the company is concerned to get customers to buy the product for the first time as it is by no means certain that the product will have a market. The issues to address are:

- What sort of new product is it: is it just a re-vamp (*i.e. this year's model*), a new and/or better way of delivering benefits for which there is an already established market (*i.e. a one button, pre-set number dialling facility on a telephone handset*), **or**
- Is it something so radical that it will alter customer's purchase and/or consumption behaviour (*e.g. colour printers, e-mail, out-of-town shopping areas, chartered jets for holidays in the guaranteed sun*),

and depending on the above...

- Who are the 'innovator' customers and the 'early adopters', and how can the company clearly identify them (*see the Technology Adoption Curve following*).

Pricing considerations for 'Gestation and Introduction'

Here the focus is on the type of innovation contemplated. Pricing these types of totally new products, i.e. **DI**'s and/or **DDI**'s (*particularly the latter*) will need careful consideration. At this stage of the PLC, it is vital to have a good assessment of how and how much the 'intended target group' of customers value the innovation. And perhaps price above that value (*"Any fool can lower a price, it takes real skill to put it back up again" Anon.*). A suitable pricing strategy is known as 'skimming' – which we will examine a little later.

At 'Introduction' **CI** type products will probably need a 'penetration' pricing strategy to get that essential initial foothold in the market, which is another way of saying a low price to start with – but then how does the business intend to get the price back afterwards?

Growth

At this stage the potential of the product starts to be exhibited. More and more new customers are drawn to the product and sales volumes start to rise dramatically. Word starts to spread amongst customers and competitors alike. If the new product is of the CI type, by the latter part of this stage competitors start to realize that it is taking some of their business, and if they don't react it could well take all of it. Others, not in the market, are also noticing the success and are forming the intention to enter what is now a proven marketplace so that they too can enjoy this new source of profit.

Pricing during 'growth'

By definition, this market should be a monopoly or at least an oligopoly. SO – It usually doesn't matter what category of innovation the business is dealing with. At this stage the customer is choosing to buy or not to buy and the pricing manager (*product manager*), rather than mess around with the pricing point established at introduction, will be best advised to spend their time and budget on research designed to track the take-up of the product. And also on 'non-price' promotional activity such as advertising and sales offers etc.

Maturity

Several things typify this stage:

- At the beginning of the stage, repeat customers become a significant part of the market, at the end they are the main type of customer in the market
- Customers are getting to know enough about the product to specify exactly what they want
- The rate of entry of new competitors to the market reaches its peak, and so does the intensity of competition. This creates a downward pressure on margins. Even if there is no price war – which can break-out
- The pressure of having to compete will force extra expenditure to be made on promotion of one sort or another
- Discerning people in this market can, if they bother to look, often espy the seeds of what will eventually supplant their product, e.g. the railways and Henry Ford and/or the Wright Brothers; IBM and Apple etc. This is the point in time (*point 'A' in Figure 2.12*) at which plans for re-positioning the product, or launching a new one, should start to be laid. It is dangerous (*as IBM found*) to ignore these thunder clouds on the horizon, or to wait until they start to have an effect on the business (*point 'B' in Figure 2.12*) before taking action. (**NB.** *The chief reason IBM was able to survive was its size and the depth of its purse.*)

PRICING DURING 'MATURITY'

A characteristic of this stage of the PLC is that direct competition starts to emerge, it is a threat, but it is also a compliment. The more professional and wiser competitors will be aiming at the same price point as the innovator has established. After all, why give away margin – they will compete on features (*more benefits, different benefits, easier to use etc.*). However, don't count on it, there are not too many of these sorts of competitor about. In our experience the majority of firms will be seduced by the ease and speed with which they can attract the customers via using a lower price.

In this phase, the real danger for the innovator is that, by this time, they may not have recouped their original investment (*i.e. all the costs during gestation and promotion etc. during the introduction and growth phases*).

Saturation

Nearly every customer here is a repeat customer. The main source of new customers is maturation, i.e. those that move into the market by virtue of where they are on some family or business life cycle (*e.g. prams and pushchairs are acquired for mothers or mothers to be, usually not before; computer servers and intranet systems are acquired by companies that have reached a certain size, before this they offer few benefits worth the cost etc.*). During 'saturation' competition is at its most intense, there is only one way to grow for any player in this market, and that is to take business from their competition.

PRICING DURING 'SATURATION'

At this stage, any extra business must be obtained at the expense of the competition. As we will discuss in Chapter 7 on Price Wars, if by this stage the market is 'structured'[ii] (*sometimes referred to as orderly*) the chance of a price war breaking-out is minimal – all in the market have a lot to lose, and few if any have anything to gain by it. However, an 'unstructured market', i.e. where the average firm, at best, has a relatively small share of that market, is still a hunting ground which offers growth potential for the aggressive firm. To avoid price erosion, the best defence is a strong fortress which comes in the form of a well constructed market segment.

Decline

A product's 'life cycle decline' is caused by its market disappearing. New products now better satisfy the former customers' needs. Or the needs:

- no longer apply (*e.g. tin baths and 'buggy whips': people have hot water systems and few drive horse-drawn buggies etc.*) or
- are now being satisfied via a product that, in some way, is more attractive to customers (*e.g. with the exception of Holland, cars have largely replaced bicycles as a means of getting to and from work in western Europe. A car keeps you dry when it rains, warm when its cold, and is less tiring. Thus it allows you to reach a place of work many more miles from where you live, or to live many miles from where you have to work*).

Pricing in 'decline'

Some life cycles are long (*e.g. generic steel*) others short (*e.g. pop music, female fashion etc.*). One thing they have in common is that at the decline stage, customers are deserting this market because they have found a more attractive way to satisfy the needs which were previously satisfied by the products in the old life cycle.

Structured market or not, price competition can get very intense here – many businesses, still in products of the old life cycle, will believe that a lower price can yet turn the market around. Wiser heads start to leave for pastures new, some to totally new markets – others (*traditionally very few*[iii]) to take-up the new technology that is replacing the old. For many firms, particularly the larger ones, the advice is to either get with the new or get out all together.

For the smaller firms, however, there could be gold at the end of this rainbow. As we will see in the 'Technology Adoption Curve' (*at the end of this chapter*) many customers take a much longer time, than most, to leave the old market. The costs and trouble of switching to the new may not be seen as worth it. Newer technologies may pose real and psychological barriers – so they stay on as long as they can. Other suppliers may even take up the old products for either nostalgic or collector's reasons (*see the 'Classic Connection' who have 'cornered the market' in tyres for vintage and classic motor vehicles*). However, as more of the previous suppliers leave, the shrinking proportion of suppliers remaining to customers may often return the market to an oligopoly, where prices can be 'hard' again.

Strategic focus and the product life cycle

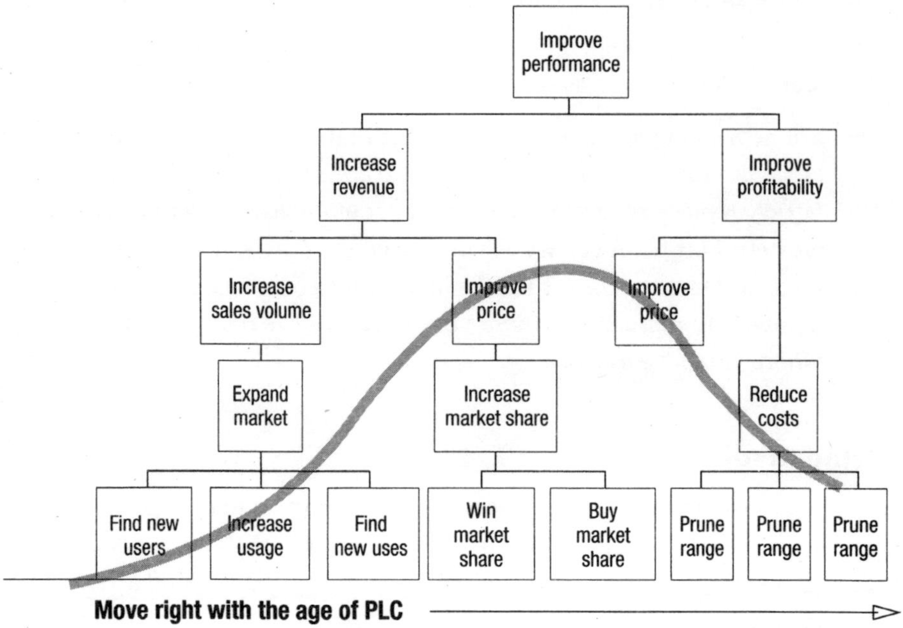

FIGURE 2.11: STRATEGIC FOCUS – MANAGING THE PRODUCT/S

Taking the organogram in Figure 2.11, but now with the product life cycle superimposed as in Figure 2.13, we can see that 'expanding the market' is a suitable emphasis for the early stages of a product life cycle. During the following growth and maturity phases (*where competition gets quite intense*), the business emphasis moves towards defending and/or increasing one's market share. This can be attained by either beating the competitor in the marketplace, e.g. the launch of 'Orange' in the British market, or, if that's too expensive, then it might be worth considering buying the competition.

This last option is perhaps more suitable for the saturation stage of the life cycle when there might be companies available for sale because they are more geared up to exploit growth, than to manage themselves in a steady state market, and are thus vulnerable.

At the saturation and decline stage the emphasis of the company must be to reduce costs to the absolute minimum. The market is not going to go anywhere and the emphasis therefore is to milk as much profit as can be obtained from static and eventually declining sales.

Figure 2.11, the cost reduction exercises normally fall into four basic areas – the reduction of:

- inventory carrying costs
- production costs which accompany the reduction in the size of the range
- fixed costs and
- variable costs.

Extensive attention is frequently paid to the reduction of fixed costs. In many cases that means reducing the size of the workforce, which is perhaps the largest single fixed cost a company may have. It may also involve getting rid of production facilities and deciding to 'outsource' during this particular stage of the life cycle. Out-sourcing is a very potent way, if employed wisely, of making dramatic reductions in the cost of facilities. It is also interesting to note that outsourcing can also have the effect of reducing the amount of capital employed, i.e. the fourth area of improving financial performance as mentioned on page 33.

Lastly the reduction of variable costs should be addressed, assiduously. Actions to do this will range from:

- re-engineering the product, (so that it can be produced more cheaply), and/or bringing great pressure to bear on suppliers (so that they reduce their prices to the company), to –
- rationalizing the company's logistics so that the costs of transportation are reduced to the minimum.

Possible pricing policies/strategies to consider

For the SME that is really innovative (*i.e. aims to launch new products as a major part of their business model*), two particular pricing policies/strategies are worth considering:

- **'Skimming'**
- **'Barrier'**

Price skimming

What this illustrates is a launch at a (*very*) high price, which comes down in a controlled manner, a little during the latter stages of the 'Introduction', most during the latter stages of the 'Growth' phase with some 'trimming' during the early parts of the 'Maturity' phase of the life cycle. Note also the point at which the product enters profitability.

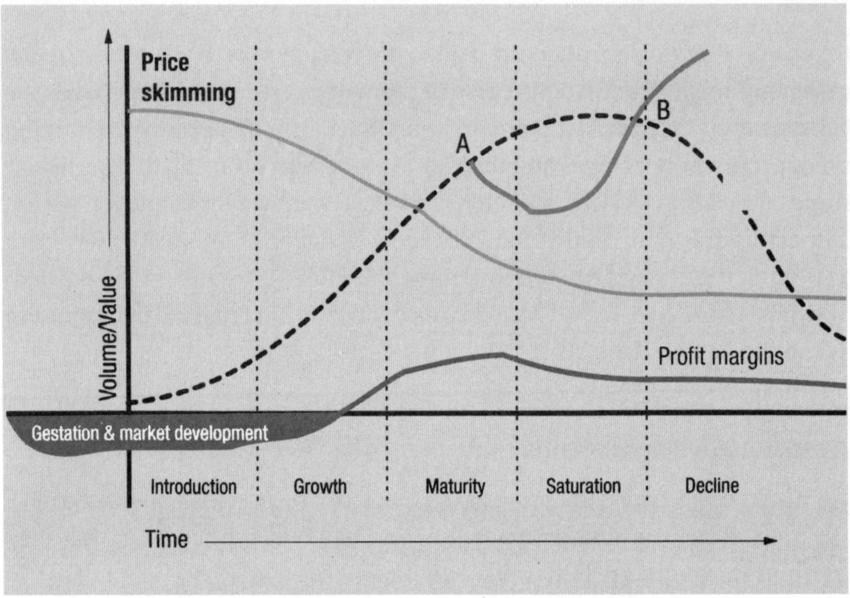

FIGURE 2.12: PRICE SKIMMING

This strategy is the reserve of those firms who aim regularly to launch new products as a central theme of their business model.

It aims to do several things in the early stages of the life cycle to:

- Recoup the costs of research and development well before the competition enters (*after which the ability to do so will be severely constrained*);
- Establish a good understanding of the new products:
  - real target market
  - elasticity of demand and
  - optimum the price point, and thereby –

- Determine the size and character of the resources of production and distribution required for the full roll-out of the product.

A good example of this was Sony's launch of the walkman. Akito Morita, the founder of Sony, did not know what the best 'price point' should be, what the probable take-up or market size could be. So he launched the product at a high price to constrain demand, and with very limited production facilities thus reducing risk by not investing in a full-blown factory until he knew they had a winner. By then, bringing the price down in small stages, he was able to evaluate the best price point, re. volume and profitability.

The downside of this was that the very high price and initial take-up of the walkman lured the competition to the market Sony had created – long before Sony had the capacity to meet the volume being demanded. Nonetheless Sony made a lot of money, and the product became a 'generic', i.e. no matter who made it, the customer knew this type of product as a 'walkman'.

Barrier pricing

This strategy is intended to keep the competition out of the innovator's (*new*) market. It does so by pricing very low from the start – thus making the market unattractive to potential new entrants.

There are not the short-term margins to warrant making the necessary investment in technology, or plant. The intention is that the profit foregone by the business in the early days, will be recouped by having the market to themselves for a long time to come, if not eternity. If this strategy can be re-enforced with copyright and/or patents so much the better. Consider Figure 2.13:

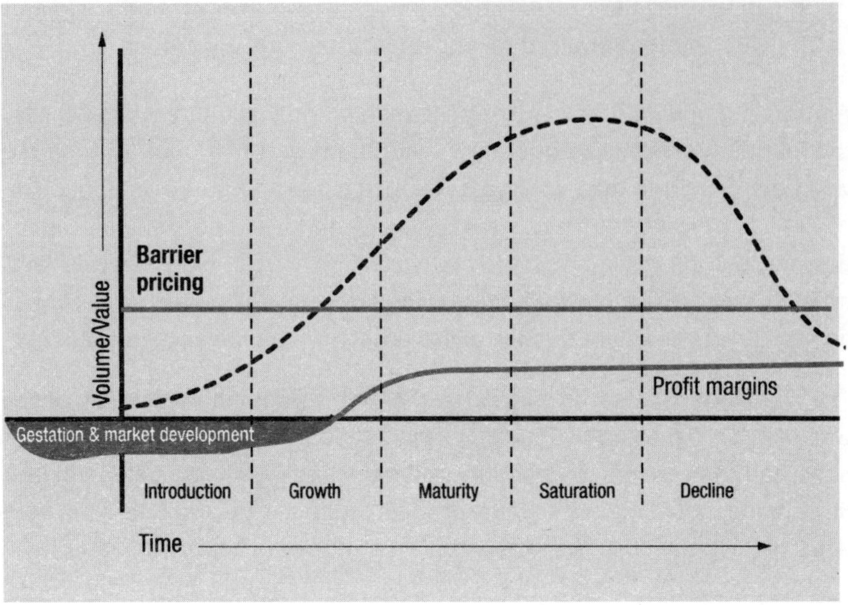

FIGURE 2.13: PRICE SKIMMING

Note the lateness of recouping the R&D (etc.) but also note that the profit margins after this are also long-term – by this time the capital costs of machinery, plant etc are all paid for.

To employ this strategy it is vital that the decision-makers in the firm have dominant control of the business over the long-term. Capital, in the form of stocks and shares, is too mobile nowadays and such investors are too often looking for short-term results, thus this strategy is not often enacted by the normal large-scale operation. It is a ploy best suited to firms that are family firms so to speak. That is to say a few people who are in the game for the long-term and own the majority of the equity.

A good example of this pricing strategy being employed is Pilkington, the world's dominant producer of fenestration glass (*i.e. that which goes into windows*). They were the inventor and[iv] the main innovators of what is known as the 'float glass production method'. This is the process where, to produce glass for (*say*) windows and the like, molten glass is drawn over a bed of molten tin, gradually cooling as it goes. The firm makes much profit from licensing this technology to firms in other countries. These firms and the original innovator all sell their fenestration glass at barrier prices, and, although margins on fenestration glass are slim, because of the volumes that come from being a sole supplier, they also make much money.

Now and then, when specialist glass, such as armoured glass for banks, armoured cars, fighter cockpits etc. products are required, because they are the only firms with the technology and the plant to produce to these requirements, they again have the monopoly. Thus this 'specialist glass' is not cheap to buy, and although demand may be sporadic, it is a very profitable business for those few who can make it.

Price and the technology adoption curve (TAC)

The TAC is a subset of the PLC which we have just examined.

Formerly, and academically known as the diffusion of innovation curve, it is a child of many studies conducted in the early part of the last century, which aimed to understand how new farming methods and new crops were taken-up in a fundamentally conservative community. The TAC curve deals with just the 'rising' part of the product life cycle, i.e. the curve from 'introduction', through 'growth' and 'maturity' to 'saturation'.

The TAC curve was popularized in the early 1990's by Geoffrey A. Moore in his first book *Crossing the Chasm* (Harper Business, 1991). Here he showed that the behaviour of business people adopting the huge waves of innovations in IT (*which were so novel as to cause what some people referred to as 'Technology Shock'*), closely modelled that of farming communities when it came to dealing with a perceived risky innovation. Geoffrey, via his second book *Inside the Tornado* (Harper Business, 1994), added to the understanding of this type of behaviour by showing that, when adopting risky innovations, there was an obstacle, a disconnect, between those in the market who were driving the innovation, and those who were responsible for making money out of it (*often by the innovation reducing internal costs*). This 'disconnect' was termed the 'chasm' (*i.e. a canyon to cross*).

The implications for pricing mainly arise from the best way to cross this chasm and how best to price the product at the other side – when the vendor has to deal with a very turbulent and chaotic marketplace, which is likened by Geoffrey to being inside a 'tornado'.

Briefly, if the rate at which people are adopting the i nnovation is plotted against time, the curve created very closely resemble: a so-called 'normal distribution' like so:

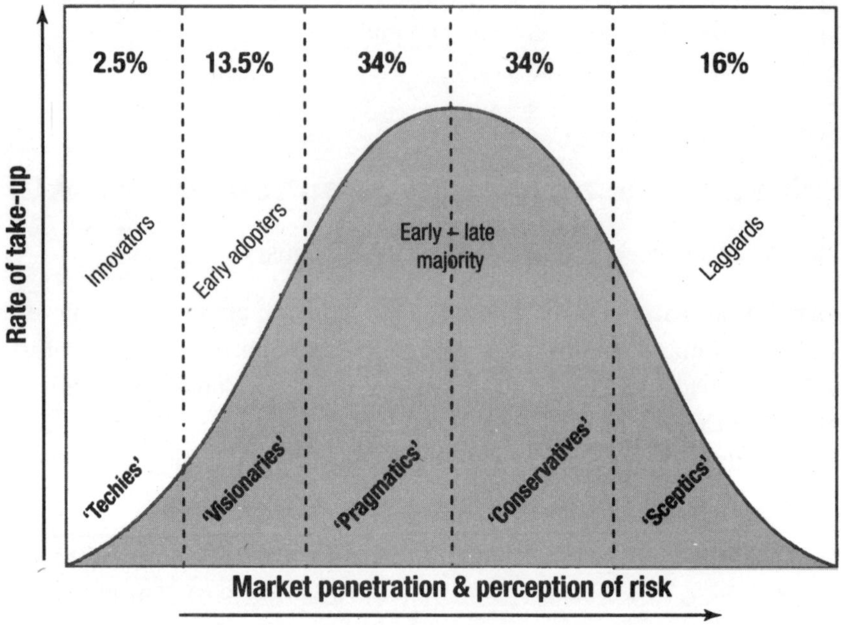

FIGURE 2.14: THE TECHNOLOGY ADOPTION CURVE

A very useful insight by Geoffrey was to propose that the buyers psychology, re. risk tollerance, was different at different stages of the 'take-up' process, and he accordingly relabelled the types of people so involved. This way innovators became techies, and early adopters became visionaries. These 'visionaries' are the Bill Gates, Steve Jobs and Steve Wosniak's of this world. They can bring all the technical innovations together and can have a vision of how this can shape the future. The Early and Late Majorities, Pragmatics and Conservatives are more risk aware, it is their job to earn money via these innovations – not fritter it away. Thus they must deal with the contemplated change so as to manage the risks responsibly.

Laggards, aka Sceptics, really don't want to know the new technology, they are technophobes. They will use it only when events and progress force them to.

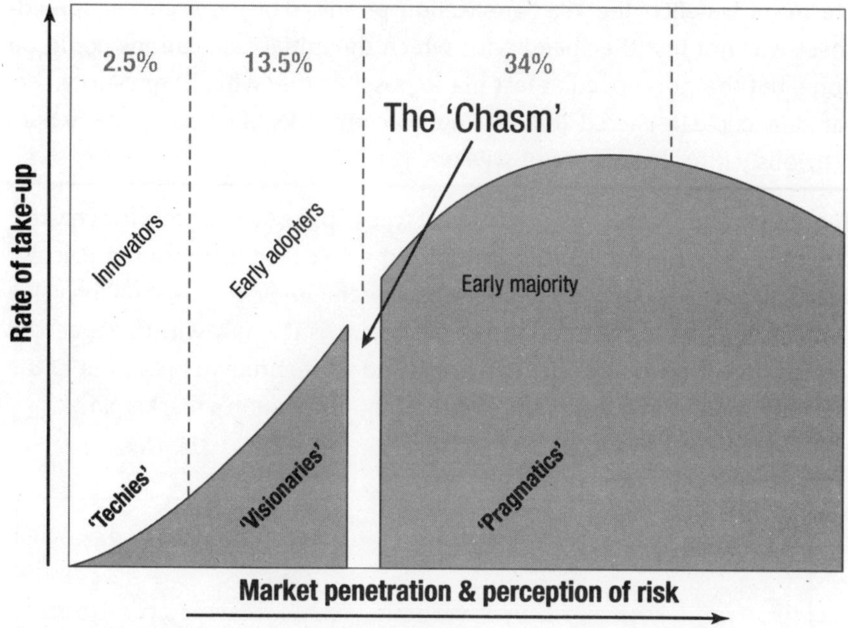

FIGURE 2.15: THE CHASM THE INNOVATION MUST CROSS – OR FAIL

The chasm is the main barrier to an innovation accessing the volume market. This is said to be caused by the differences of perspective mentioned above, and also by the perceived rates of failure that the Pragmatics believe to be the case. Buyers have a responsibility to their employer to resist expensive and risky change, for changes sake.

From the research that Geoffrey did for his first book, those technologies, which had succeeded in getting across the chasm, had done this via an 'intense, marketing led, sales invasion'. For which he used the simile of the Normandy landings. The main issue is that the technology has to promise a so called 'killer application' and the process must be focused on this and not diluted or distracted by other targets of opportunity at this stage.

A good example of this 'killer application' ('killer app.')concept is the way that the 'Apple Two' (*then known as a 'micro computer' and a hobbyist's machine*) became a business tool via the addition of VisiCalc the world's first electronic spreadsheet. The visionaries were not the two Steve's of Apple, they were the 'techies' in this case. The visionaries were two college professors Dan Bricklin and Bob Frankstone (*visit their website, it's fascinating – www.bricklin.com/visicalc.htm*).

The major benefit of the 'killer application' promised by the electronic spreadsheet was not just the speed with which the initial calculations could be done, but that this speed at last made possible the 'what if' questions, i.e. variables could be altered and resultant outcomes identified in minutes, where previously it took days, if not weeks.

The pricing issue that arises is 'with what type of price do you cross the chasm?' The naive see this challenge as requiring a so called 'penetration pricing' strategy, whereas experience shows that a premium price, based on the value of the 'killer app' to the intended target group, is the only way to get across the chasm with enough pricing margin and momentum to break-out of the 'beachhead' and invest the hinterland of the innovation's marketplace.

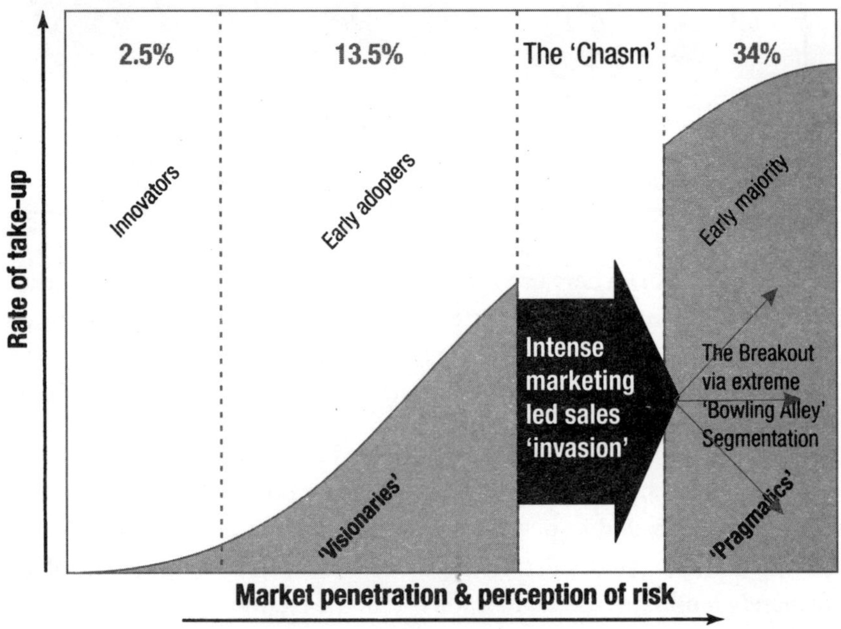

FIGURE 2.16: 'CROSSING THE CHASM' AND THE SUBSEQUENT 'BREAK-OUT'

A value based pricing strategy is vital for this type of situation. Not only are there all the costs of development to re-coup, as in the skimming strategy like the Sony Walkman case mentioned earlier, but additionally, using value based pricing the vendor's business will be coming from the 'high-ground' when it commences the 'break-out' into the potentially very profitable green fields of the market hinterland.

Geoffrey's research cited within *Inside the Tornado* clearly shows that this 'break-out' is best accomplished by quickly developing additional applications for the technology. During the break-out the Apple +VisiCalc now also becomes a database tool for one stream of prospects; then Apple + WordStar + Database becomes a word processor and direct mailing tool for another distinct stream, and so on.

Another way of looking at this issue and its implications for pricing is that in all probability the new product will be a 'Dynamic Discontinuous Innovation' and the value to the customer will be out of all proportion to the costs of production (*don't factor in R&D, here it's an unrelated consideration*). If for no other reason but this last, then the business MUST set prices high. Over time the price will be eroded (*look at the cost of PC's today compared to when they were innovated back in the late 1980's*) but by then developments will most probably enable lower costs of production to lead to still acceptable margins.

[*Another interesting and useful source of light on the issue of when and how a 'sea change' takes place in human behaviour, is offered by Malcolm Gladwell's book 'The Tipping Point', Little, Brown and Company, 2000*]

Exercise 2.1 commentary

Have you done a search of the web? At the time of writing an internet search of the main speakers bureaux will give you a figure for a daily rate of between $3,500 for an expert but non professional speaker, to in excess of $40,000 for the expert celebrity (such as Tom Peters). The average for the first of these categories is from $4,000 to greater that $8,000 (*mainly for the lower end of the celebrity spectrum*).

Do you know who else has been invited to speak, and at what fee?

IF the price you were contemplating for this exercise falls outside this range, and/or what other speakers are charging – ask why. You are either being too cheap or too expensive.

If too cheap – your customer could consider that you are either desperate or very inexperienced.

If too expensive – your customer may consider that they have inadvertently contacted a professional speaker outside their intended range.

IF YOUR CONTEMPLATED FEE WAS IN THE FIRST LOWER PRICE CATEGORY: You may not get the job, or if you do, imagine how you would feel if, at the pre-conference speaker's dinner the night prior, you discovered in casual conversation that you were the cheapest speaker there and that others were charging some three or four times your fee.

IF YOUR CONTEMPLATED FEE WAS IN THE LATTER UPPER PRICE CATEGORY: You risk not getting the job, and thus missing a tremendous networking opportunity. You will also miss the prestige that comes from putting such an occasion on your résumé.

You must do your research:

> **If you don't know the market, the market price and what you are up against, you will either:**
>
> - Not get the business
> - Or – Get screwed if you do!
>
> Either way you will damage your long-term standing in the market-place...
>
> *(after John Winkler, 'Pricing for Results')*

Exercise 2.3

Take your main products (*goods or services*) and plot where they are on:

- The supply and demand cycle,
- Their product life cycle

Say what action you will take in the light of the findings you make. And if early on in the PLC:

- Are they CI's, DCI's or DDI's – why do you say this?

If they have yet to 'cross the chasm':

- What will your 'killer app' be?

If you have already crossed:

- What would you do differently next time, re price and the activities that support price?

The Price Elasticity of Demand

All the above assumes that price and volume have a 'straight line' relationship – but that may not be the case in your market. Consider the following, say your firm sold x-ray film and the basis of pricing in the healthcare industry was by the square metre or sub-section thereof.

Exercise 2.4

Say that:

- The variable cost was $4.00 per square metre ('sqm').
- Your fixed costs were $1,000.00 for weekly volumes up to and including 1,500 sqm.
- For all subsequent volumes fixed cost rose to $2,000.00.

Using the price to volume relationship shown on the table overleaf calculate:

- The net profit at each price point
- Which price produces the most contribution
- The optimum price

And when this is done, venture an opinion as to:

- What is happening?
- What are the possible lessons we can draw from this?
- What factors could lead to the price being set higher or lower than the calculated optimum price?

Please don't read ahead at this point.

THE X-RAY FILM BUSINESS

Price Per Unit	Forecast Sales	Sales Revenue	Variable Costs	Fixed Costs	Net Profit
$12	517				
$11	600				
$10	740				
$9	910				
$8	1,120				
$7	1,410				
$6	1,800				
$5	2,500				

The issue is that different products and different markets respond to prices in different ways. Some markets are 'elastic' others are not. In fact there are recognized to be some four different types of 'price elasticity' as shown below:

Price Elasticity's of Demand

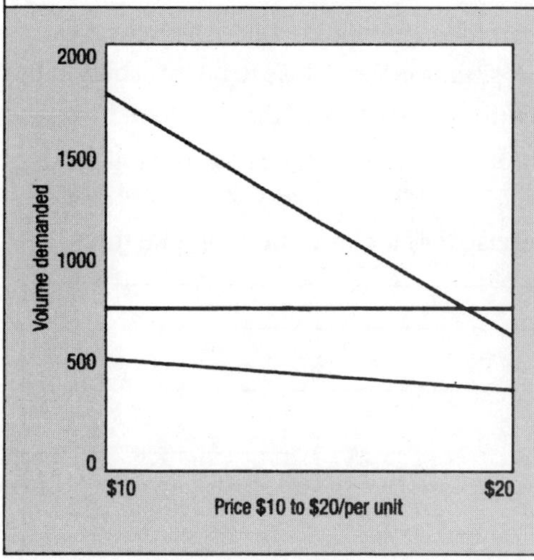

Price $10 to $20	Quantity in Units	Revenue Change
Elastic	1,800	18,000
	600	12,000
Unit	1,000	10,000
Elasticity	500	10,000
Inelastic	500	5000
	400	8000
Zero	750	7,500
Elasticity	750	15,000

FIGURE 2.17

These price changes are shown as straight lines, but they rarely are. Price elasticity will change over a wide range of prices – at some point it may be inelastic, at other times elastic, and all points in between. That is why we refer to the phenomena as an 'elasticity curve'.

In the above graphic, consider the change in volume demanded when the price changes from $20 to $10, or vice versa.

In the first case this increase in price results in a dramatic drop to one third of the previous volume – the market for this product is **'elastic'**. On the other hand, if the product was originally at $20 and the price dropped to $10 volume would increase to three times the size and the revenue would increase by 50%.

In the second case we have 'unit elasticity'. The price doubles and the volume halves, the net effect on revenue is zero.

In the third case the market is said to be inelastic. Some 20% of the business drops away if the price doubles, and the price change produces an increase in revenue of 60%. Only a few of these customers appear to have any alternative to the product – this models public transport in many big cities, frequently only those who have no alternative use it, all those who have an alternative (motor car, bicycle, walking, distance working etc) have already left.

Finally we have zero elasticity. Even this dramatic doubling of price produces no change in volume demanded. A situation very close to heating bills in the frigid northern winters, or air-conditioning costs in the developed tropical areas of the world such as Singapore, Texas, Florida, UAE, Kuwait etc.

The curve for the x-ray film (Exercise 2.4) looks something like this:

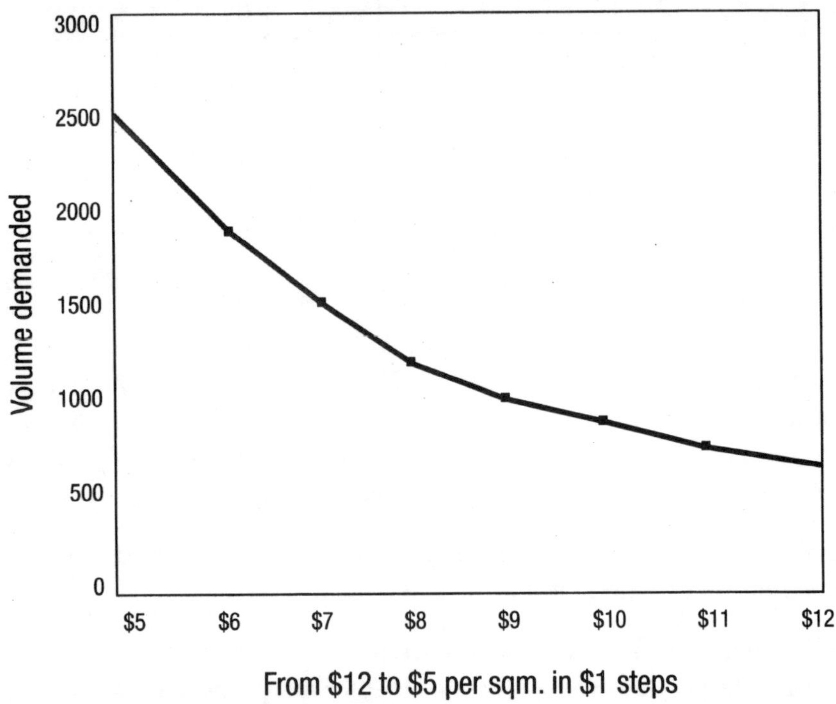

FIGURE 2.18

Discovering price elasticity's is either from keeping good records and now being able to conduct an historical regression on this data – as we will discuss a little later, or via so called test marketing or via market research – employing conjoint analysis – a technique we discuss later in Chapter 5, Value Based Pricing.

Moves within the 'demand curve'

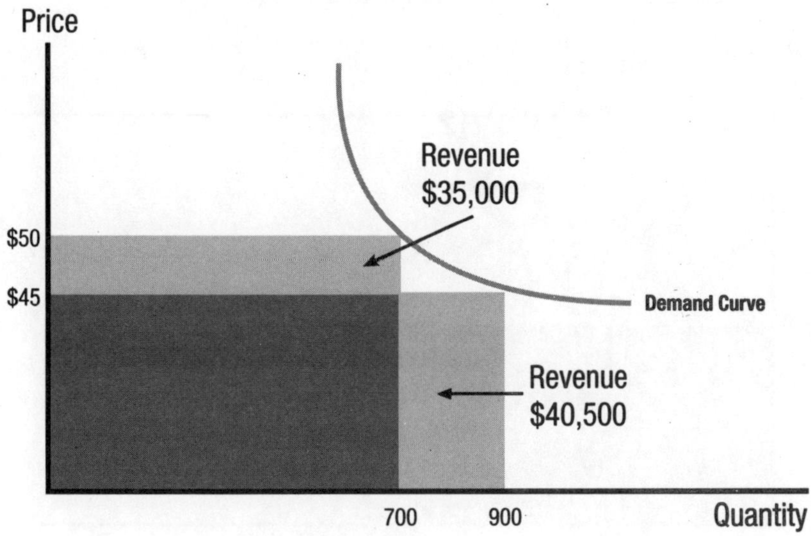

FIGURE 2.19

The situation here is that by dropping the price by some $5.00 we can increase our revenue by $5,500.00. However, this may be only half the story. The questions we must address when evaluating this option, and before we make the decision on price, are:

- How does this extra volume effect the cost of production? For example the x-ray film exercise above, here we saw a step-change in the overhead at 1,500 sqm. per period This was probably caused by having to take on an extra shift to meet the volumes in excess of that figure. If this is the case more volume does not equate to more profit.
- The business must also consider the effects on the product's position in the market – in many cases there is evidence to show that customers use price as the most frequent indicator of a products' quality (see Pricing Tactics in Chapter 6). This lower price could also provoke a price war which is the last thing any sane business wants. One way or the other it could be detrimental to our market share.

What if the demand curve can be shifted?

We could have a situation similar to the following:

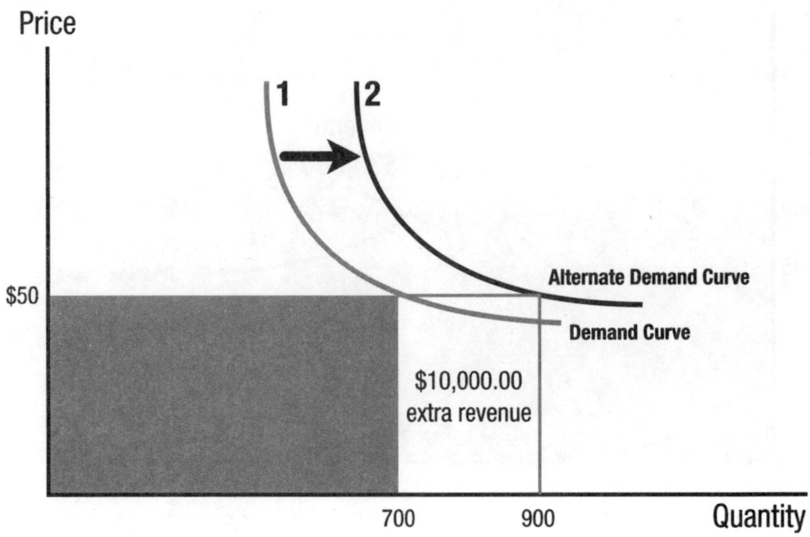

FIGURE 2.20: SHIFT IN THE DEMAND CURVE

Figure 2.20 shows the effect of other changes when all things are not equal. Things that can shift the demand curve fall into two categories:

1. MOVES WITHIN THE CONTROL OF A COMPANY

- Advertising
- Non-price promotion
- Product improvement
- Distribution

2. MOVES BEYOND THE CONTROL OF A COMPANY

- The 'economy'
- Changes in customer perception of the product or service
- Competitive changes either by the competition itself or because of legislation
- Business cycle (ref Chapter 1) and where we are in this process
- Demographics, etc.

The Figure 2.21 clearly shows the phenomena when markets are in short supply, i.e. they are hard sellers markets. The possible downside could be that the costs of production, (*supplies and/or labour etc*) could also be increasing. In that case, we too have to move our prices higher and forego the chance to make more money and grow market share through higher volumes.

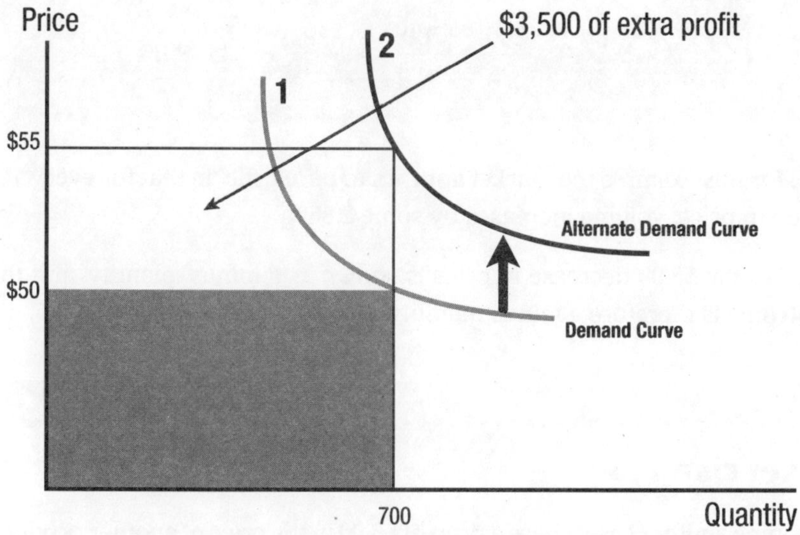

FIGURE 2.21: SHIFTS IN THE DEMAND CURVE

So what could move the demand curve upward as shown in Figure 2.21? This can be accounted for via either:

- Deliberate moves on the firm's behalf such as adding extra value and / or
- Moves in the overall marketplace resulting in shortage of this commodity. For example, the rise in the prices of commodities that occurred in the early years of the 21st century when China's industry sucked in huge quantities of oil, copper, etc.

$$E = \frac{\Delta Q/Q}{\Delta P/P} \text{ i.e.}$$

% Change in Quantity demanded divided by the original Quantity

All divided by

% Change in the Price Charged divided by the original Price

FIGURE 2.22: THE FORMULA FOR PRICE ELASTICITY

EXAMPLE

So calculating the price elasticity for a situation where a drop in price of \$5.00 for a product normally sold for \$50, produces an increase in volume of 200, where normally 700 were sold at the original price.

$$\text{ANS} = \frac{200 \div 700}{-5 \div 50} = \frac{28.6\%}{-10\%} = -2.86$$

So, for this example the market appears to be 'elastic' in that for every 1% drop in price, volume increases by some 2.86%.

NOTE: the \$5.00 decrease in price is shown as a minus quantity, and the outcome is therefore a minus quantity.

Exercise 2.5

Imagine another case where a drop of \$5.00 in the price of another product, again normally sold for \$50, this time produces an increase in sales of say 300, where normally some 700 are sold at the original price – what then is the elasticity of price? (Answer in Appendix 1.)

Be aware that historical data may be incomplete; things could have been going on in those markets, which were not recorded, such as competitor stock shortages or rumours thereof. Consequently, most experienced people involved in pricing decisions have strong reservations about any elasticity of price that may be greater than '4'.

References

i A 'PROSPECT' is a member of the population toward whom the 'business' is targeting its sales efforts, but who has yet not purchased.

ii A market is said to be 'structured' if 80% or more of the business in that market is done by 20% or less of the firms in it. An 'unstructured' market is obviously the reverse.

iii Where are the firms that used to make slide rules, none of them are in PC's; Where are the railroad firms in an age of cheap flights? We only know of one that made the transition 'Canadian Airlines' born from the loins of the 'Canadian Pacific Railroad'.

iv Today the Pilkington's global empire is fast being acquired by Japanese business. How far they will be able to consolidate this acquisition strategy aimed at the worldwide market for fenestration glass before they are accused of becoming a monopoly is anyone's guess.

HOW OTHERS PRICE

HOW OTHERS PRICE

Synopsis

In this chapter we will examine the main body of practice in relation to pricing today. Most current pricing is based on the oldest methods known to commercial man, i.e. 'cost plus'. In many cases such practice may be appropriate – however in the vast majority of situations it must be remembered that, *"The customer is not the least concerned about the vendor's costs – what customers want is their specification fulfilled at a competitive price*[i]*"*.

This chapter looks at the various appendages to this methodology, some good, some contentious and some the cause of much unnecessary internal conflict within the firms employing them.

On the way we will examine the issue of the 'elasticity of demand' and the calculations necessary to foresee the impact of this issue on volume and financial outcomes.

The chapter will conclude with an examination of the principles of 'activity based costing' now available to the majority of businesses via software such as SAP.

The current situation?

Consider the following illustrations which show the results of a major but informal study carried out at a European business school in the mid 90's, and cited by Richard Collier in his product management courses and publications:

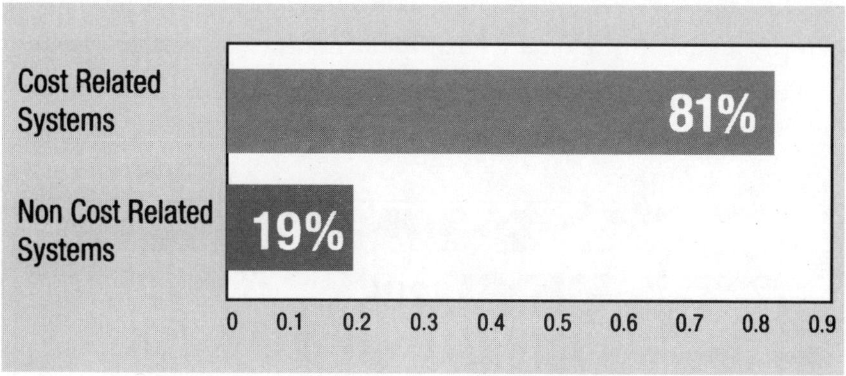

FIGURE 3.1: THE INITIAL BREAKDOWN RE COST BASED VS. NON-COST BASED SYSTEMS

Unfortunately we don't have a breakdown as to how this was distributed between the sizes of firms. Smaller firms, say from the 'corner store' to the smaller 'builder' etc are well advised to keep this as a sound basis for deciding their prices (***note****: we say basis for deciding, not* ***the*** *basis for setting the final price they will charge*).

When the 81% who were using cost as their main basis for setting price, were asked how frequently they subsequently amended their decision, the breakdown was as follows:

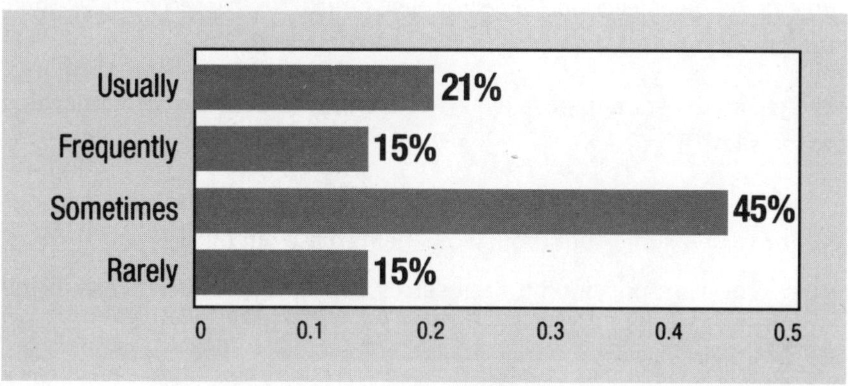

FIGURE 3.2: THE EXTENT TO WHICH COST RELATED PRICING SYSTEMS ARE LATER MODIFIED

When the data is extrapolated we find that some 48.6% of the firms in the survey based their prices on their cost and, more or less, ignored the market.

Whilst it is wise for the medium to large enterprises to keep their costs constantly under surveillance and control, cost based systems are definitely not the best way for setting price in highly competitive markets.

What about the 19% in Figure 3.1 who did not use cost related systems? The breakdown as to how they approached the process of setting their prices was as follows:

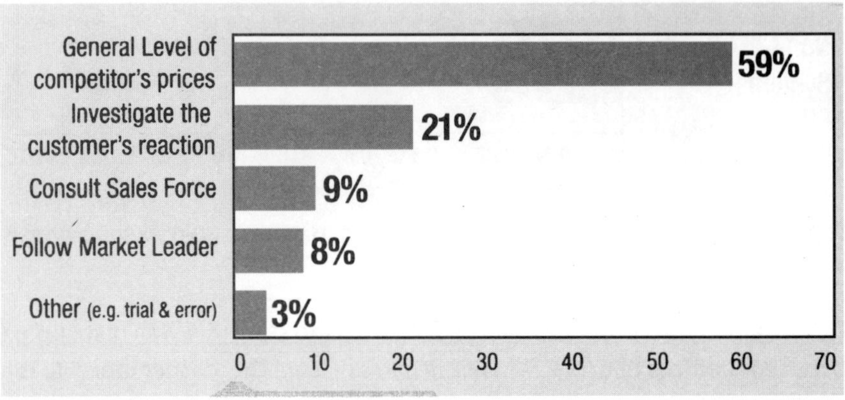

FIGURE 3.3: THE 'NON-COST RELATED SYSTEMS' USED BY THE REMAINDER (19%)

The largest proportion here is the 59% of those not using cost as a basis for setting price (*i.e. just over 11% of the total sample interviewed*). These people are running with the herd! No skill there. At first glance it seems a smart thing to do BUT if most of their competition do the same thing (*we know it will be at least one in ten if these figures are representative*), their market will rapidly be commoditized (*see Chapter 2*).

The second question to pose is, 'What are they to do if the profit margins are too slim?'

At least those firms that said they set prices by following the market leader (8%) are using some cunning. Two benefits arise out of this:

1. They are positioning themselves and their products close to the market leader, maybe even at the top end of their market – no bad thing to do.
2. They will be more profitable than most in their market, always assuming that their costs are fairly similar to the rest of the field.

Those firms that consult the sales force as a way of setting price walk a really thin tight-rope. Although the sales team are often the closest people in the firm to the customer, it must never be forgotten that they are influenced by the easy option. It is frequently easier to sell something at a lower price. Buyers continually bring pressure on the sales team to lower their prices (*see below*) and in many cases, if not most, sales performance is measured and incentivized, by the volumes achieved (*or some equivalent*) not by the profit obtained. So any manager investigating the suitability of their price via consulting their sales force must take whatever they say with a large pinch of salt before they can be sure that they have something useful with which to act.

The really smart thing to do is to follow the 21% (*c.4% of the total responding*) who say they investigate their customer's reaction to price. As we will see when we discuss Value-Based Pricing (Chapter 5), this is no easy task. In Business to Business (B2B) markets for example, ask the buyer what price they are willing to pay, and by-and-large they will quote the lowest in the market if not lower. It is their job to do so – they would be atypical buyers if they did anything else.

In B2B and in B2C (*i.e. Business to Consumer*) markets we must get behind the buyer, and be able to influence the Decision Making Unit's (DMU – *see 'Mastering Marketing'*) for whom that buyer is sourcing. To do so we will need to know how best to use the tools of qualitative research, the value/price grid, the Levitt construct, a spidergram and conjoint analysis and even then there is still no certainty that we will set the 'right' price.

How does cost plus work?

This discipline is sometimes known as 'mark-up' and that phrase aptly describes how this ancient[ii] way of setting prices works. It is summarized as follows:

- **Find the full cost of the good or service[iii]**
- **Agree a profit ratio**
- **Multiply a) by b) = profit**
- **Add c) to a) = price**

So simple it has worked for some 4,000 years or more, so why not now?

The answer is quite clearly a combination of three things. Mainly that from 4,000 years ago until quite recently:

- Most businesses' product line portfolio was fairly simplistic.
- In the great part, until the flowering of the Industrial Revolution's enhanced production capacity, the world was to a great extent characterized by hard markets in that the supply of most goods fell well short of demand.
- Since the Great Britain Exhibition of 1851 on the one hand, and end of the American Civil War on the other, there has been a tremendous growth in the number of businesses that are very big, complex and possessed of large and multifarious product ranges. These types of business are, by and large, fairly run of the mill firms today. On top of that we have the mega-businesses, the global players such as Dell, HP, IBM, General Motors etc.

That is to say, it ain't so simple nowadays. Compound all the above with the birth of modern accountancy practice and cost plus can be a nightmare.

The main issue in large organizations is identifying the real cost of anything that they produce or deliver (*good and/or service*).

Consider the following situation:

Assume a company produces two products 'H' and 'L'. Both of these are produced on the same equipment, and both use the same processes. The products differ by the volumes in which they are sold, and therefore the volumes in which they are produced. Product 'H' is the high volume product and product 'L' is the low volume item. Details of product inputs and outputs and the costs of activities involved are as follows:

	Machine hours Per unit	Direct Labour hours Per unit	Annual Output units	Total Machine hours	Total Direct Labour hours	No. of purchase orders	No. of 'set-ups'
Product 'L'	2	4	1,000	2,000	4,000	80	40
Product 'H'	2	4	10,000	20,000	40,000	160	60
				22,000	44,000	240	100

The cost of these activities is as follows:

	$
Volume related	110,000
Purchase related	120,000
Set-up related	210,000
Total =	**440,000**

A traditional volume based costing system would handle it this way:

Cost centre allocated costs	$440,000
Overhead rate per machine hour	$20 ($440,000/22,000 hrs)
Overhead rate per direct labour hour	$10 ($440,000/44,000 hrs)
Therefore, Cost per unit of 'L' =	$40 (2 machines hrs @$20 or 4 DLH's)
Therefore, Cost per unit of 'H'=	$40 (at $10 per hour)
Thus total cost allocated to product 'L' =	$40,000 (1000 X $40)
And total cost allocated to product 'H'=	$400,000 (10,000 X $40)

(after *Management and Cost Accounting* by Colin Drury.)

Is this the reality?

What about the situation as cited in the following discussion?

Have a look at it and see what you think is the reality – answer in Appendix 1.

Exercise 3.1 'What price peanuts?'[iv]

This is the story of Joe, a restaurateur who added a rack of peanuts to his counter to make some extra profit. He was visited by his accountant and this is the conversation that followed:

Accnt. Joe, you said you put in these peanuts because some people ask for them, but do you realize what this rack of peanuts is costing you?

Joe *It ain't gonna cost. 'Sgonna be a profit. Sure I hadda pay 25 dollars for a fancy rack to holda bags, but the peanuts cost 6 cents a bag and I sell 'em for 10 cents. Figger I sell 50 bags a week to start. It'll take 13 weeks to cover the cost of the rack. After that I gotta clear profit of 4 cents a bag. The more I sell the more I make.*

Accnt. Joe, that is an antiquated and completely unrealistic approach. Fortunately, modern accounting procedures permit a more accurate picture which reveals the complexities involved.

Joe *Huh?*

Accnt. To be precise, those peanuts must be integrated into your entire operation and be allocated their appropriate share of business overhead. They must share a proportionate part of your expenditures for rent, heat, light, equipment depreciation, decorating, salaries for your waitresses and cook.

Joe *The cook? What'sa he gotta do wit'a peanuts? He don' even know I go' 'em.*

Accnt. Look, Joe. The cook is in the kitchen, the kitchen prepares the food, the food is what brings people in here, and the people ask to buy peanuts. That's why you must charge a portion of the cook's wages, as well as part of your own salary, to peanut sales. This sheet contains a carefully calculated cost analysis which indicates the peanut operation should pay exactly one thousand two hundred and seventy-eight dollars per year toward general overhead costs.

Joe *The peanuts? 1, 278 dollars a year for overhead? The nuts?*

Accnt. It's really a little more than that. You also spend money each week to have the windows washed, to have the place swept out in the mornings and keep soap in the washroom, that raises the total to one thousand three hundred and thirteen dollars per year.

Joe (thoughtfully) *But the peanut salesman said I'd make money. Put 'em on the end of the counter he said. And get 4 cents a bag profit!*

Accnt. (sniff) He's not an accountant. Do you actually know what the portion of the counter occupied by the peanut rack is worth to you?

Joe *Ain't worth nothing – no stool there – just a dead spot at the end.*

Accnt. The modern cost picture permits no dead spot. Your counter contains 60 square feet and your counter business grosses fifteen thousand dollars a year. Consequently, the square foot of space occupied by the peanut rack is worth two-fifty dollars a year. Since you have taken that area away from general counter use, you must charge the value of the space to the occupant.

Joe *You mean I gotta add 250 dollars a year more to the peanuts?*

Accnt. Right. That raises their share of the general operating costs to a grand total of one thousand five hundred and sixty-three dollars per year. Now then. If you sell 50 bags of peanuts per week, these allocated costs will amount to 60 cents per bag.

Joe *WHAT!!*

Accnt. Obviously, to that must be added your purchase price of 6 cents per bag, which brings the total to 66 cents. So you see, by selling peanuts at 10 cents per bag you are losing 56 cents on every sale.

Joe *Something's crazy!*

Accnt. Not at all! Here are the figures. They prove your peanut operation cannot stand on its own feet.

Joe (brightening) *Suppose I sell lotsa peanuts – thousand bags a week 'stead of fifty?*

Accnt. (tolerantly) Joe, you don't understand the problem. If the volume of peanut sales increases, your operating cost will go up. You'll have to handle more bags, with more time, more depreciation, more everything. The basic principle of accounting is firm on the subject: "The Bigger the Operation the More General Overhead Costs that Must be Allocated." No, increasing the sales won't help.

Joe *Okay. You so smart, you tell me what I gotta do.*

Accnt. (condescendingly) Well – you could first reduce operating expenses.

Joe *How?*

Accnt. Move to a building with a cheaper rent. Cut salaries. Wash the windows bi-weekly. Have the floor swept only on Thursday. Remove the soap from the washrooms. Decrease the square foot value of your counter. For example, if you can cut your expenses by 50%, that will reduce the amount allocated to peanuts from one thousand five hundred and sixty-three dollars down to seven hundred and eighty-one dollars fifty per year, reducing the cost to 36 cents per bag.

Joe (slowly) *That's better?*

Accnt. Much, much better. However, even then you would lose 26 cents per bag if you charge only 10 cents. Therefore, you must also raise your selling price. If you want a net profit of 4 cents per bag, you would have to charge 40 cents.

Joe (flabbergasted) *You mean even after I cut operating costs 50%, I still gotta charge 40 cents for a 10 cent bag of peanuts? Nobody's that nuts about nuts! Who'd buy 'em?*

Accnt. Joe, that is a secondary consideration. The point is, at 40 cents you'd be selling at a price based upon a true and proper evaluation of your then reduced cost.

Joe (eagerly) *Look, I gotta better idea. Why don't I just throw the nuts out – put 'em in the trash can?*

Accnt. Can you afford it?

Joe *Sure. All I got is about 50 bags of peanuts – cost about three bucks – so I lose 25 dollars on the rack, but I'm outta this nuts business, and no more grief.*

Accnt. (shaking head) Joe, it isn't quite that simple. You are in the peanut business! The minute you throw those peanuts out you are adding one thousand five hundred and sixty-three dollars of annual overhead to the rest of your operation. Joe, be realistic, can you afford to do that?

Joe (completely crushed) *It'sa unbelievable! Last week I was a-make-a money. Now I'm in-a trouble. Just because I think peanuts on a counter is gonna bring me some extra profit. Just because I believe fifty bags of peanuts a week isa easy.*

Accnt. (with raised eyebrow) That is the object of modern cost studies, Joe. To dispel these false illusions.

So, what do you think? See Appendix 1, Exercise 3.1 for the discussion.

Simply put, the methods of spreading the firm's fixed costs', i.e. their overheads, are legion, complex and open to much argument. Therein lies the problem.

First lets see that different ways of allocating overhead will produce different outcomes. Do the following exercise – again the answers will be found in Appendix 1.

Exercise 3.2 'What is the cost?'

The typical formulae for 'recovering' overheads and profit include the following factors:

1. Percentage on direct labour (i.e. O as a % of L)
2. Rate per labour hour
3. Rate per unit produced (i.e. O ÷ 20K units)
4. Percentage on 'prime cost' (i.e. direct materials, plus direct labour and other direct expenses)
5. Rate per machine hour
6. Separate rates applied to various elements of the costs (e.g. materials, machine hours etc.)

The resultant cost will be quite different according to the formula used! For example, take the following situation:

An Outline Budget $000	Supporting Data	
Materials (M) $60	Planned labour hours	50,000
Labour (L) $40	Planned machine hours	40,000
Overheads (O) $84	Planned output (units)	20,000
Total $184	Labour Rate per hour	$2.40

	Product A	Product B
Materials =	$3.00	$3.00
Labour =	1 hour	½ hour
Labour Cost =	$2.40	$1.20

So, calculate what will be the full costs for each of the above formulae.

i.e. formulae 1 to 5 (inclusive).

Is there a 'right one'?, If so, why do you believe this to be the case?

	Product A	Product B
Using Formula 1 or 2		
First what is the rate (R) = ________%		
Per labour hour		
Materials	$3.00	$3.00
Labour	$2.40	$1.20
R x Labour =	____	____
Therefore Full Cost =	____	____
Using Formula 3 (O/H per unit)		
Now what is R? as $________		
Materials	$3.00	$3.00
Labour	$2.40	$1.20
$ R =	____	____
Therefore Full Cost =	____	____
Using Formula 4 (% of 'Prime' cost)		
(i.e. [M+L] +O = R%)		
Prime Cost	$5.40	$4.20
x R =	____	____
Therefore Full Cost =	____	____
Using Formula 5 (rate per machine hour = O + ? = $R)		
Labour	$5.40	$4.20
R x 1½ hrs =	____	2¼hrs ____
Therefore Full Cost =	____	____

So, not only is this approach capable of producing a wide range of results, all of which are capable of being contentious but, in addition, the method that is adopted is, more often than not, the result of whichever department is in the political ascendant at the time. The managers and/or the directors in that part of the firm will be most happy with a method that puts their part of the business into a favourable light. This will create more freedom to manage without the 'Board' breathing down their necks, better access to internal investment, bonuses, more attractive careers etc.

But it can be disastrous for the firm in the medium to long-term. Do the following exercise to illustrate the danger – before we have a look at a real life example where such shenanigans brought a mega company to its knees and nearly destroyed it.

Exercise 3.3 'Spreading the unspreadable'

Materials	90	30	150	270
Labour	10	130	100	240
Other Direct Costs	20	40	150	210
Totals (prime) =	120	200	400	720
Contribution therefore =	50	120	270	440
Central overheads #				360
Thus Profit/Loss =				80

To keep it simple there are three products in this firm's range, A, B and C. So far they are making a nice profit of some £80,000.00 per period (say quarterly).

Say that a new CEO has taken over the running of the business and has called on his management team to propose how the overhead of £360,000.00 should be allocated. This has brought rivalry to the fore with one team (case i.) who have come from a traditional manufacturing background proposing that overhead should be attributed according to the cost of the labour being consumed by that product. Whilst another set, who have a marketing background say that because labour is no longer a 'variable cost,' overhead is best attributed according to the prime cost of production (case ii.).

So who is right? what would be the outcomes for each method? when you have done the arithmetic turn to Appendix 1, Exercise 3.3.

The central issue is that as long as the firm is profitable, and all products in the range are either making a healthy contribution directly, OR are supporting those parts of the business that are, overhead attribution IF it is necessary, should be done with great care.

In the late 1980's and early 1990's a major global corporation (let's call them 'HAL' inc.) worked itself into a position to make the largest loss in the then annals of corporate history (well over $32bn). One of the factors that brought this about was the way internal accounting systems favoured the old technology over the new.

The people at the top of the business in the late 1980's had come up through the Old Technology, and (*being followers of Machiavelli*) looked after their old constituencies by ensuring that the way costs were attributed, always put those 'alma mater' departments into a good light. To do this they shovelled unfair levels of overhead onto the 'up-and-coming' new technologies. The net result was that their retail prices for the new technology were very uncompetitive like for like. For some years, they were able to get away with these higher prices because of their well-known and respected HAL brand. However, over time hard-hitting competitors such as 'Bell' arose with superb new business models that reduced costs dramatically. These savings were passed on to the market via very competitive prices. At the same time customers became very technology literate and realized that although HAL's brand was good, the extent to which it was superior did not justify the price premium being asked.

After a dramatic decline in volume and market share, the top people in HAL looked at the margins (*after overhead attribution)* they would have to accept if they were to match the competition. As a result they decided that HAL should get out of the new technology (*which they had effectively pioneered only a short while before*) and leave it to the likes of Bell etc.

A later study within HAL, when it was too late to reverse the decision to quit the market, found that a very good portion (*c.80% the author has been given to believe)* of the components that Bell used, were in fact sourced from HAL. They also concluded that the main reason HAL could not compete with a reasonable price against Bell was purely the size of the overhead attributed to the new technology side of the business.

So if we re-visit the principles of cost-plus pricing:

a **Find the full cost of the good or service**[v]

b **Agree a profit ratio**

c **Multiply a) by b) = profit**

d **Add c) to a) = price**

We find that, even in a moderately-sized business, that using traditional methods (*we will be taking a brief look at activity based costing later in this chapter*) it is extraordinarily difficult to actually know with any reliability what is the true cost of any product ('good' or 'service'). And the larger the business, the more the difficulties compound.

But what about item **b) agree a profit ratio?** The main methods employed here are based on issues such as:

- **Tradition**
- **Industry norm**
- **Target profit per annum**

Take 'tradition'. Some crafts, such as tailoring, up until quite recently used the 'yardstick' of 'The cost of the cloth times two'. In other words, they 'marked-up' by 100%, and achieved a 50% profit on the return (*i.e. the sale price*). Out of that had to come all overheads before any net profit could be made. Thus, traditionally, the tailor tried to sell to their client the most expensive suiting material they could.

The hardware retailer (*almost a vanished breed today*) did something very similar – in their case there was not so much intimate connection with producing the product, but turnover in hardware was traditionally slow – thus the profit retail margin had to fund that capital lying idle for so long. (*The business model of the ubiquitous out of town DIY store overcomes this aspect of the business with strong merchandising plus low stocks and 'just in time delivery', and thus a more rapid turn-over. This in turn results in much lower retail prices than the traditional hardware store could ever manage.)*

As to 'target profit per annum' a nice trick if you can do it, but the modern business is more often operating in 'soft' if not actually 'commodity' markets. Frequently the business is faced with the situation where it has to trade-off margin against the probability of losing the sale.

> **Remember:** ***'The customer is not the least bit interested in our costs, what they require, nay even demand, is obtaining the product they want, at what they perceive to be a 'competitive' price'.***

The pricing tools associated with cost-plus

However, even though the technique of cost-plus is one that the author does not recommend as the sole methodology for setting a price, there are some tools associated with this approach that should be in the repertoire of everyone in business.

The first of these is break-even analysis. At what point in the business will a given price recover all its (*assumed*) costs?

There are two approaches: one graphical – which is a great help in communicating the concept, but not to be used by the professional business today; the other, which is recommended, is numeric. Let's consider the graphic method first.

Calculating break-even

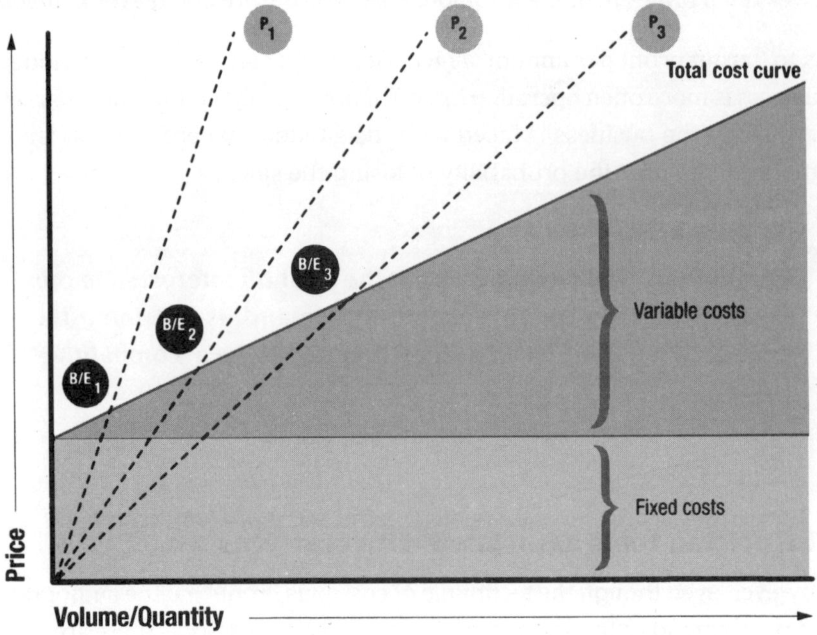

FIGURE 3.4: GRAPHIC BREAK-EVEN ANALYSIS

The vertical axis 'price' is set against the horizontal axis showing volume/ quantity. It is conventional to set the fixed costs on top of the horizontal axis, and the variable costs on top of the fixed costs as shown.

At this point, it is worth making an observation about the extent to which the graph reflects reality. In reality, there is no such thing as a truly fixed cost. Consider:

Say a given business, such as a manufacturer, is doing well. So much so that they have the option of either adding to their plant and machinery, and/or going into a second, or even a third shift. Or say they need to take on an extra sales person, with all the costs of that person's salary, car, pension plan etc. At the point of volume where either of those scenarios happen **the overhead costs go up a step**. Neither is the variable cost a straight line. Take the previous situation – as business improves, one would imagine that the firm would need to purchase extra supplies of whatever they require to serve their market. Larger volumes should attract (extra?) discounts, so, at that point on the volume axis, **the variable cost curve rises less steeply.**

As can be seen the 'total cost curve' is the sum of the overheads and the variable costs at any given volume.

FOR EACH PRICE, a sloping line 'Pn' can be drawn which describes the revenue generated at any price/volume relationship. Revenue is the product of price multiplied by volume. So these lines, P1, P2, etc. are usually called 'price/revenue' curves.

At the point where a given price/revenue curve intersects the total cost curve the business is said to break-even. Before that intersection the business has still not covered all of its costs, afterwards it has covered its costs and the revenue generated is (*almost pure*) profit.

Assuming for the moment that there is no price sensitivity (*i.e. the volume purchased is not constrained by the price asked – wouldn't that be great!*), then the higher the price, the sooner the firm will break-even.

Figure 3.4 is a useful way of visualizing the business situation, but as a management tool it is too crude to be of real use. The best way for any business to discover it's break-even is by calculation, i.e. a numerical means.

By definition, break-even is when all costs have been covered. From Figure 3.4 we see that revenue must cover more than the variable costs of the product. The amount remaining after the variable costs are covered is known as either 'gross profit' or 'contribution' (*i.e. a contribution toward paying-off the overhead/fixed costs*)[1]. Thus 'unit price' less 'unit variable costs' equals 'contribution margin'.

To express this as a formula let:

- 'VC' stand for (unit) direct variable costs
- 'FC' stand for total fixed costs (in a given period)
- 'P' stand for (unit) selling price
- 'BeQ' stand for break-even quantity
- 'BeR' stand for break-even (sales) revenue.

Thus:

$$BeQ = \frac{FC}{P - VC}$$

$$BeR = \left(\frac{FC}{P - VC}\right) \times P$$

So, calculating break-even is relatively simple[2]. However, the intelligent use of this calculation and everything else that comes from it, is an invaluable business tool. Take the following hypothetical situation, for example:

Exercise 3.4

Imagine that you are running a small one product business that every month, as regular as clockwork, sells 2,000 items at $60.00 each. Your fixed costs are $40,000 per month, and the variable costs per item equate to some $25.00 each.

Firstly, what would your monthly budget look like?

What would be your:

- Trading profit?
- Percentage return on sales?
- Break-even quantity (BeQ as above)?
- BeQ as a percentage of sales?

But before turning to Appendix 1 consider the following conundrum:

Say a fast talking, silver tongued marketing agency approached you with the following proposition:

They could offer to run a month's promotion for you, which, for a fixed fee of $20,000.00 would increase your sales by at least 700 items that month.

The question is – 'Is it worth doing this promotion?'

Now, in order to make your decision, do steps 1 to 4 again, factoring-in the promotion and then compare the two situations.

When you have completed this task, please refer to the Appendix for our analysis.

Back to methods of break-even analysis:

Another way of calculating break-even where there is a 'product-range' being investigated, and that range is fairly consistent in the proportions of each line in the total volume, is to use a so called Profit Volume Ratio (PV).

Using the same nomenclature as above:

$$BeR = \frac{FC}{PV}$$

So, for example, say a single product, priced at \$10 each, with a variable cost of \$8 each, had a profit volume ratio of 0.20 calculated as follows:

$$PV = (\text{Price} - \text{Variable Costs}) \div \text{Price} \qquad \frac{\$10 - \$8}{\$10} = 0.20$$

Thus, if we sold a thousand of these 'products' the profit would be:

$$BeR = \frac{\$10{,}000}{0.20} = \$50{,}000$$

For a given mix of products we can even create a 'composite' PV thus:

Product	Each product's own PV	Proportion of Total Volume		Weighted PV
Col (1)	Col (2)	Col (3)		Cols (2) X (3)
X	0.40	40%	= 0.40	0.16
Y	0.30	25%	= 0.25	0.075
Z	0.35	35%	= 0.35	0.1225
Thus the composite PV for this range is =				**0.3575**

However, perhaps the most useful application of break-even analysis is in being able to calculate either:

- How much more volume the business has to sell in order to maintain profitability in the face of having to reduce a product's price, or
- The acceptable volume decrease before profitability is harmed by a product price increase.

Lets take the first one, as often today this is the most likely to happen in the face of very aggressive price competition.

In general, for a **price decrease** the necessary **volume increase** required before profitability is enhanced is given by the following formula:

$$\text{Volume Increase (\%)} = \frac{X}{PV - X} \times 100$$

Where 'X' is the percentage price decrease expressed as a decimal.

So that, assuming that PV is 30% (expressed as a decimal = 0.30), and that the price decrease being contemplated is 9%, then:

$$\text{Volume Increase (\%)} = \frac{0.9}{(0.30 - 0.90)} \times 100 = 42.86\%$$

What this is saying is that to accept a price decrease of 9%, we must be able to obtain some 43% **extra** business **just to stand still.**

Similarly, what if we needed a price INCREASE, what would be the maximum volume we can afford to **lose,** before our profitability suffers? The following formula applies:

$$\text{Volume Increase (\%)} = \frac{X}{PV + X} \times 100$$

Note that all that has changed is the sign which is now a plus (+) versus a minus (-). Using the same numbers, the calculation looks like this:

$$\text{Volume Increase (\%)} = \frac{0.9}{(0.30 + 0.90)} \times 100 = 23.08\%$$

In this case, in the face of a price increase we cannot afford to lose more than 23% of our previous volume or our profitability will suffer.

Break-even and price elasticity

As we have seen in Chapter 2, the fourth issue when analyzing the market is the elasticity of price and this should be factored into any break-even analysis.

Reverting to the classic graphic representation (see Figure 3.4) the one question not asked is will we sell enough at each price-revenue curve to actually break-even?

To answer this quandary we can factor in the elasticities via a spreadsheet application, but the situation is best illustrated via the following diagrams:

Explaining Figure 3.5 below, in a fictional case, we have combined both the graphics from the break-even analysis and the demand curve. First the break-even: Here we show only the total cost curve, and we super-impose some five price-revenue curves which intersect it. Underneath, we show the demand curve for this fictional product, but upside down.

NOTE: the volume demanded axis MUST be of the same scale (synchronizing the scales for the two price axis does not matter) so that we can project upward the point on the demand curve for each price. The point where a given upward projection intersects the relevant price-revenue slope for that price indicates the volume that will be sold at that price.

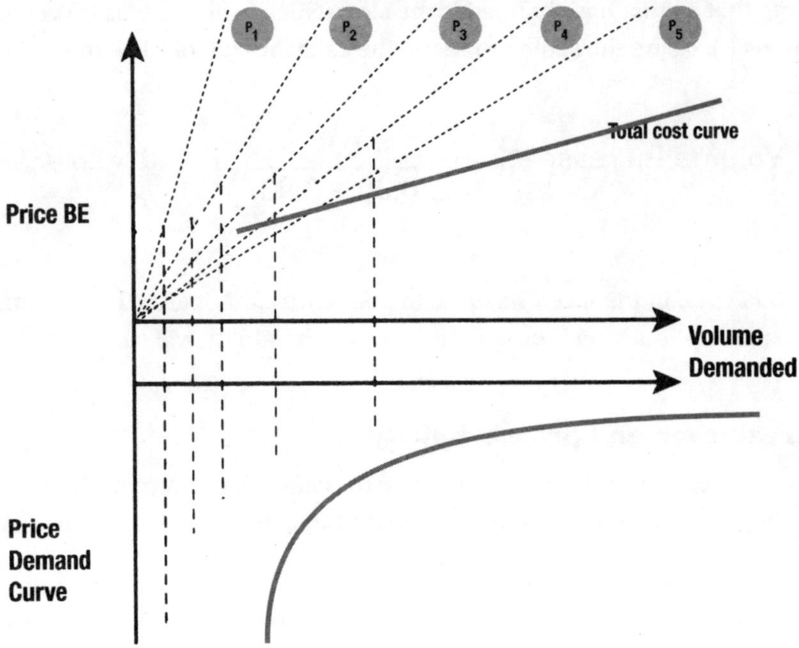

FIGURE 3.5: COMBINING THE DEMAND CURVE WITH THE BREAK-EVEN GRAPH

Thus we see that in this case the sales of product at P1 and P2 will not actually re-coup their total costs, the product breaks-even somewhere between P2 and P3. If we continue these projections we will produce a curve as shown below, stripped of its projection lines for clarity:

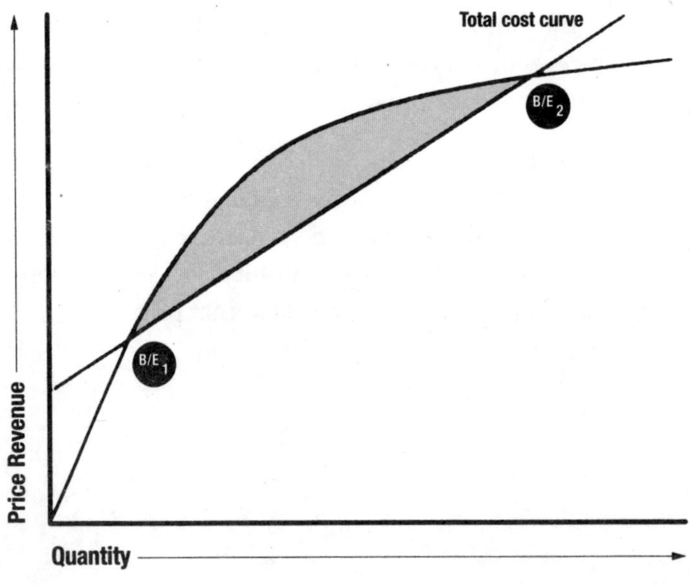

FIGURE 3.6: COMBINING THE DEMAND CURVE WITH THE BREAK-EVEN GRAPH

Here we can see an illustration of what can be revealed when we combine the two graphics. The two cones at either end show where the product is not covering its costs, and the central dome-like space between them where the product is making profit. The ultimate price being where the vertical distance between the top of the dome and the total cost curve is at its greatest, as shown in Figure 3.7.

The most important lesson from this analysis is that it is possible to sell too much. Consider in Figure 3.7 the curve which plots the intersections of the price revenue curves with the upward projection of volume demanded at that price, is showing positive growth throughout, but there comes a point where its rate of growth diminishes and eventually there is a re-entry at BE2 after which the product is no longer profitable.

For any business to continue to price low after BE2, there must be good tactical reasons. However, whatever the imperative, the business must never forget that it is easy to bring price down; the skill is in being able to put it up again afterwards.

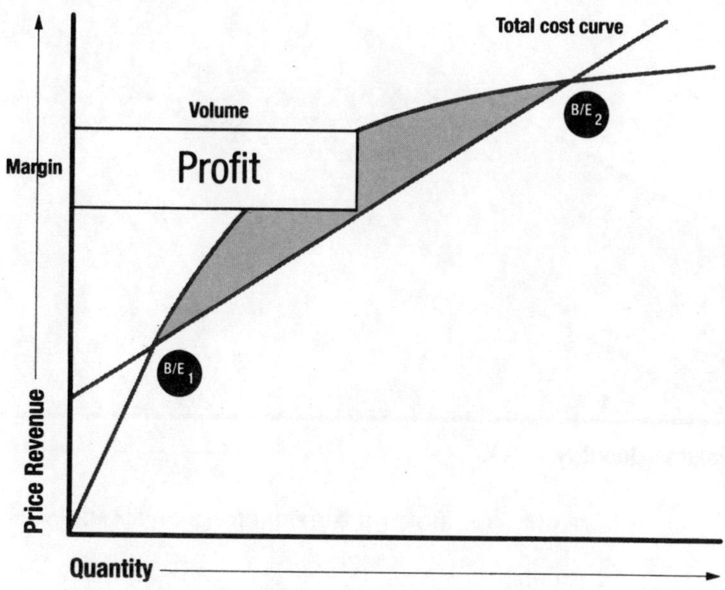

FIGURE 3.7: SHOWING WHERE THE OPTIMUM PRICE WILL BE 'PROFIT-WISE'

Again, such analysis should only be used for the 'guidance of the wise', there are many good tactical, strategic and marketing reasons why a business may wish to price above or below the optimum price point shown in this form of analysis.

Marginal pricing

In the years immediately after the Second World War most of Europe was suffering from shortages of almost every commodity in both business and domestic life. By the mid to late 1950's this situation had more or less abated, and with the easing of shortages grew the intensity of competition (*see Law of Supply and Demand Figure 2.6*) and many businesses were hunting for the holy grail of pricing – how to be competitive whilst at the same time being profitable. Out of this quest grew the insidious ogre of marginal pricing.

The philosophy of marginal pricing is simple – it holds that as long as the price asked is greater than the variable cost, then the firm is making a margin, i.e. the difference between the two. Consider Figure 3.8:

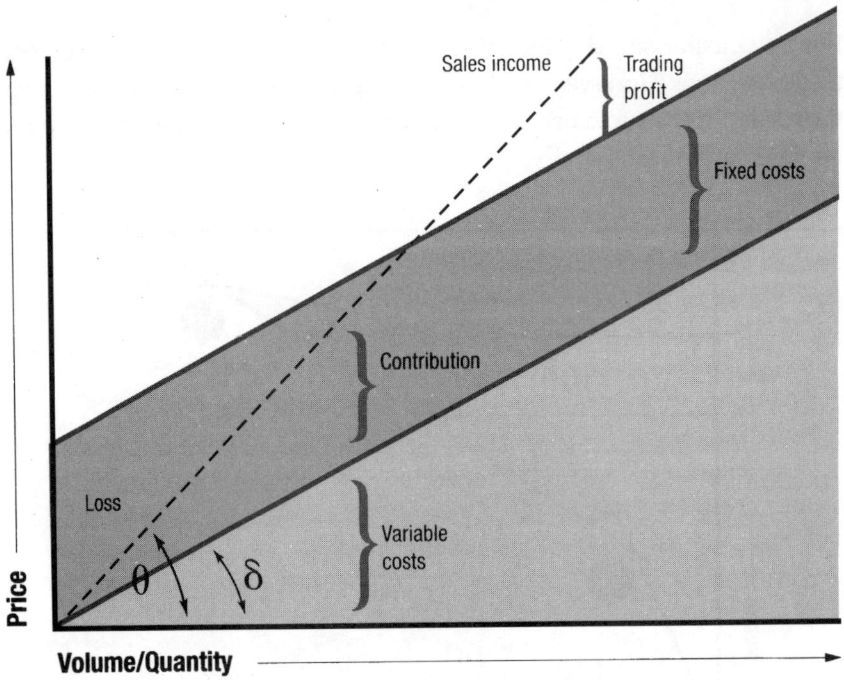

FIGURE 3.8: SHOWING THE PRINCIPLES OF 'MARGINAL PRICING'

The principle is that as long as the angle **'q'** (*theta*) is greater than the angle **'d'** (*delta*), then the difference (***q*** *minus* **d** *= the 'margin'*) is the contribution being made by the sale. (*Contribution toward recovery of overhead, and then toward the eventual profit; contribution, many accountants argue, is not the same as gross profit but for the ordinary folk like you and I, the difference is so slight as not to be worth considering.*)

The problems with this model were not discovered until the first of a series of recessions which began in the late 1970's. Everything is fine as long as there is plenty of business to be had, even though the market may be 'competitive'. The trouble starts when firms are experiencing close to commodity market conditions. Here prices may be forced so low that the sum of all the margins do not add-up to the total fixed cost of the organization by the end of the financial year. Banks may be willing to extend credit for one more year, but not often for more. In the UK recession of the early '90's, which was precipitated by the George Sorus Hedge Fund's run on the Pound Stirling, many British businesses of all types and sizes went bankrupt which, in many cases, could be directly traced to employing marginal pricing (*see Chapter 7 for the Rules for Using Marginal Pricing*).

Activity based costing

In the late 1980's a considerable amount of attention was being paid to the shortcomings of the traditional product (*goods or services*) costing methods.

Firms were producing wider and more diverse product ranges, and the input of labour to the production process was declining compared to the start of the century, when most product costing methods, currently in use in the 1980's had been developed.

As per the diagram in Figure 3.9:

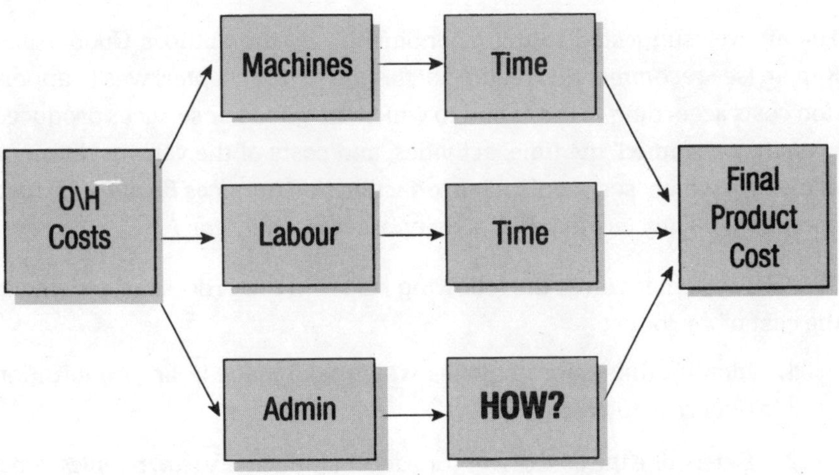

FIGURE 3.9: THE TRADITIONAL WAY OF ATTRIBUTING COSTS

Originally, machine hours and direct labour costs were the two main drivers. These were apportioned to product cost calculations, often in terms of the volume of the goods or services that were created. This was acceptable when ranges of goods or services were simple and confined to limited numbers, and labour was a major input. However, current product ranges are wide and diverse, AND firms are becoming more global and at the same time orientated toward market segmentation. So nowadays internal services, rather than direct labour, drive the costs of a firm.

Because the old methods were simple to understand and few people in the firm were in a position to challenge, these reports distorted product costs, particularly where the firm produced a diverse range of products some with high, and others with low volumes of production and consumption.

This often resulted in the over-costing of high volume goods or services and the under-costing of those with low volumes.

Thus, often the higher volume products would subsidize the low. This lead to the higher volume items often showing shrinking margins, whilst the margins of the low-volume ones appear to grow.

This creates a dangerous trap that too many firms fall into. Incorrect product mix decisions are made at the expense of the high volume products in the range. Decisions are taken to expand the low-volume parts of the range, resulting in a growth of overhead costs and a decline in long-run profitability. Strategically this often lures the unwary into dangerous product range extension.

The answer suggested to this phenomenon by the authors Cooper and Kaplan (*see recommended reading at the end of this chapter*) was to apportion costs according to the extent to which the goods or services produced actually 'consumed' the time, activities, and costs of the various divisions of the firm which 'serviced' their production (*for 'Services Businesses' read operations*). They termed this 'activity based costing' (or ABC).

An ABC system involves the following stages in the process of arriving at the cost of a product:

1. Identify the major activities which take place in an organization (*Figure 3.10 below*)
2. Determine the cost driver for each major activity (*e.g. peoples' time, capital tied up, area of the warehouse etc.*)

3. Create a cost centre/cost pool for each major activity
4. Trace the costs of activities to products (*goods or services*) according to the products demand for, or consumption of, these activities (*using the extent to which the cost drivers are consumed as a measure of this demand*).

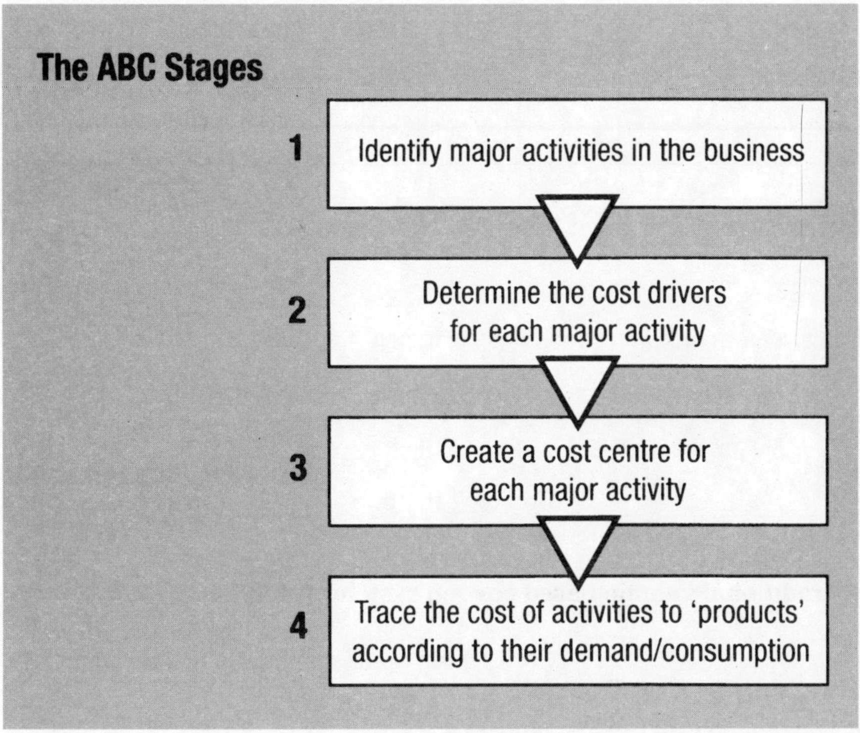

FIGURE 3.10: THE STAGES OF ACTIVITY BASED COSTING

To illustrate with a simple situation:

Assume a company produces two products 'H' and 'L'. Both of these are produced on the same equipment, and both use the same processes. The products differ by the volumes in which they are sold and therefore the volumes in which they are produced.

Product 'H' is the high volume product and product 'L' is the low volume item.

Details of product inputs and outputs and the costs of activities involved are as follows:

	Machine hours Per unit	Direct Labour hours Per unit	Annual Output units	Total Machine hours	Total Direct Labour hours	No. of purchase orders	No. of 'set-ups'
Product 'L'	2	4	1,000	2,000	4,000	80	40
Product 'H'	2	4	10,000	20,000	40,000	160	60
				22,000	44,000	240	100

The cost of these activities is as follows:

	$
Volume related	110,000
Purchase related	120,000
Set-up related	210,000
Total =	**440,000**

A traditional volume based costing system would handle it this way:

Cost centre allocated costs	$440,000
Overhead rate per machine hour	$20 ($440,000/22,000 hrs)
Overhead rate per direct labour hour	$10 ($440,000/44,000 hrs)
Cost per unit of 'L' =	$40 (2 machines hrs @$20 or 4 DLH's)
Cost per unit of 'H'=	$40 (at $10 per hour)
Thus total cost allocated to product 'L' =	$40,000 (1000 X $40)
And total cost allocated to product 'H'=	$400,000 (10,000 X $40)

An activity based costing system would handle it this way:

	Activities		
	Volume related	Purchasing related	Set-up related
Costs traced to activities	**$110,000**	**$120,000**	**$210,000**
Consumption of activities	22,000 machine hrs	240 purchase orders	100 set-ups
Cost	$5 per machine hr	$550 per order	$2,100 per set-up
Thus cost traced to the product =			
'L'	$10,000 (2000 X $5)	$40,000 (80 X $500)	$84,000 (40 X $2,100)
'H'	$100,000 (20,000 X $5)	$80,000 (160 X $500)	$126,000 (60 X $2,100)

Thus cost per unit under ABC =

Product 'L' $134 ($10,000 + $40,000 + $84,000) / 1,000 units

Product 'H' $30.60 ($100,000 + 80,000 + $126,000) / 10,000 units

Quite a difference??

ABC systems try to recognize the activities that are unrelated to the volume of the product, by using cost drivers that are independent of volume. Activities are divided into three major categories. At the product level these are:

- Unit level
- Batch-related
- Product sustaining

Product costs are accumulated by these three categories. Facility-sustaining expenses (Head Office, PR etc) are incurred to support the entire firm, and are therefore a common and joint activity – thus they should not be assigned to the product's cost.

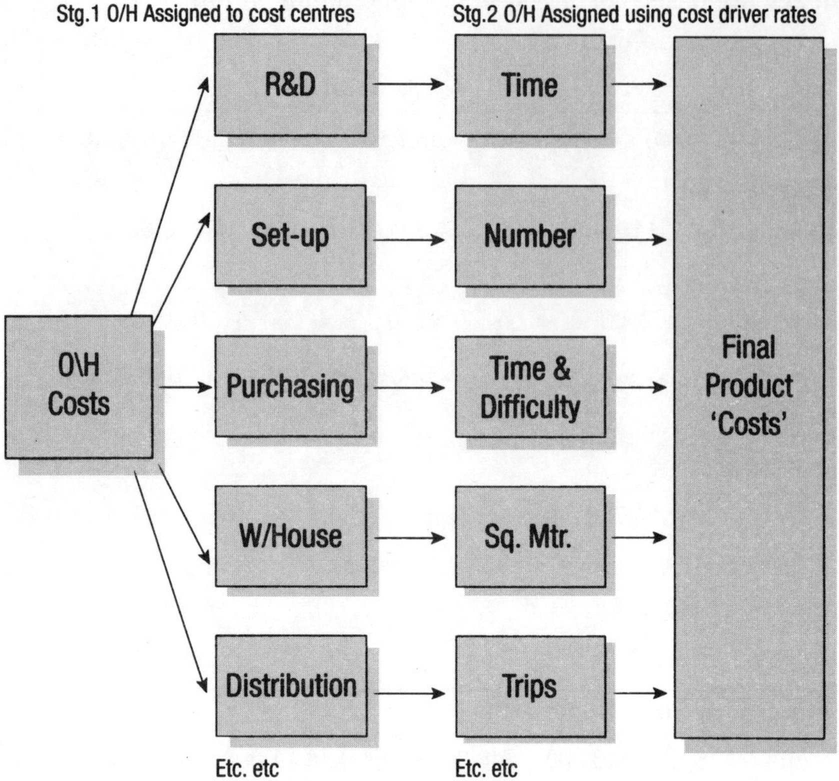

FIGURE 3.11: THE ACTIVITY BASED COSTING MODEL

ABC systems are therefore models of the firm's consumption of resources, not their spending. The system attempts to measure all of the organizational resources required to produce a good, or perform a service (*i.e. the product*).

It must be stressed that ABC systems are intended to identify priorities for managerial attention, and NOT, on their own, to provide the basis of decisions relevant to costs.

ABC has attracted a considerable amount of interest in businesses because it not only provides the basis on which product costs can be calculated with a higher degree of certainty but it also provides a way to manage overhead costs in general. By collecting and reporting on the significant activities in which a business engages, it is possible to understand and manage costs more effectively. Perhaps the area of cost management, rather than product costing per se, is the system's forte.

Yet even today, more than twenty years after the system was first developed, too few firms go to the extent of employing this approach to establishing more realistic costings of their products[vi].

Exercise

So what are the cost drivers in your business?

- Cite these activities, and
- The possible cost centres,
- The basis for apportionment.

For all of your chosen product (goods and/or service) range.

Assessing profitability

This is not as straightforward an activity as one would normally assume. Most businesses would elect to use a 'return on sales' criterion, but is this the best way?

Say we have a situation as shown below:

Example 1.	**Product 'A'**	**Product 'B'**
Selling Price	$11.00	$12.00
Total Cost	$7.00	$8.00
Gross Margin	$4.00	$4.00
% return on Sales	36%	33%

Which is therefore the better business? Both make $4.00 profit, though product 'A' appears to be more profitable percentage-wise.

However, if we look on the above in terms of return on investment we may see a different picture, such as below:

Example 2.	Product 'A'	Product 'B'
1 Selling price	$11.00	$12.00
2 **Costs:**		
3 Raw materials costs	$2.00	$4.00
4 In-house direct value added	$5.00	$4.00
5 Gross margin therefore =	$4.00	$4.00
6 % Return on sales =	36%	33%
7 % Return on total costs =	57%	50%
8 **% Return on total VA* costs**	**80%**	**100%**

* VA = Value Added (row 5 as % row 4)

The important point here is that we assess the profitability of products as a return on the investment made – which can be argued as being just the in-house direct costs of adding value, the 'overhead' of the organization being a sunk cost, and any attribution of these are more often than not totally arbitrary.

In short, the final figure (Figure 3.12) in this chapter:

	Product – Good / Service						Total
	1	2	3	4	5	etc.	
Net Selling Price							
Variable Cost per Unit							
Unit Contribution							
Units sold							
Sales in $							
Contribution Ratio							
Contribution in $							
Fixed Cost							
Profit							

Measure cost NOT price as a means of setting profitability

By-passes the problem of the attribution of FC (overhead)

FIGURE 3.12: A BETTER WAY TO ASSESS PROFITABILITY?

References

i After John Winkler, *'Pricing for Results'* Butterworth Hienemann 1991.

ii According to David Sacks in his book *'The Alphabet'* (Arrow 2004), the great majority of the 'cuneiform' script bearing clay tablets unearthed from Ancient Ur and Summer [the Greek Mesopotamia now known as Iraq], are business documents, contracts, books of accounts, bills of sale etc. etc. AND Cost Plus was the main, if not only pricing method that appears therein.

iii Note not 'Product' or service, what a customer buys when they acquire a 'product' is a 'bundle of benefits' thus a product can be either a good and/or a service.

References

iv This story, whose origin is unknown, is reproduced by courtesy of the New York Certified Public Accountant and Frank P Smith, Director of Education and Personnel, Lybrand, Ross Bros. & Montgomery, New York, and has been adapted from an original by, and with the consent of: Roy H. Hill, OBE FCMA FCIS FinstAM(DIP) MCIM, FIMC FITD.

v Note not 'Product' or service, what a customer buys when they acquire a 'product' is a 'bundle of benefits' thus a product can be either a good and/or a service.

vi RECOMMENDED READING re ABC

For a detailed description of activity-based costing systems, including case studies relating to three UK companies that have implemented ABC, you should refer to Innes and Mitchell (1990), Cooper (1990a,c,d;1991) has also written a series of articles discussing some of the practical issues relating to the implementation and operation of ABC. For a discussion of the criticisms of activity-based costing see Piper and Walley (1990, 1991) and also Cooper's (1990e) reply to these criticisms. Finally you should refer to Kaplan (1990) for a discussion of activity-based profitability and analysis and a comparison of resource consumption and spending models.

FOUR

PRICE POSITIONING AND STRATEGIES

PRICE POSITIONING AND STRATEGIES

Synopsis

This chapter examines and explores the process of choosing and applying a pricing strategy in a given marketplace. It starts by stipulating that the best pricing strategies are not a 'one-size fits all' affair but are targeted to specific populations of customers via the use of segmentation, different customers, different price strategies. The chapter then goes on to expound the process and the procedure for optimum segmentation practice in a pricing context. From here it proceeds to show how the 'price grid' and its derivative, the 'price landscape', can be very useful in analyzing the target markets in which the pricer may wish to do business – this part culminates by showing how the price landscape is the starting point for generating a value based pricing strategy. The chapter concludes with a basic list of generic pricing strategies, their working, their role in the business and where they can best be used.

Where it all begins

Like most of the marketing decisions we take, it all begins with the modern '**P1**', i.e. 'segmentation, targeting and positioning' as per the second edition of *Mastering Marketing*[i]. The start of this chapter is concerned with defining 'P1', i.e. identifying one's source (or sources) of business and it has two stages:

i ***Segmentation*** – i.e. deciding how best to divide the market into groups of customers so that customers within a given group have more in common between themselves, in terms of the way they perceive, use, purchase etc the product, than they have with the customers in other groups. (*This is so that the whole of each offering that the company makes to its market can be specifically tailored to those segments in which the company chooses to do business.*)

ii ***Targeting*** – i.e. defining which particular group/s of customers (segments) will be addressed.

Segmenting for price

Why segment?

Consider the following illustration, Figure 4.1.

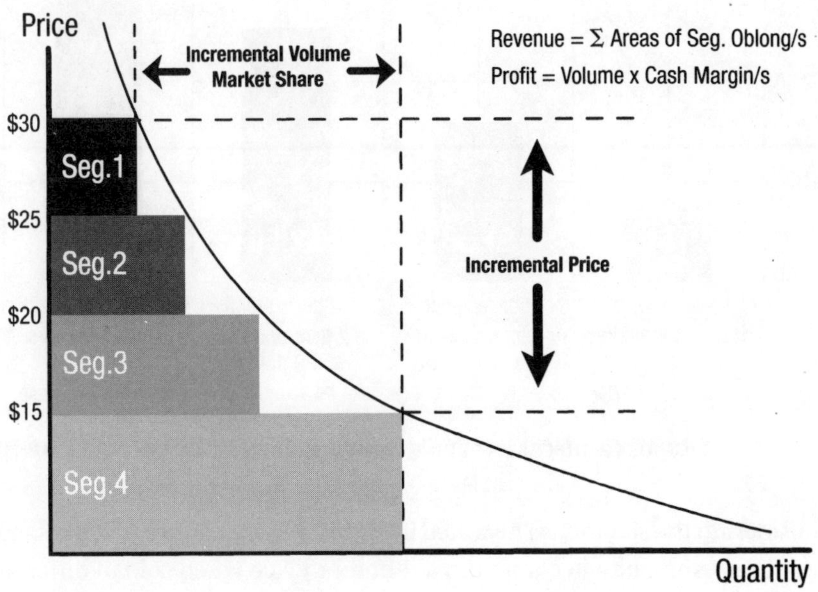

FIGURE 4.1: IMPROVING PROFIT MARGINS (1)

The illustrative situation shown in Figure 4.1 is of a business that can clearly segregate its market in to (say) four distinct segments, and has been able to employ multiple pricing. Each of these segments will demand different quantities. Segment No.1 the least, segment No. 4 the most. But each of the segments are at different prices, so the total of the revenue from each will be substantial.

A good example of this happening in everyday life is the price differential people are usually willing to pay for the same product but at different times, and in different circumstances.

Take some canned refreshment such as a cola or even beer as in Figure 4.2:

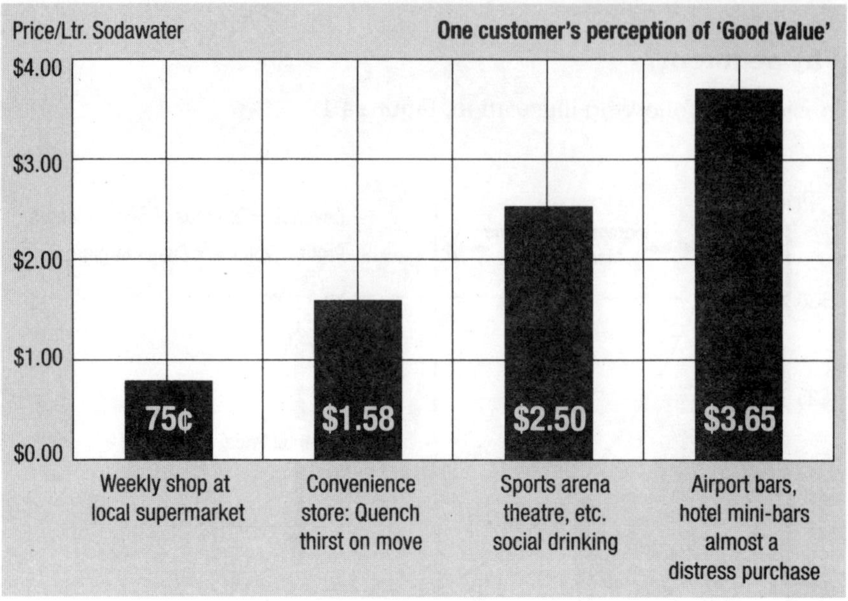

FIGURE 4.2: DIFFERENT PRICES FOR DIFFERENT (OCCASION) SEGMENTS

Considering the situations illustrated in Figure 4.2, we can see that the same can of refreshment will command a different price when sold in different situations (a valid segmentation variable). On the left where there is a great deal of retailer competition, often including local supermarkets for example, a low retail price can be expected, especially when the customer may well be buying as part of their weekly or monthly shopping[ii].

At the other end of the scale, the segment that can be charged the most is the one that is essentially a captive market. Customers can't go elsewhere; they have few options apart from bringing their own supplies to the situation, not impossible, but a bit impractical when you are a travelling business person.

Segmentation

This is the strategic process of defining the specific groups of customers toward whom the firm will focus its marketing efforts in order to generate revenue (*these are often known as the 'target group'*); whilst simultaneously discerning that target groups' specific needs and deciding which of these needs will form the core of the product benefits to be offered to them.

'Segmentation' is the process of defining the target group and 'positioning' per se, is the process of aligning product benefits with customer needs.

Thus the marketer will:

- **'focus'**, so as to get closer to the customer and by so doing:
- **'outflank'** the opposition. (*It is important for the marketer never to fight on the ground of the competitor's own choosing.*)

Taking the last point first:

On the basis that the larger the market share the greater the chance the company is a **price maker**, and the smaller the market share, the greater the chance the company is a **price taker**[iii], companies that do not dominate the market find themselves having to consider a 'head-to-head' confrontation with the major player in their market in order just to survive.

Market segmentation is a means of stepping out from underneath the dominance of market leaders. It does this by redefining the marketplace in which the company operates, the marketer targets those customers the opponents have neglected.

Put simply, segmentation is the process of:

- Dividing a market into smaller, more homogeneous groups of customers **on the basis of the customers' needs**.
- Selecting from these groups those which the marketer believes:
  a) have needs which so far are not properly addressed (*'gap in the market'*),
  b) his/her company can address them to the improved satisfaction of customers (*'competitive differential advantage'*),
  c) the sub group is large enough to be profitable for his/her company (*'market in the gap'*).
- So that the firm can establish effective communications and address each group selected with a marketing mix unique to that group.

Segments can come in a range of sizes (refer to Figure 4.3 following). In simple terms, if a market is sliced into fairly large groups, where each group can support two or more average size suppliers, it is called a 'market segment'. If, however, those groupings are smaller and are only big enough to support one average size supplier, then it is referred to as a market 'niche'.

If the division goes smaller still, the name used is 'micro segmentation' or 'cherry picking'. Cherry picking is the practice of addressing small groups of 'high value – low volume business'. Cherry pickers present a considerable threat to the larger players (*size and share*) in most markets (*see 'Mastering Marketing'*).

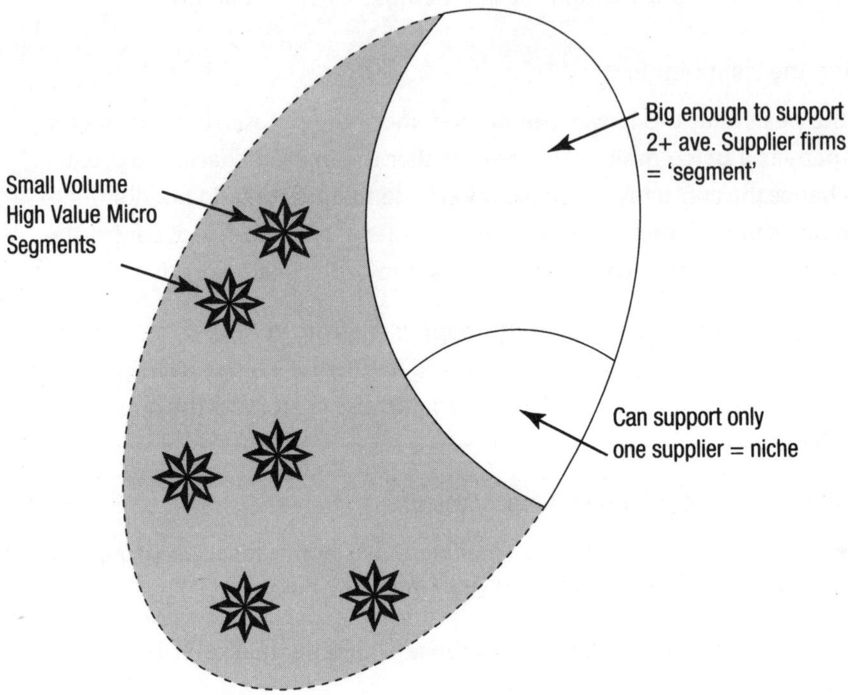

FIGURE 4.3: SEGMENT VARIANTS BY SIZE

By segmenting a market, the company increases its understanding of its customers' needs, it improves its ability to identify market opportunities and provides a clearer idea of what strategies and implementable actions need to be taken. The process of segmenting effectively locks out the competition. Segments (*cherry, niche etc.*) are homogeneous in the sense that customers within that group have more in common between themselves when it comes to behaviour towards the products in question (re. *their purchase and use*), than they have with people in other segments. Marketers refer to this as 'intra-segment homogeneity' and 'inter-segment heterogeneity'. Ideally, a good segmentation strategy should result in their being no more than two competitors (three at the most) vying for any one customer's business – more competition than this means the inevitable errosion of price.

The conditions

The conditions for successful price oriented segmentation are:

- **A cluster of prospects at a particular price point.** It is very wise to start here, many markets may appear to be homogenous in a range of factors, only to later fragment into diametrically different groups when Price comes into the equation – doing this differentiation by price sensitivity first avoids trouble later on, when you may think you have a viable segment, but on Price issues it is not homogeneous.

- **A 'gap' in the market.** There should be needs (as we will see when examining the order of things in the segmentation process) that are seen by the potential customers as not as yet being fulfilled/ addressed. OR, not being addressed adequately – this is the gap to explore.

- **A market in the 'gap'.** This asks the 'segmenter' to determine whether the gap above is big enough for their business. That is to ask whether there are enough potential customers with the requisite spending power to warrant making the necessary investment of time, talent and resources to cater to their needs. Whether there are enough buyers in a market depends on the size of the potential vendor firm. Small firms such as Morgan Cars (*at one time reputed to only make and sell nine cars per month, but to have a nine year waiting list*) can make a nice living out of micro segments (see Figure 4.3) where the larger players, say Fords or General Motors, cannot![iv]

- **We can communicate with it.** This in the sense of will it be possible to research the market more fully (*i.e. to explore their needs and buying behaviour etc. in depth*) and will it be possible to 'target' any marketing promotion at this group of customers, and do this efficiently and without contaminating the vendor's regular market.

The segmentation process

The various strategies for segmenting a market are presented by the cascade diagram, Figure 4.4. The dotted arrows show non-ideal paths, the solid arrows show the ideal path toward obtaining a segment which is the most difficult for your competition to attack.

The 'cascade' (*as shown by the arrows*) is the 'process' by which a market is segmented. To separate out the different types of customer – one from the other – discriminating variables must be used. For example, gender separates out and discriminates males from females. These variables are shown at the 'decision nodes', i.e. the shaded areas.

Stage one of the process commences with an analysis that searches for unfulfilled demand (*current or potential*). In other words, segments related to what the customers require and are willing to pay a 'profitable' price for (*i.e. not just 'need' or 'want'*). These requirements can be sub-divided into objective needs versus subjective needs. Objective needs are those that can be measured to a commonly agreed standard.

Whether or not the 'objective needs' draw a blank the wise market/pricer will now look toward subjective needs to continue to define the potential segment.

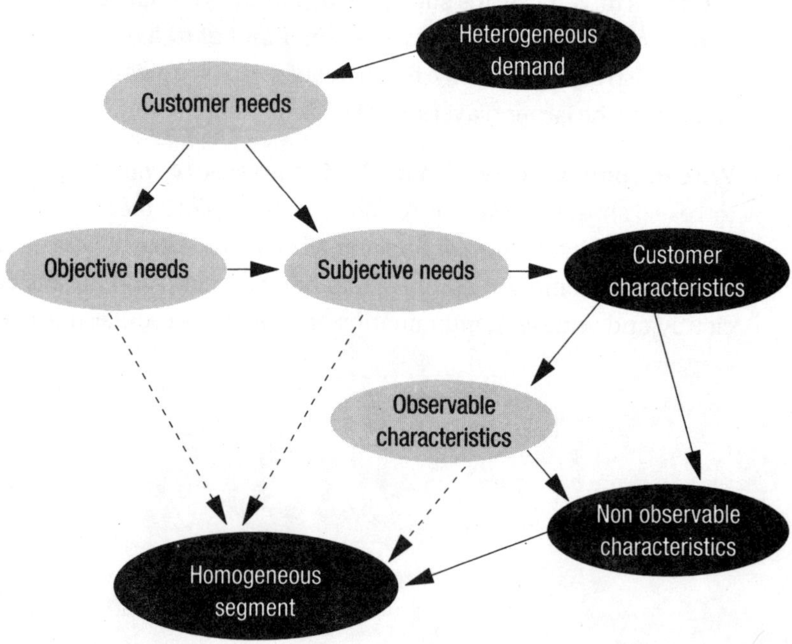

FIGURE 4.4: THE OUTLINE OF AN IDEAL SEGMENTING PROCESS

One of the advantages of market pricing for a product where the key benefits are coming from a service (versus a 'good') is that a given 'core' service has the potential to be almost all things to all customers. Thus, the product/ service pricer would have to appraise subjective issues such as the:

- Customer's status
- Social visibility
- Political respectability of the supplier (*e.g. does his/her bank exploit the poor in third world countries?*)

The pricer should next identify what types of customers exhibit these particular objective or subjective requirements (*i.e. we now need to know who wants what*).

i For the purposes of segmentation, customers can be described using two sets of criteria, that which:

- can easily be seen: for example, their observable characteristics, and
- can't be so readily seen: for example their personality traits, cultural norms, psychology etc.

The easiest of these elements to examine are the observable characteristics, i.e. the marketer/pricer is able to tell by looking.

In consumer markets, for example, this would perhaps include the customer's:

- age
- gender
- race
- location
- socio-economic class etc.

In other words their demography.

In business to business markets the vendor would need to ask: Are the customers:

- large or small companies?
- in high-tech or low-tech?
- the service sector or manufacturing?

And

- What sort of industry are they in, e.g. chemicals, utilities, agriculture etc.?

The business must then proceed to examine customer characteristics for non-observable phenomena.

ii In a consumer market this will mainly be along the lines of the personality (*sometimes known as psychographics*) of the prospects. There are numerous ways of defining personality – many of them have proved useful when defining segments[v].

Additional variables in this category include people's opinions, beliefs, leisure activities, level of education etc. All of which are difficult to see at a glance but, with the right skills, can be elucidated and used to segment.

In a business to business situation this might be 'company culture'[vi].

Whilst it is possible to form a viable segmentation strategy from just customer demand (*objective or subjective measures*), i.e. just to go down one route, the more of these variables that are included in the definition of the market segment (i.e. *the route shown by the solid arrows*), the stronger, more stable, more defensible is that segmentation.

The types of market segmentation for consumer and business markets consist of:

- **Benefit segmentation alone,** as we have discussed above.

- **Situation** – the situation company staff may find themselves in at particular times such as, for example, a business traveller needing to change travellers cheques or obtain currency after bank closing hours, is the ideal target market for Bureau de Change.

- **Psychographics segmentation** is all about defining people by their personality. As there are over 650 personality traits this can become cumbersome. So what most marketers do is to cluster these together into psychographic segments and put labels on them which will serve as a short-hand (*such as 'yuppy' – young upwardly mobile urban professional; 'woopy' – well-off older person; 'dinky' – dual income, no kids/children- yet*). Personality is of tremendous importance when segmenting the consumer market for IT.

- **Geographic segmentation** exploits the location of the customer – wherever they may be.

- **Usage segmentation** is about what the customer does with one's product. So, for example, mobile phones can be used either for:
  - Incoming and outgoing calls, texts etc. whilst on the move (*normal pattern?*)
  - Outgoing calls only (*trainers can't take calls in a seminar*)
  - Data transmission (*i.e. either stand-alone or linked to notebook/ laptop*)
  - Personal administration, e.g. managing one's diary
  - Taking and sending photographs
  - Accessing the Internet
  - Accessing entertainment (e.g. video and music on-line)
  - Any combination of the above, and more to come: nationally and internationally etc.

Segmenting via B2B buyer behaviour

Segmentation in some business to business markets feature benefits such as company loyalty and buyers' motives (*in other words the buyers previous purchase behaviour*). Therefore businesses buyers (*i.e. the procurement department*) are not just concerned with physically obtaining supply but also with:

- earning a bonus based on cost reductions achieved;
- making a statement in the organization about their buying abilities; or
- playing a political game to guard themselves against future recrimination (*see Value-Based Pricing, Chapter 5 and Negotiation, Chapter 8*).

- **Suitable technology** is also a means by which we can segment in a business to business market. The question is "do our customers have the technology to be able to use our products?" Someone marketing software packages designed for the intranet for example, would have to focus on those organizations that have the necessary hardware to support that software's requirements.

The remaining segmentation types for locating business to business segments are:

- **Type of end use**, i.e. the actual use for the IT and/or service. For a vehicle maintenance supplier it may be to keep customers' vehicles on the road, via regular or preventative maintenance, or it could be to train people to operate a hotline for example.
- **The type of industry** as a means of segmenting the market would address the service sector, rather than the manufacturing sector; local authority, rather than financial services and so forth.
- **The job function of the user** – is the user a manager, a manual worker, a financial director, a designer etc?
- **Not all customers behave the same way**

There are considerable differences emerging in how some B2B customers, compared to others, will choose to approach their relationships with their suppliers.

Generally, B2B customers employ one of three likely purchasing agendas, as shown in Figure 4.5 when dealing with suppliers.

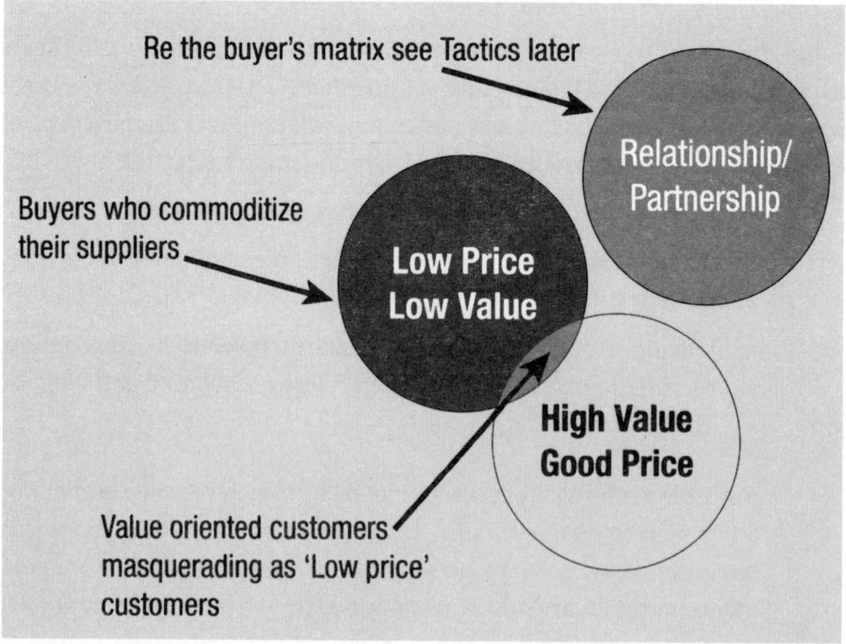

FIGURE 4.5: SEGMENTING BY B2B BUYER ATTITUDE

- **Low price:** Buyers are driven to obtain goods and/or services at the lowest possible prices. This includes qualifying many vendors to ensure an aggressive price battle for their business.
- **High value:** Buyers are willing to trade off different vendors based on the value they bring to the table and are willing to pay more for higher value offerings.
- **Relationship/partnership:** Buyers actively seek vendors who can help them understand and optimally apply their offering, and who, in addition, are able to help the buyer's firm better exploit the downstream elements of the 'value chain'. In consequence customers are willing to pay higher prices for access to those skills and expertise[1] (*see Value Based Pricing, Chapter 5*).

Unfortunately, when it comes to the boundaries between the low price buyers and the high value buyers not all customers want to, or will, be loyal. Nor will every customer be willing to pay suppliers vendors for the value/s they provide. Instead, a considerable portion of buyers in almost every market will put high-value suppliers into the same negotiating 'meat grinder' as low-value suppliers (*i.e. like the preying mantis, B2B buyers will disguise themselves as something that they are not, so as to gain the advantage*). They intend that the high-value vendors should surrender under the competitive pressure so produced, and provide their higher value offering to the buyer at the lower price. Given such an environment, it is certainly very important for salespeople to be able to recognize such behaviours and develop the appropriate approach for each customer type.

Finally you need to know

Are your target group:

- Price conscious?
- Price aware? – or –
- Price sensitive?

Price conscious?

By this we mean, do they ever consider price in their decision to buy? It may surprise you that this may never be the case, but there are certain purchases which often fall below the spending horizon – so to speak. A good example of this is the relationship which the Author's family once had with a milk-delivery business. In those days in England, milk was delivered in pint bottles to the doorstep very early in the morning say between 04.30 hrs and 07.00 hrs latest. At that time, the Author had four children in his family, and the family took delivery of five pints per day. The milkman usually called later on Saturday morning to collect the money for the previous week's deliveries. A new milkman somehow stopped doing this and the Author soon forgot this habit – until that is, some four months into the new man's tenure this milkman's boss threatened to fire him unless he collected what our family owed their business. So, very early one Saturday morning the Author was awakened by that milkman who was demanding that he should be paid what was owed. The bill was a fantastic £146 (i.e. c.£9 per week for 16 weeks) which at the time was nearly 12.5% of the Author's monthly post-taxed pay from the university at which he lectured. Result – a total change of our milk buying behaviour. The new milkman's failure to get us to pay weekly as before had now made us price aware:

Price aware?

This means that the customer actually knows the price they pay – hidden costs and all, but chooses not to alter their buying and/or their consuming behaviour. So back to the milk saga: Now the family were price aware, we suddenly realized that there could be some great savings to be had if we were to:

1. consume less each week, and
2. shop around.

Thus we started to consider the policy of buying milk weekly from the local supermarket. This in turn made us price sensitive:

Price sensitive?

This is a state where the customer will alter their buying and often their consumption behaviour as a result of a change in price – this is a very dangerous state of affairs for the pricer: Once more – back to the milk saga: Now the Author's family actively started to shop around for the best in milk deals and other groceries. In the long run, by the act which caused him to lose a customer, that milkman changed a family's whole weekly-shopping/ buying behaviour and consequently saved us quite a fortune over the years.

SO – Look at the situation from the sellers point of view: if your business can make the customer's payments fall below the customer's spending horizon, say – by collecting the payment automatically via Direct Debits for example, then your business will suffer far less price sensitivity[vii].

What constitutes price to your 'target group'?

Is it capital cost, total repaid, or monthly instalments?

When people are involved in large purchases for themselves or their family, what is it about the finances of that purchase that features large (or largest) in their considerations? It often depends on the amount of money involved. For perhaps the most extreme example take the purchase of a home.

TOTAL CAPITAL COST?

From the sellers point of view, the purchase price of the home (*be that a house or an apartment*) is an indicator of the quality of the property and the value of the investment the buyers will be acquiring. This especially applies to those parts of the world where the scarcity of land, or the proximity of employment (*i.e. near a busy city like London, New York, Paris, Hamburg etc.*) means that the prices of such accommodation can reasonably be expected to appreciate faster than inflation over the years, and thus a profit can be made when that home be sold at some later date. **But the value of that home is in its 'asset value', not the price of purchase but the degree to which it will appreciate over the years.**

TOTAL REPAID?

Many years ago, the author was a keynote speaker at a conference for Marketing People in the British Financial Services sector. To make this point, each of the audience of several hundred people were asked to put their right hand in the air, if they knew exactly how much the acquisition of their home would cost them by the time they had completed the instalments. To the Author's surprise (*bearing in mind that these were savvy people in the financial community*), only two people raised their hands. Of those who had not raised their hands, when the author asked them for the reason why, the almost unanimous response was that they preferred not to know, the financial number was so large. To tell the buyer exactly how much they will pay to complete the purchase can scare them off the purchase – so unless the law of your land specifically mandates sellers to do so (*as it does in many parts of Europe*) don't needlessly scare the customer away by disclosing this figure when you don't have to.

MONTHLY/WEEKLY REPAYMENTS?

In the early 1990's a major innovation occurred in the UK's motor insurance market. This mainly happened via the use of telephone selling, and some very astute segmentation using the home location of the customer to assess the risk to the underwriters. Additionally, by making the premiums payable via a monthly Direct Debit the sales pitch was able to soften the financial blow. The premiums ceased to be (for example) £356 per year, but a pound a day. ***"What's the matter John, can't afford a pound a day****?!?"*

This brings us back to the really large purchases, specifically the capital purchases of the consumer market, e.g. motor cars, homes, home improvements, private medicine, private schooling, that second home in Spain, Italy or Cyprus, even some exorbitant 'once in a lifetime' holidays – they can all be purchased on an instalment plan, designed specifically to make it affordable to their target group, i.e. their market segment.

General segmentation principles

To conclude this section on general segmentation, it is important to note four basic principles of segmentation:

- It is always more effective to use several variables (*to differentiate one prospective customer from another*), rather than just one.
- There is a trade-off – between the desire to know and the cost of obtaining that information, i.e. the principle of the law of diminishing returns.
- Market segmentation and product differentiation are joint decisions but it is also important not to forget that a segmentation strategy involves the whole marketing mix (*all five P's*). Thus, not just the product will be differentiated, but so will the price, the promotion, the physical evidence, the process, the distribution and, in the service industry, the people who are delivering the service during those moments of truth.

- The largest market segment is not always the most desirable. Many companies have made good money addressing small segments (*cherry pickers, niche players*) sometimes with products which are even at the end of their life cycles. Larger companies stay away because they often believe these small and perhaps declining markets represent very little opportunity (*i.e. for them there is 'no market in the gap'*). This leads to fewer competitors which also means that there is little or no price competition and thus profitability can be very healthy[viii].

The essential ADDITIONAL steps in price segmentation:

- Segment by price first, then via the other four routes as per Figure 4.4.
- Examine existing price strategy and structures that exist in your (intended) market.
- Understand where and how price sensitivity varies within the customer base (*to determine segments*).
- Identify segments that are not as yet fully realized due to current pricing practice by your competition.
- Develop pricing levels and structures that will leverage customer perceptions, preferences and behaviours in your favour.

Price positioning

The following three maxims the 'pricer' should always bear in mind:

- Price is the most prevalent shorthand way by which customers assess a good or service;
- Pricing exactly to the competitor, will 'commoditize' your product;
- It is important to understand your own product and its value versus your competition.

The best way to address the analysis of these three points, particularly the last, is to use a tool often referred to as the 'price position matrix', and it's (*slightly more sophisticated*) 'price landscape grid' (*or 'price landscape' for short*).

Following this we see the basic price positioning matrix (Figure 4.6). In many circles this positioning matrix is often oriented so that the top left is the ultimate position, i.e. it is high in value and high in price, i.e. Hi/Hi. However, because of what follows, the author prefers to use the common (i.e. mathematical) convention when plotting a graph, i.e. the Hi/Hi position will be at the top right, and the Lo/Lo position at the bottom left.

The scale for both the positioning matrix and the landscape grid is linear, i.e. not logarithmic etc.

Value \ Price	Low	Medium	High
High	1 Suberb Value	2 Penetration	3 Premium Contact
Medium	4 Good Value	5 Average	6 Overcharging
Low	7 Cheap Value	8 Skim the Cream	9 Rip-off Price

FIGURE 4.6: THE BASIC PRICE POSITION MATRIX

This matrix sets out a very basic grid on which the pricer/marketer can visualize where their product stands (or should stand), price position-wise, in their marketplace. In Figure 4.7 the grey filled cells show how the 'orderly' (i.e. stereotypical) pricing hierarchy should be in any market.

Also in Figure 4.8 we see how this would pan-out in a 'normal' marketplace, i.e. if all players observed the conventional approach – this way there would be a place/position for everyone in the market. If the pricer has segmented the market effectively there should be no more that three players in that segment including the pricer's product/s (i.e. goods and/or services). If there are more than three and if the pricer's firm is not the biggest player, they will sooner or later come under attack. So they will need to either re-segment, and/or prepare for a price war (see Chapter 7).

Value \ Price	Low	Medium	High
High	1 Suberb Value	2 Penetration	**3** **Premium Contact**
Medium	4 Good Value	**5** **Average**	6 Overcharging
Low	**7** **Cheap Value**	8 Skim the Cream	9 Rip-off Price

FIGURE 4.7: POSITION NUMBER ONE 'HOLDING'

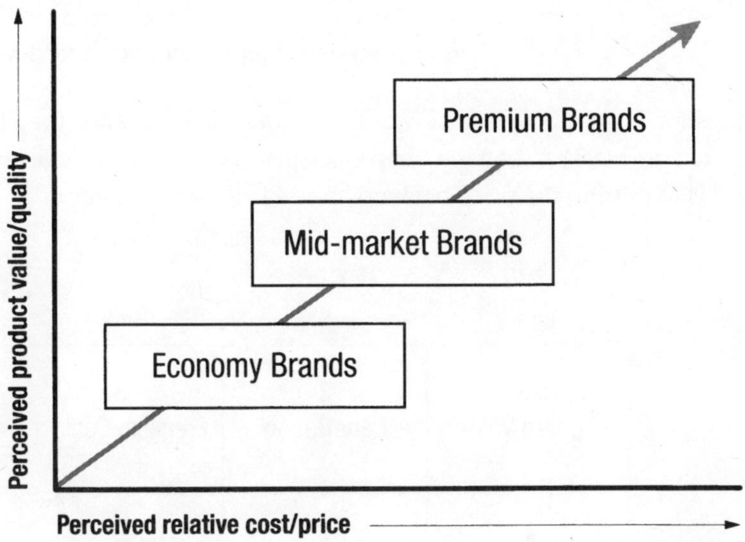

FIGURE 4.8: THE 'THREE-TIER' VALUE POSITIONS.

Figure 4.8 shows how these positions pan-out in the minds of your customers, be they business to business or consumers.

However, the above is an orderly market, and things do not always go the way we wish. A new player can enter our market, with the intention of establishing a presence which they can use as a platform from which to expand, i.e. they intend to penetrate the incumbent's customer base. If that market is structured,[ix] this is probably the only way they can enter.

Value \ Price	Low	Medium	High
High	1 **Suberb Value**	2 **Penetration**	3 Premium Contact
Medium	4 **Good Value**	5 Average	6 Overcharging
Low	7 Cheap Value	8 Skim the Cream	9 Rip-off Price

FIGURE 4.9: POSITION NUMBER TWO 'PENETRATION'

The question is how do these new entrants make a profit after they have penetrated the market? Anyone can reduce price, which needs little talent, the skill is in putting the price back up afterwards (see Chapter 6).

Value \ Price	Low	Medium	High
High	1 Suberb Value	2 Penetration	3 Premium Contact
Medium	4 Good Value	5 Average	6 **Overcharging**
Low	7 Cheap Value	8 **Skim the Cream**	9 **Rip-off Price**

FIGURE 4.10: POSITION NUMBER THREE 'SKIMMING'

A price skimming position is the absolute opposite of penetration. The three positions shown here in Figure 4.10 assume that there can be little or no competitive entry expected, i.e. the customer will have little option but to pay the price asked. This was the strategy employed by the private companies who took over the running of British Rail networks in the 1990's. If you lived outside the big City and wanted to get to work in the mornings, you had no option other than rail, except to drive to and from work, which for those working in London, Birmingham, Manchester, Leeds, Glasgow etc. can be, and often is a nightmare.

However, as low-cost airlines have demonstrated, operating on what is known as the South Western Airline's model the high premiums for low'ish value (in this case from National Carriers) will attract the entrepreneur who is determined to exploit these overblown margins, via the application of a more economic business model.

Prior to the formation of South Western in the USA, the airlines had been tightly regulated, in a way that was designed to protect the indigenous 'carriers' from competition. This resulted in a low quality of service and high costs, all fenced in via extremes of protectionism, elements of which still persist. For example, the 'cabotage' regulations which mean that very few countries will allow foreign airlines to land in one part of their country to pick-up passengers for another part of their country, for example, the USA. A British Airways plane (say) whose final destination is Los Angeles and which makes an interim landing in New York cannot pick-up passengers from New York for the onward flight, nor can they pick up passengers in Los Angeles for New York on their return home.

The price landscape

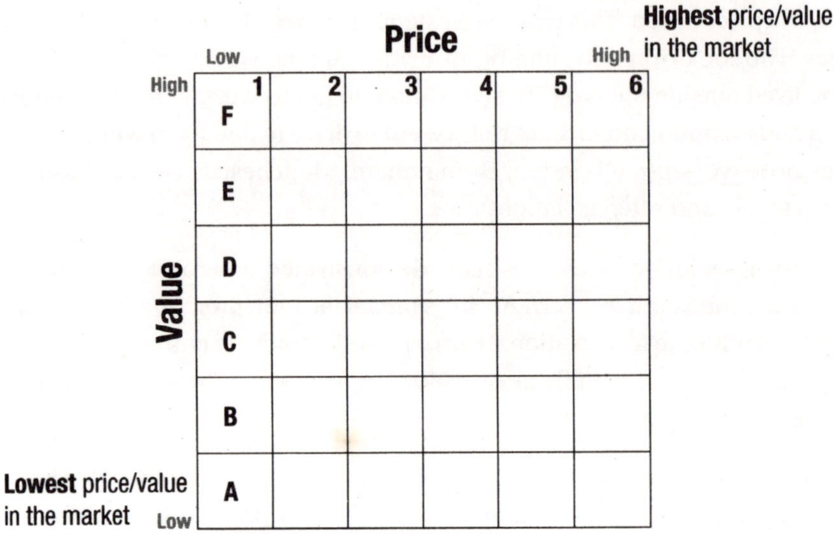

FIGURE 4.11: THE 'PRICE LANDSCAPE'

This price landscape is more than just the price matrix with four times more squares, it is a tool that:

- Allows us to position ourselves versus the competition with more finesse – and
- Provides us with the means to analyze more precisely where we stand versus the other players. Take Figure 4.12 for example, if we were 'C' it indicates that:
  - For the same price as 'B' we are adding considerably more value than 'B' and 'A', and
  - We are not capturing the extra margin that these extra values could command (*however we may be growing our market share – but that could threaten a price war*).

As we shall see in Chapter 5 we can also use the landscape grid to visualize the competitive gap between players both in terms of price **and** value, not only relative positions but also the direction and extent of the 'gaps' between us and the other players in our market – see Figure 4.13.

By arbitrarily positioning ourselves centrally on the price landscape grid, we can visualize where the main competitors stand relative to us, using our price and our values as the datum.

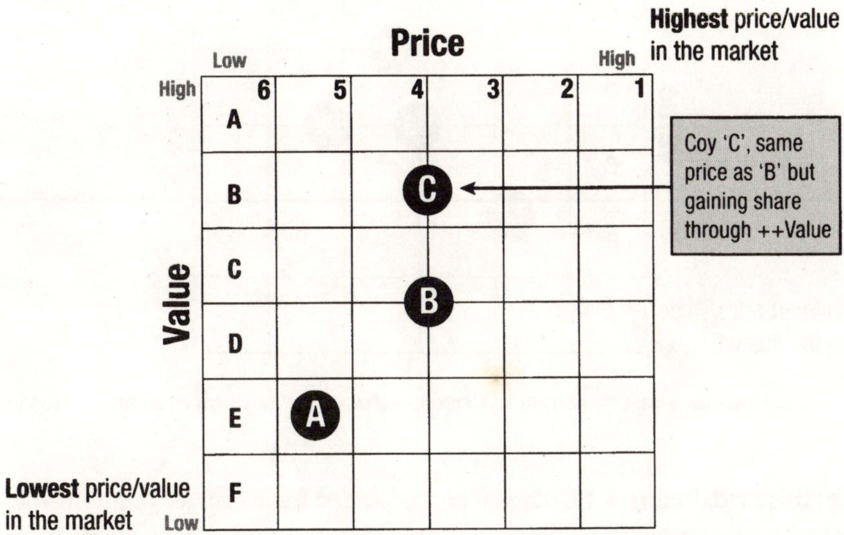

FIGURE 4.12: PLOTTING WHERE OUR COMPETITION STAND COMPARED TO YOU

Ideally the positions of competitors **should not** be subjective guesses on our part but should be derived via marketing research – which is examining that segment's type of customer's perceptions of that specific market's players (*customer's perceptions drives customer behaviour – in business it is the only reality when they buy*). In a consumer market this can most ideally be done via the use of the 'Hall Test' type of data gathering, in business to business markets this will require semi-indepth interviews with the main customer decision-makers and specifiers.[x]

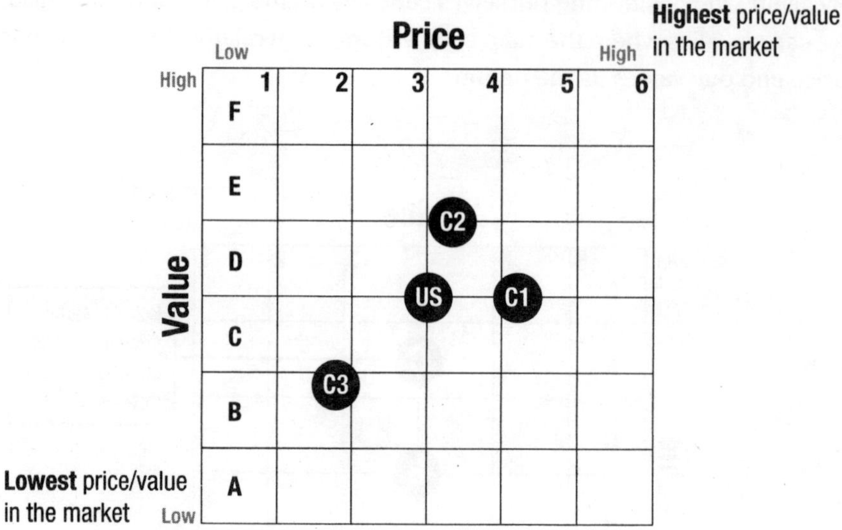

FIGURE 4.13: USING THE LANDSCAPE TO ANALYZE COMPETITOR POSITIONS

On this grid, Figure 4.13, the pricer has placed their firm as 'piggy-in-the-middle'. So reading the above landscape, C1 and C2 are capturing higher prices than us, whereas C3 sits well down on the diagonal running from top left to bottom right, i.e. the perceived 'rational positions'. It would now be useful to know what the market shares are i.e. the relative volumes of business each of the competitors enjoy. This will then allow us to identify who has the advantage in this marketplace, i.e. who is gaining most from their position.

Exercise 4.1

Draw in fairly large scale, a price landscape for one major segment of your market.

Place your business at the centre of this landscape (i.e. at the intersection of lines that lie between columns 3 and 4 and rows D and C). Explain the concept of this grid to some of your colleagues, then work with them to identify the three major competitors, and plot them on this landscape where you and they believe these competitors to be in relation to your business on the continuums of price and value to your customers. If you have some friendly customers to hand, you can also ask them to comment on your team's opinion, versus how they see the marketplace. (*However, don't believe everything they say, they not only have a different perspective, but they will also have an agenda to 'improve' your prices to them – but it is good to see the business from their perspective now and then.*)

Price as an indicator of quality

Under the right conditions price can often be a major indicator of the quality of the products for sale. Nowhere is this more true than where service is used to add value. The basic conditions for this situation exist in services because the product is not only intangible and therefore prone to a great deal of subjective appraisal, but in addition it cannot be sampled. Thus, prior to purchase, much of the offering is a promise which can only be evaluated after commitment.

The basic conditions that must exist for customers to use price as an indicator of quality are if one or more of the following apply:

- There is little or no product information available to the customer. In other words the customer is essentially naive about the product and is unable to make an informed judgment. If the purchase is important enough, it is also important to make sure that they get it right. Therefore, customers will use price to inform their behaviour.
- There may be no other evaluative criteria available, OR there are perceived to be major quality differences between brands. The issue is the word 'perceived'. The marketer's battleground is in the mind of the customer and it is their perceptions. As we have seen elsewhere, it is these 'perceptions' that govern their behaviour.
- If the cost consequences of making bad decisions are great, and/or if the product has a high level of socio-economic significance. In both these situations the customer is apt to perceive a high level of risk.
- The buyers and/or other important members of the decision-making unit have confidence that price in their marketplace is an indicator of quality.

Taking consultancy services as an extreme – they are located towards the intellectual property end of the service spectrum and are considered to have a high requirement for credibility. In these areas price remains an important factor as an indicator of quality after consumption. The greater the perceived risk and cost of a product going wrong, the greater the chance that a price reduction can damage the image of the product.

Any business should give a great deal of thought when contemplating price reductions. These can detrimentally affect the image of the product and hurt the egos of those who have already purchased.

If service is employed, either as the main way value is added, or is the whole product in its own right, and is of relatively short duration (*i.e. it doesn't take a long time to deliver*) but it yields benefits over a much longer period, for example in terms of training or consultancy, the business, as a means of supporting price, must also include strategies to drive home the long-term investment nature of the product.

Objectives for pricing and pricing strategies

Like everything else in life – 'if you have no aims and/or objectives then any road will get you there.' So it is with setting pricing strategies.

Here follows a short generic list of the sorts of objectives that could lie behind your price strategy decisions.

Via pricing, businesses may wish to:

- **Achieve a given target profit:** for example, in the 1960's a major tea blender and marketer (lets call them 'T. Tiger & Co.') had a brand leader called Premium Tea. One year they wanted to corner the market for a scarce high quality tea central to the blending of their top quality brands. They did not want to borrow money from the bank in order to bid at the forthcomming tea auctions in India, so they sold their 'Premium' at knock-down prices to raise cash quickly, even if at no actual profit. This 'sale' raised a good deal of cash money and that year T. Tiger & Co. cornered the market for that exceptional tea. What they did not use themselves they sold on at a huge profit to other blenders. This episode well and truly made-up for the loss of profit on its earlier consumer brand promotion, they ended that year well ahead of any previous profit forecast, and incurred no bank charges in the process.

- **Support a planned market position:** for example, if you intend to be seen as 'top of the range' then your prices had better be congruent with this.
- **Manage demand:** for example, commuter trains at so called 'rush hours' (getting to and from work in the city). The operator does not want to invest in more capacity which would only be employed for some 20 hours a week on average (*5 days with two rush hours of two hours each*), so they use higher prices to deter people who don't have to travel during the rush hours from doing so, and lower prices outside these times to encourage those that can travel outside the rush hours to do so.
- **Pre-empt/meet or follow competition:** Some time ago the author was looking to aquire his first digital camera and lusted after the then Sony Cyber-Shot which was leading the world with more than 'three megapixels' (3MP), and at a high price. The model the Author wanted came with a 'Carl Zeiss' lens and was priced at c.£700.00. Far too much for his first digital camera, so the Author aquired a two megapixel Kodak to learn with (*still cost more than £300.00 in those days*). Nonetheless he kept looking and lusting after the Cyber-Shot. Suddenly, when passing through Madrid airport and browsing the camera shop, he noticed a dramatic price reduction in the 3MP Cyber-Shot – and this was later confirmed at other camera shops in the UK – was it a faulty camera? – surely not, it was a Sony! Some three weeks later all was revealed – Fuji launched its 3 MP 'FinePix' on the market at the same price point that Sony had formerly occupied. Sony had pre-empted Fuji and it must have taken Fuji quite some time to re-coup the losses it had thus incurred having to re-price quickly after launch.
- **Differentiate product or company image:** The original two seater 'Smart Car', in the Author's opinion, is a superb idea. At the time of writing they are appearing all over the world and for what it is (*i.e. a two seat town car with easier parking than a saloon*) they are charging a superbly positioned price. Its resale value is also very healthy. However, the mistake has been to launch the Smart 'ForFour' which is a four seater saloon like any other, but at the same sort of price premium over non Smarts. The four seater Smart

has no parking or other real advantages compared to any other small four seater saloons on the market.

- **Achieve the stabilization of price:** This is an objective open only to dominant players in the market. The brand leaders of dominant players can be used to bring sanity to the marketplace by being priced at a point that gives competitors a reasonable profit at the same price point, but not so much that they can build a 'war-chest' with which they can later attack the leader.

Checklist issues to consider when setting objectives for price are:

- **Capacity utilization** – your own and the competition's
- **Fixed cost base** – ditto
- **Profitability of the product** – ditto
- **Percentage of total sales represented by this product** – ditto
- **Percentage of total profit represented by this product** – ditto
- **Price sensitivity (elasticity)** – ditto
- **Price visibility in the marketplace** – ditto
- **Perceived value** – ditto
- **Relationship between price and perceived value by customer(s)**, i.e. is the price seen as an indicator of quality? If so it is foolish to lower the price without very serious thought.
- **Value of the product as a component of total customer purchase(s)**, i.e. is it miniscular or substancial?
- **Substitute products**, i.e. if the typical customer does not buy your type of product, what would they (normally) be expected to buy instead?
- **New entrants to your market/s**, real and potential?
- **Customer concentration**, i.e. how easily can they communicate one with the other and spread the word as to where and from whom the best bargains are to be had?
- **After market potential**, i.e. how much future business is to be had from replacing worn-out parts, re-training, maintanence etc. all of

which can bring in a long-term revenue stream? For example, the motor manufacturers, every one of their vehicle sales, from saloon cars to lorries will continue to bring in profits for as long as the vehicle is maintained by their dealerships.

Some useful marketing pricing strategies

Finally lets look at the classic marketing pricing strategies together with brief explanations as to their workings and benefits.

Penetration pricing

A low price which helps the business get into a new marketplace. (See the issues with promotional pricing below.)

Premium pricing

A high price designed to reinforce strategies that put the product at the top of its marketplace. Specifically used in markets where price is seen as an indicator of quality, such as in the early days of mobile phones for example.

Price skimming

This strategy starts off as premium price, but is deliberately designed to come down over time to anticipate or react to competitive or other pressures in the market. As its name implies, it takes the cream from the top of the market, it can also be used as a means of 'shepherding' demand and thereby relieving the pressures on resource capacity (*see Chapter 2*).

Promotional pricing

This will involve special price deals that support other marketing activities involved in a particular promotion, such as, advertising, public relations, special deals at distributors and so forth. The skill here is not so much in giving discounts or reducing the price during a promotion, BUT in getting the price back-up after the promotion has done its work. Any fool can reduce price, it takes real talent to be able to put it back-up afterwards. Look for ways where the value given when on promotion is not monetary but 'in kind'. An example of this is where beer brewers and soft drink bottlers/canners, will use slightly larger cans during a promotion such that they can announce on the can that the buyer will be getting some 15% more drink at the same price. The product's price-point has not been damaged and the drinker feels they have enjoyed the extra volume.

Line pricing

This is designed to reflect the position (*say in terms of the product's quality, or the status of the buyer*) of a product in the range on offer from that supplier, so that at the top of the range the prices would be premium, and at the bottom of the range they would be at their lowest. Products between these two extremes would be priced pro rata (this is seen in the pricing of motor vehicles and pet foods).

Bait pricing

This is designed to make it relatively cheap for a customer to enter the market by offering a very low price for the very basic and standard version of the product. The customer is then free to (*indeed, may be encouraged to*) add extras, at an increased price from a menu of optional extras. A good example of this would be a chain of hotels designed specifically for the business community. The quoted price for a room would give the occupant a basic level of accommodation, but no more. If guests wished to watch the television, that's extra; if they wished to have breakfast in the hotel, again that's extra. Another good example is the retail price of small colour printers for the home or the 'home office'. The retail price is just to cover the costs of distribution, the real profit is made on the sale of the ink cartridges – that's why they hate users re-filling them with another makers inks.

Dual or Multiple pricing

This is where the same product is sold to several different markets, each at different prices. The 'core' and the 'expected' parts, and maybe even for a substantial proportion of the 'augmented', are identical. But these products are marketed to **different segments** and each segment has its own price, which will differ from any other segment, some higher, some lower.

This strategy can only be successful if it is very difficult, if not impossible, for a set of customers in one segment to communicate and/or compare their product offering with customers in a different segment. Hampering inter-customer communications can be brought about by ensuring that one set of customers cannot even meet up with any other segments, or if they do, it is very difficult for them to compare the offering in their segment with the offerings in others.

A good example of this is the segmentation policy that airlines employ. All passengers are accommodated within the same aluminium tube when flying from one airport to another, hopefully they all take off and land at the same time. However, the airline marketer has made it possible to charge substantially more for those people who sit in the front of the aircraft compared to those people who sit in the back. They can do this because business class and first class are usually provided with substantial augmentation to the product, i.e. VIP lounges at airports, wider seats, free drinks, more space etc., all with a lower probability of being 'bounced' (i.e. moved to a later flight).

Finally, a business can use dual pricing when it develops a 'fighter brand'. A fighter brand is a product launched specifically to do damage to a competitor via the use of low, sometimes even predatory prices (*see Pricing Tactics, 'fighterbrands', Chapter 6*) .When the objective is accomplished and the competitor either withdraws or is reduced to bankruptcy, the business will kill off the fighter brand and resume business with the main product that stayed aloof during the price war and whose image is thus not contaminated with a lower price. 'Any fool can reduce their price, the real skill and genius is in being able to put them back up afterwards.'

Predatory pricing

This is a policy designed to put competitors out of the marketplace. In some countries this is illegal, but not everywhere (*e.g. in the United Kingdom*).

A good example of the employment of predatory pricing was the battle in 1996 between *The Times* and *The Daily Telegraph* (on the one side) and *The Independent* (on the other). *The Times* and *The Daily Telegraph* aimed aggressive predatory pricing strategies against *The Independent* in the hope of driving it out of the market. However, after some dramatic reorganization, the Board of *The Independent* were able to link up with a syndicate of other European newspapers for support and thus increased the size of its war chest. When faced with the prospect of a long and costly war of attrition, *The Times* and *The Daily Telegraph* ceased their preditory pricing policy.

It is interesting to note that this price war episode served to increase the overall circulation of all broadsheet newspapers in the United Kingdom, whilst at the same time proving a salutary experience to *The Independent* who, by the fall of 1997, had repositioned their paper out of the segment that put them head to head with *The Times* and *The Daily Telegraph*, and into the segment occupied by *The Guardian*, one of the only national broadsheet newspapers (the other being *The Financial Times*) that had not been adversely affected by the former predatory pricing war (*for more detail see Chapter 7 Fighting a Price War*).

Barrier pricing

As we have seen when we examined the effect of the product life cycle on pricing strategy, this is a pricing policy that, by being potentially very unprofitable, is designed to make the marketplace unattractive for the competition.

Price as a shepherd

The marketer may be required to relieve pressure on resources, or to channel customers into one segment rather than another. For example, for business travel services, a premium price can be used at peak times and a highly discounted price for other times of the day/week/year.

In those services, where a great deal of social interaction takes place, varying the price of a service can vary the types of people that use it. In those services which are characterized by having high levels of inter-customer contact and involvement (*and/or where customers use other customers as an indicator of the quality of the service that they are contemplating*), to mix the wrong sorts of people on any one occasion in any one service, can have a very negative effect on the perception of its quality.

So the business will use price to move one set of customers to the 'up-market' end of the product range, whilst deterring, via the use of price, those who would not be accepted in this segment. A good example of this being the segregation of those attending a horse racecourse where the 'Silver Ring' enclosure is cheaper than the 'Members' enclosure, and a lot less 'select'.

Value-based pricing

This is a generic pricing strategy which we will look at in more detail in Chapter 5. However, essentially this is where the total package of the relationship with the customer is designed to foster long-term business between two or more organizations. Although it is not the 'be-all-and-end-all' of the Japanese Kiretsu system, it is something which is at the heart of it. A powerful business to business variant is:

RELATIONSHIP/PARTNERSHIP PRICING

The intention of this variant of value based pricing, is to build longer-term and deeper relationships with the customer businesses. The strategy itself comprises several objectives, one being to raise the barriers to entry for competitors and the other, ironically, is to raise the hurdle of the pain at leaving what would have to be overcome by customers who may be contemplating placing their business elsewhere.

The relationship/partnership pricing strategy consists of four main parts:

1. Firstly, a 'service level agreement' between the two (*or more*) parties. This would set out agreed delivery times, speeds of response, levels of availability, cleanliness of vehicles, frequency of meetings etc.
2. Secondly, it would include open book accounting between the parties involved, so that the service provider can charge all agreed and certifiable costs as incurred.
3. Thirdly, there would usually be a management fee (frequently negotiated on an annual basis), which is sometimes negotiated as an agreed ratio of overall expenditure, as for example, in several large and famous advertising agencies, or a fixed monetary amount as perhaps might be the case for a company providing haulier services.
4. Lastly, there is often a performance bonus, this again would be negotiated, also perhaps on an annual or some other periodic basis. The bonus being tied directly to the suppliers performance against the service level agreement as above.

The principle behind the following structure is that:

- with the cost (bullet 2 above) and management fee (bullet 3), the business can only break-even.

- to make any profit at all, they will have to earn the bonuses negotiated by performing up to and beyond the service level agreed to (bullet 4).

The instance of relationship pricing is on the increase, particularly amongst those companies providing business to business services for which the customer would have a constant requirement. A particularly good example of a relationship pricing strategy is cited in the BBC video of the Tom Peter's presentation *'Management Imagination': the case of Lanes Transport of Bristol and their pricing arrangements with the Body Shop organisation.*

The profit centre?

Add to all the foregoing the question as to what is the actual profit centre of a business that has a wide range of products and activities. Should it be the branches for example, where the product (*good and/or service*) is actually delivered? Should it be the transaction itself, like cashing a cheque, or using a credit card? Or perhaps it should be the product, like insurance or breakfast cereal? Or yet again, should the total customer relationship perhaps be the centre of profit?

All of these options for pricing strategy should be carefully considered in the light of the company's marketing objectives, so as to discover which are the most appropriate.

Exercise 4.2

Please examine the table following:

In the left hand column you will see seven real life situations from the recent past that required the product to be priced. See if you can determine which pricing strategy from those we discuss above, would best apply to which situation(s) (*i.e. you may want to use a strategy more than once*). Some of these situations could have been given several pricing strategies, so its worthwhile stating what would have been your pricing objective first, and then trying to keep the strategy to address these situations and objectives to a focused two (no more). When you have done this, turn to the answers in the appendix and see if you and the real life Pricers made the same decisions and/or whether you would have made a better decision than they did.

There are seven products – they are more than they seem – so to explain:

CLASSIC FRENCH PERFUME

The product is a sampler that will provide some 5 to 10 applications only. The dispenser is very small and is designed to fit in the smallest handbag or evening bag. It can be had in any of the most popular top perfumes. The product is aimed at busy metropolitan working women who may wish to freshen-up either for a special meeting at work, or before going on to a rendezvous in the evening straight from work, without having to carry the normal bulky bottle of their favourite perfume with them. The obvious price strategy is 'premium pricing' yet for so few applications the purchase price would be very low. ***So what pricing strategy should the entrepreneur who thought of this concept choose?***

SMALL SCREEN (14"/35CM) PORTABLE TV FOR THE KITCHEN

This product is designed for the smaller apartment or house (i.e. starter homes – a growing trend especially in urban areas). This TV saves having to have one in every room. It is about the size of an average laptop, i.e. 35cm square (13" by 13") with high quality stereo speakers built in. The TV has a flat LCD screen which can either be flipped upward in the fashion of a laptop, or it fits into a bracket fixed under the kitchen cupboard, over the worktop, in which case the screen flips downward and the picture automatically re-orientates. The product has powerful batteries which will give some five hours play time or more, the bracket is also its charging base. The product takes its wireless TV signal from the set-top-box which delivers the satellite or cable channels to the home. This TV will operate anywhere irrespective of whether there is another TV in the home. In the case of two or more of these in the home, at any one time each can be displaying different channels. ***So, what pricing strategy or strategies, would you recommend for this product?***

NEW TYPE OF PORTABLE DATA STORAGE FOR PC'S, LAPTOPS ETC.

Solid state and up to 250 times the memory of anything currently available. The physical attributes of this device are that it is small enough to fit into the average mans wallet or ladies regular purse – so is exceedingly portable. In terms of memory it can store some 250 times more data than anything that small currently available in the market. It comes with its own internal and external software which enables it to read and write data some three times faster than currently available equivalent data storage. It can interface with the data source via USB, fire-wire, wireless etc. ***So, who would be your target group for this product and what pricing strategy would you recommend to the makers?***

BULGARIAN RED WINE (CEPAGE = MERLOT) ENTERING YOUR COUNTRY'S MARKET FOR THE FIRST TIME

Bulgaria's traditional market for its wine industry was the Russian federation. Before the fall of the Berlin wall in the early 1990's, the Russians would take all the wine Bulgaria could produce. Now however, Russians are taking to sobriety wholesale and Bulgaria has to look for new markets.

Assume they are trying to enter your country's wine drinking market, and that so far they are unknown, what pricing strategy would you propose? ***And if you choose 'promotional pricing', how do you propose to get the price back-up afterwards?***

A RANGE OF TOP CLASS MEN'S FASHION SHIRTS (NOT TAILOR MADE)

These shirts are not for casual wear, they are fashionable shirts to wear to the office if the owner is a manager, or at special occasions such as christenings, weddings, dining out at select restaurants etc.

They are well made, from good quality fabrics, and come in a wide range of colours to suit all occasions. They are complete with a spare collar and spare buttons (one of each size used) sewn on to the bottom right front of the shirt. ***You were thinking of giving a pair of these to a favourite male relative, how much do you think it would be reasonable to pay? i.e. what would be the best price strategy for the makers to adopt?***

AN AFFINITY GOLD CARD THAT CAN BE USED FOR EITHER DEBIT OR CREDIT

This unique type of card (see below) is to be launched by a major domestic utility provider (*i.e. they provide gas, electricity, water and cable TV to homes*). Every purchase made with this card will earn points for the cardholder, which they can redeem as a discount on their utility bills as and when they want to, just by paying their utility bills with this card. The card is unique in that it is both a credit card AND a debit card. At the point of purchase the cardholder can elect to have the money for the purchase transaction drawn from their current account OR, with this card they can choose to fund the purchase via the credit card facility.

The utility company will only provide the card to customers with very good credit ratings. ***So (in terms of the charges for the card, i.e the interest rates and the card fees), what should be the utility's pricing strategy for these gold cards?***

A CHAIN OF HOTELS SPECIALIZING IN PROVIDING OVERNIGHT ACCOMMODATION FOR TRAVELLING BUSINESS PEOPLE

This chain has newly acquired hotels throughout Europe and will be re-launching the business under new management, a new banner and new facilities. The décor and facilities in the rooms and the common rooms such as reception, the bar and the dining rooms etc, will be stylish in the mode of Ikea. The bedrooms are fully equipped and with comfortable beds with en-suite but again in a very minimalist mode. **As they see it they have two pricing problems:**

- **What is the best pricing scheme to build regular customers, who only stay away for some 4 nights in the week? – and –**
- **How best should they ensure that the business at least breaks-even during the weekends?**

Product	Strategy/ies	Reasons
A: Classic French perfume		
B: A small screen (14") colour TV		
C: New type P.C storage (250 x more)		
D: Bulgarian red wine		
E: Range of men's fashion shirts		
F: A 'gold' charge credit card		
G: Room hire in a 3-4 star chain business-traveller hotels		

When complete, turn to the Appendix and check the comments on Exercise 4.2.

References

i Chapter 3 of *'Mastering Marketing'*, 2nd edition, Thorogood 2007.

ii Don't have any sympathy for the Supermarket, if they are not using this product to attract customers, i.e. it is not a 'loss leader', the high volumes well and truly make-up for the low margins per can. Not only that but via 'just in time delivery' these retailers can keep very low buffer stocks, and via their bargaining power, they may well not pay their suppliers for eight or more weeks. This means that the real profit obtained is not from what they sell, but from what they do with the money obtained via the sale, before they have to pay their suppliers. This is why so many large supermarket chains are also in financial services.

iii An early finding of the organization known as PIMS (The Profit Impact of Marketing Strategies. Inc.).

iv Refer to the BBC series in the mid 1990's called the 'Trouble Shooter', featuring Sir John Harvey Jones – in the episode where he examines the 'Morgan Cars' business – it makes a nice case study of very successful Micro-segmentation and Pricing. In those days they were getting upwards of £50,000 for just the basic car.

v See Schifman and Kunuk, Prentice Hall, 1978.

vi The reader should also consider Psychographics in Business to Business as per *'Crossing the Chasm'* by Geoffrey A. Moore.

vii We are now renovating another house – our fourth. A large DIY store from which we buy most of the building supplies, has given us a credit card to shop with in their stores – we now don't even bother to take a note of how large a bill we have racked up on any particular visit to them. We know that every month a Direct Debit will be taken from our bank account and there are more things to worry about than the cost of timber.

viii For a more detailed discussion of Segmentation and Positioning, please refer to *'Mastering Marketing'*, and *'Marketing your Service Business'* both by this Author and this publisher.

ix A 'Structured Market' is one where it takes less than 20% of the players to command 80%+ of that market's business – entering this market is a very difficult task, there are profound barriers to entry. As opposed to an 'Unstructured Market' where the market shares and the customer bases are very fluid – here there are fewer barriers to any newcomer's entrance.

x For a discussion of the DMU see Value Based Pricing, Chapter 5.

FIVE

VALUE-BASED PRICING

VALUE-BASED PRICING

Make sure whatever you offer is unique and wanted by your customers, ***a strong competitive differential keeps the discounter at bay!***

Synopsis

This chapter examines and outlines one of the most powerful pricing strategies available. Frequently known as 'value-based pricing' it is exactly that – we price our goods or services according to the values we deliver to the consumer (B2C), or the customer's business (B2B).

The chapter first cites two examples (*one B2C and the other B2B*) to illustrate the power of the idea. It then takes us through the basic concept of how to derive the value proposition for your customers step-by-step.

Two Cases: 'Value-Based Pricing'

1. Castrol v. the Rest

For those who are unfamiliar with do-it-yourself motorcar maintenance, Castrol is a well respected brand of engine oil – i.e. it keeps the moving parts of the car engine lubricated and also assists in the cooling process. For many years it was the product of a company that was independent of the oil majors such as British Petroleum (BP), Shell, Chevron, Exxon etc.

During the fiscal year 2000/2001, the amount of money that Castrol spent advertising its product in the USA was 167% more than its nearest rival by volume Exxon[1].

Bearing in mind that the volume sales of Castrol in the USA during that period were only an extra 500,000 gallons more than those of Exxon[2], this initially looks like crass over-kill.

However, examine the following table and you will see a different perspective:

Lubricants World Motor Oil Retail Price Survey: Houston*								
	May 2000				January 2001			
Brand	Wal-Mart	Target	O'Reilly	Autozone	Wal-Mart	Target	O'Reilly	Autozone
Castrol	$1.53	–	$1.59	$1.54	$1.66	–	$1.69	$1.69
Pennzoil	$1.53	$1.44	$1.59	$1.54	$1.53	$1.49	$1.69	$1.69
Valvoline	$1.47	$1.69	$1.49	$1.47	$1.62	$1.54	$1.69	$1.64
Havoline	_	$1.09	$1.37	$1.29	$1.27	$1.24	$1.49	$1.39
Mobil	$1.04	$1.04	–	$1.04	$0.92	$1.14	–	–
Exxon	–	–	$1.19	$1.07	–	–	$1.29	$1.19
**Retail prices for American Petroleum Insitute SJ-quality 10W-30 1-quart bottles of motor oil*								

TABLE 5.1: LUBRICANT PRICES COMMANDED 2000/2001

The above prices were for a 'Quart', i.e. 25% of a US gallon – and it can be seen from the above that Castrol was commanding a premium price of some $1.50 per gallon more that its two main volume rivals in the USA: Exxon and Mobil. This equated to an extra profitability of $140m more than these two rivals (assuming that the costs of production were the same).

The emphasis of Castrol's promotion being that *'An expensive oil, is a cheap mechanic'*, i.e. the better oil means your engine will last longer and not break-down so often. In this case customers were prepared to pay more for what they **perceived** to be a superior product.

2. Lanes Transport and The Body Shop

This is the story of the relationship that existed in the early 1990's between Lanes Transport of Bristol, and Body Shop UK.[i] Lanes transport was, and, at the time of writing still is, a logistics company whose business it is to deliver the goods of its clients to wherever they may be needed.

Lanes Transport had won the contract to deliver The Body Shop products to all The Body Shop's UK branches. And they had done this in spite of being a relatively small firm with less than £14M pa. turnover at the time of the award. They had done this via the use of a variant of the Value-based pricing strategy, called 'relationship' or 'partnership' pricing.

The heart of the contract between the above two firms covered two main areas:

1. 'Maintaining and supporting the 'image' of The Body Shop' – and –
2. 'Reducing The Body Shop's costs'

Taking the above in reverse order:

REDUCTION OF THE BODY SHOP'S COSTS

The main engine here was a service level agreement – the relevant part of which[3] stipulated the discipline for delivering products to The Body Shop's outlets. 99% of all deliveries had to be made within a window of plus or minus one hour of a stipulated time, on the stipulated day. And their performance against this standard was tied to the amount of profit that Lanes Transport would make – as we will see below.

The chief benefit to The Body Shop of this aspect of the agreement was the effect it had on their 'inventory carrying costs'. Traditionally, for each line of product, retail outlets would keep enough stock to last them between deliveries PLUS a buffer stock of about 1 to 2 cases to allow for unexpected delays. The regime, with which Lanes had now to comply, meant that this buffer-stock could be reduced to a few bottles per product line, per shop. So, if The Body Shop sold an average of 500 different lines, say each shop would have to carry at least c.750 cases of buffer stock to ensure that they could meet demand in the event of a delayed delivery. If there were say 250 Body Shop outlets in the UK at that time, this would mean that the business would have to carry an excess of 187,500 cases at all times. Assuming each case represented an average of some £50 worth of product at production costs (*these being cosmetics*) then this stock represented some £9,375,000 of capital tied-up – doing nothing, not even earning interest.

At an interest rate then applying to businesses of some 10-12% pa this represents an annual cost to the company of some £1.25m. So, if Lanes were successful in fulfilling these conditions, they would save The Body Shop a large amount of money.

Consequently the Partnership Agreement rewarded Lanes Transport with a bonus tied to the level of their success in exceeding this '99% deliveries on time' aspect of the contract.

"Just over 14,000 deliveries per year, and they can't afford to have more than 140 of them late."[4]

MAINTAINING AND SUPPORTING THE 'IMAGE' OF THE BODY SHOP

All the vehicles involved in servicing The Body Shop were owned by Lanes Transport but were painted in the livery of The Body Shop. These lorries were, and still are, effectively travelling posters for The Body Shop's ethos. At that time no mention of Lanes Transport was made on these vehicles (*though the Author has noted that the 'Lanes Transport' logo now does appear, but still in The Body Shop colours*). The drivers, though employed by Lanes Transport, wore The Body Shop work-wear.

And, at the start of the contract, all these vehicles were new, well maintained and chosen on the basis of being very fuel efficient and the most environmentally friendly vehicles available.

There is much more to this case than we have space to mention above.[ii]

The Heart of Value-Based Pricing

There are said to be three main areas where Value-based pricing (*VBP*) can create a platform justifying the price premium because the overall 'deal' makes some extra contribution to the customer's benefit than does the competition. These areas are referred to as the VBP Triad. They are:

i Reducing the customer's costs

ii Improving/supporting the customer's price to their customers

iii Enhancing the (customer's) product's aesthetics.

All three can apply to a Business to Business situation, and i. & ii. can apply in consumer markets. Let's elaborate slightly:

Reducing the customer's costs

Your price to your customer is their cost, and there is no getting away from that fact. However, **lowering their costs does not necessarily mean having to lower your price.**

We have seen in the above case of Lanes Transport a good example of this in action, refer also to Chapter 6 which focuses on pricing tactics, there we discuss business process outsourcing, which is another important way of reducing the customer's fixed costs via turning them into a variable cost. So that the customer only has to pay when they use the facility, when they don't use it, they don't incur costs.

But this does not always mean business to business markets – it can also apply massively to consumer markets. Some years ago a report entitled *Why the poor Pay More* was published by the Greenwood Publishing Group[iii], the central tenant of which was that people on low incomes would often spend more on their children's clothing than did people who were better paid. A good illustration of why this happened was the example given of the purchase and usage behaviour of children's shoes. Whereas the better paid families would buy one good pair of shoes for school and these would last the school year, and probably be replaced only because the child had grown out of them, the poorer people could not afford such good quality and thus would, stereotypically, buy a cheap pair of fabric based 'trainers' which would probably have to be replaced at least twice in a school year – three pairs of trainers being more expensive in the long run than one good pair of well-made leather shoes.

At the end of this chapter there are four checklists which headline the main list of VBP stratagems that we know are in common usage (*by those few firms who use VBP proficiently*).

IMPROVING/SUPPORTING OUR CUSTOMER'S PRICE TO THEIR CUSTOMERS

The question is "does a way exist where the good, and/or service[5] which makes-up our 'product', can allow our customer to charge more for their products" – and the answer is that it does exist in many cases, but is only exploited in a few.

Take the motor industry practice of installing especially tuned engines from other manufactures in their top of the range cars (*e.g. Morgan cars have often used Cosworth engines versus their standard engine sourced from Ford*).

Take the case of Intel, and their branding and the promotion which supports it "Intel Inside", which has in turn become the imprimatur of quality/reliability/functionality etc. for the IT industry, PC's, and laptops and now also Apple Macs.

ENHANCING THE (CUSTOMER'S) PRODUCT'S AESTHETICS[6]

(*The 'customer' is in brackets because we can either do this direct if we are in consumer markets ourselves, or via our customer's businesses if we are not. In which case it is said to be business to business markets.*)

The first case mentioned above, re Castrol's product's positioning as a high quality motor oil perfectly illustrates this effect in action.

The benefits of adding that extra value to your product

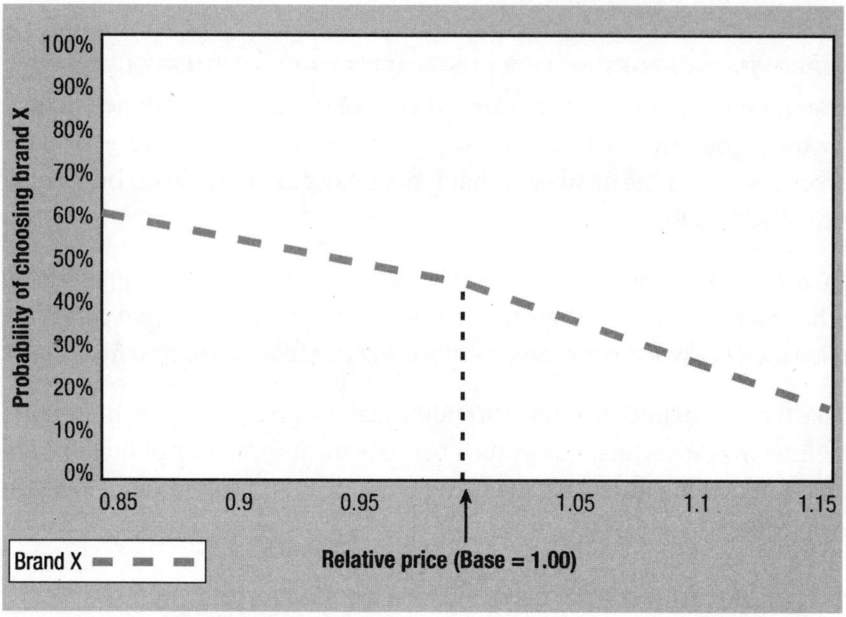

FIGURE 5.2: THE BASIC SITUATION RE. ELASTICITY WITHOUT ANY VALUE ADDED

In the above diagram we see the product at its present price which we have indicated as being the figure 1. On the vertical axis we show the volumes expected at the different prices, so that at the current price we have say c.45% of the available business. At a 15% discount (*shown as 0.85*) the probability is that we will obtain some c.60% of the available business, and at a 15% premium (*1.15*) we will sell only c.15% of the available business. In both cases, probably losing money in the process. If the price is too low, not withstanding any economies of scale, we lose margin, if the price is too high we lose volume – either way we will probably suffer. However, what if we can move the curve upward? If we do, then we can open-up a wider range of more attractive possibilities as shown in Figure 5.3 below:

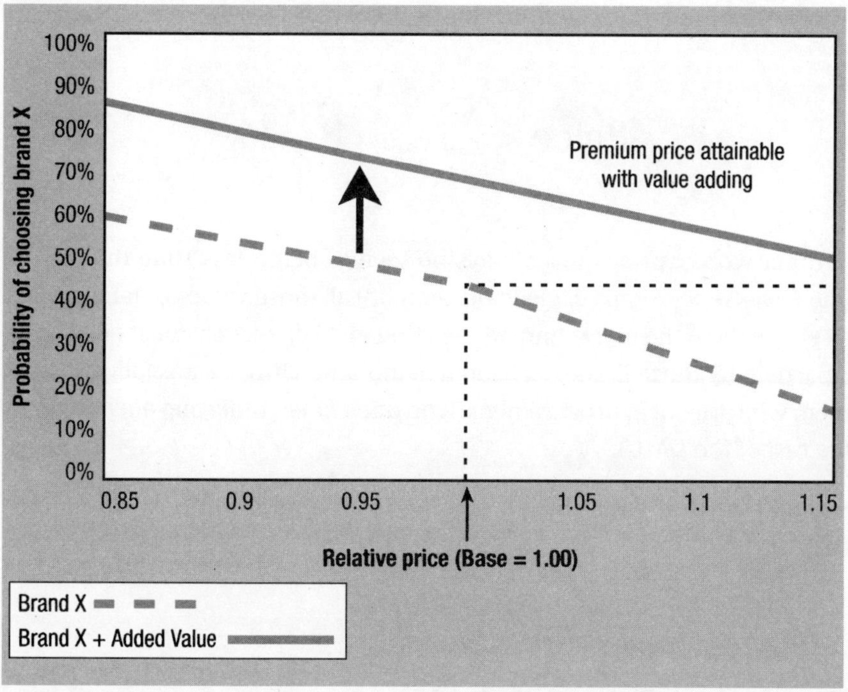

FIGURE 5.3: SHOWING THE EFFECT OF MOVING THE CURVE UPWARD VIA ADDING VALUE

By adding value that the customer appreciates, we will be moving the curve upward, we can then either sell some c.20+% extra volume, at the normal price, perhaps also reaping economies of scale in the process. Or, at the other extreme of the options available, we can command a 15% price premium whilst selling the same volume that was attained before the value addition. Between these two extremes we have any combination of those possibilities.

It is important to realize that there are two dimensions to value; Intrinsic and Extrinsic.

Intrinsic value: is a 'built-in' property of the good or service itself, whether it is a commodity or not. For example, rice, cooking ware, motor oil, bottled water, dental or medical services et. al.

Extrinsic value: is nearly all perception, i.e. it is the way customers think (*or can be made to think*) about the product (*good and/or service*) as is illustrated by such commodities as gold, or 'Intel Inside', or BMW motor vehicles, or Emirates Airlines (*say vs. Gulf Air, BA et al.*), The Maldives as a holiday destination (*vs. say Thailand or New Zealand*).

The basic equation for adding value is shown as follows:

$$\text{Price} < \sum_{\text{values}} P_1 - P_n$$

In other words, price must always be seen as being **less than** the sum of (*the Greek letter Sigma* Σ *meaning 'sum of'*) all those values obtained from all elements of the marketing mix employed,[iv] i.e. the deal must be seen as a bargain by those in the decision making unit (DMU), especially those of them who are not in procurement (*who often have conflicting agendas with the rest of the DMU*).

So, that is what value-based pricing is all about, but how do you do it?

The Value-Based Pricing process of analysis

What is the process that needs to be observed in order to be able to identify and add the values that will command the extra premium, or help resist the continual downward pressure on prices that occur in most markets which are not suffering a shortage of supply?

The rest of this chapter is devoted to outlining the answer to that question.

In short, the process consists of the following (5 or 6[7]) stages

- Monitoring our price/value situation vs. the competition, which is expressed via the 'price landscaping' tool,
- Being quite clear at all times what type of customer (*re the SPG 3 segments approach*) we will be dealing with,
- Similarly being realistic about how the customer sees us and/or our product offerings; for B2B markets this means using market research to feed into the 'McDonald buyers matrix',
- Researching and analyzing the customer's/prospect's perception of what is 'value' for them, this by the use of the Levitt construct,

- Again using market research, analyzing how the customers view us in this respect vs. the competition and their ideal configuration of benefits/values. And for consumer markets only, if relevant:
- Building a 'conjoint analysis' based model of the consumer's trade-off behaviours when faced with the purchase decision.

Knowing where we stand vs. the competition

In Chapter 4 we described the 9 cell price positioning matrix and its uses, and we also discussed the 36 cell landscape grid. It is the latter that we must use in this context. This means not so much employing market research, which is a project style operation, but adopting the practice of continuously monitoring the market via a market intelligence system, i.e. an MIS (*which is good practice anyway, not just for VBP*).

Consider the following landscape grid – your research reveals the picture below. It shows where your customers believe you stand in relation to your segment competitors in a specific market segment[8].

It is useful when plotting the research data to put your company in the middle, i.e. to use yourself as the benchmark. This leaves enough room around to scope the market compared to your own business.

Note that competitor one and competitor four are on the 'logical' diagonal, their positions re. price and value are logical, and they pose no real threat other than if you had meant to be where competitor one is today.

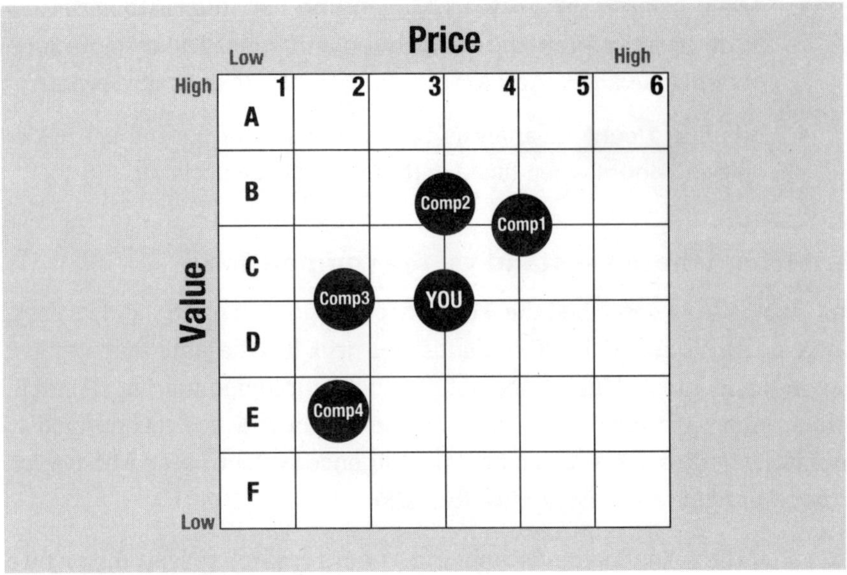

FIGURE 5.4: A HYPOTHETICAL VALUE SITUATION ACCORDING TO YOUR BUYERS

The threats come from the other two competitors.

Competitor two is at the same price as you are, but your customers believe (*and people behave according to their perceptions, not our desires*) that they offer better value than do you. Competitor three could be an even greater threat, in that they offer the same value as your business does, but at a lower price. [*A good current example of where this is increasingly the case is imports into Europe of electronic goods from the Far East – at the time of writing, specifically China.*]

Exercise 5.1: Price landscaping

Take a market that you know well and, placing yourself in the centre, as above, plot on that grid, where your two major competitors stand in that market segment. IF they are not on the diagonal – try to explain why not, and where and why they may have the edge over you!!

We obviously need to analyze how our customers perceive value. Knowing what constitutes value for them is a MUST!

However, before that we do need to know what types of customer, along the lines of the SPG's 'Super Segments' mentioned in Chapter 4 (*Figure 4.5 and re-visited below*) we are dealing with.

Just to remind you, the low price segments are buyers who are more concerned with the cost of acquisition rather than anything else, the 'high-value, good-price' are concerned with the costs of ownership, relationship/ partnership customers want a 'Kiretsue' style partnership with their suppliers (*more of this below*).

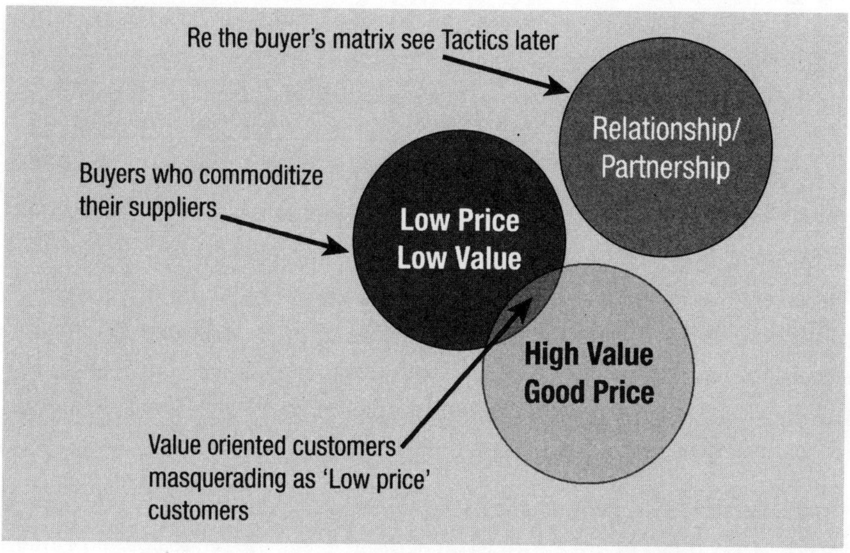

FIGURE 5.5: SPG'S B2B 'SUPER SEGMENTS'

So if we are in B2B markets, at this point, and in relationship to the price landscape situation we have established, it is important that we deal with customers who fall into either one of the latter two types of 'Super Segments' (i.e. high value or relationship). There is usually no way we can persuade the low-price, low-value buyers to see it our way – they are probably in a desperately aggressive and price competitive market. The most we can consider doing in this circumstance is to keep our competitors on their toes via the use of a fighter brand[9], to ensure that they don't have it all their own way and, hopefully, keep their attention diverted from the last two more profitable segments.

Coincidentally, in B2B markets, we need to know how the customer's procurement department view us on the buyers matrix, below:

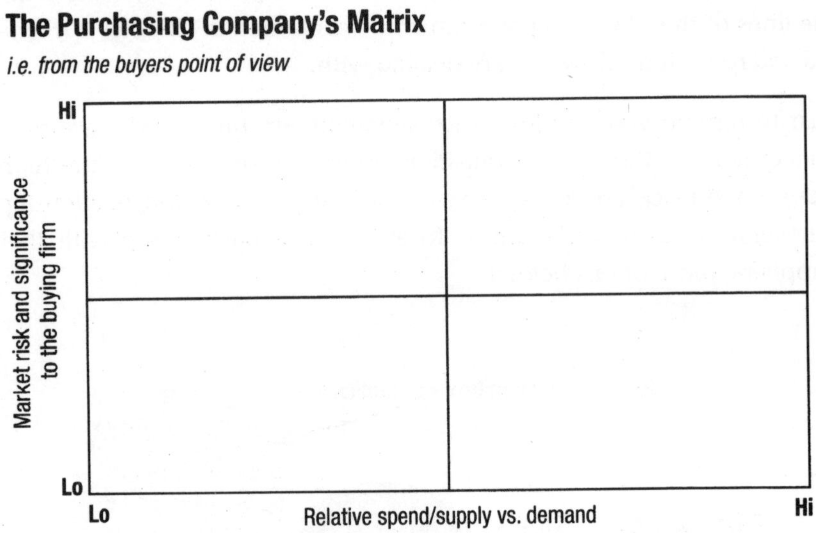

FIGURE 5.6: THE BUYERS MATRIX[v]

The axes are important, in that on the horizontal axis, the buyer spends more time and effort on the right hand side of the matrix than on the left, either there are shortages (*i.e. supply and demand situation is adverse*) and/or this is where the most procurement money is spent so a small reduction in cost per unit, will accrue large overall savings.

On the vertical axis, products in the upper row are critical to the customer's business, i.e. they cannot afford to be without it (*see the ref. to colour printers below*).

The main indications arising from this construct are that, from the supplier's point of view:

- The ideal place for them to be is in the top right-hand quadrant. Here the best strategy is to persuade the customer to accept a 'partnership' arrangement. The problem is not the cost of supplies but the danger of running out of stock. For example, most major international colour printer manufacturers, at the small printer end of their market, make their profit on the sales of toner, or ink cartridges, not on the sale of their printers per se. The retail price of the printer is mainly to cover the costs of distribution (*a good example of 'bait pricing'*). In the case of ink-jet printers it is essential that the ink is liquid until it hits the paper, and, when it hits the paper, it solidifies almost instantaneously. At one time there was only one major producer of such an additive for this type of ink, i.e. one which enabled the liquid to solidify so quickly (*at that time the chemical that would do this was referred to in the industry as a 'fastener'*). Today one would be amazed at the lengths to which printer manufacturers would go to ensure that a partnership existed, and that their security of supply was assured.

- The next best place to be is in the top left quadrant. Here the importance to the buyer is to insure there are no bottlenecks or so called 'choke points' which could interrupt production (*for example*).
- If your business falls in the bottom left quadrant you are relatively 'small fry' from a procurement point of view. The same amount of time spent negotiating with you can pay better dividends elsewhere in the matrix. The best strategy for any firm in this quadrant must be to promote a sole supplier status for themselves. This adds value for the customer at little (if any) cost to you. The customer can now invest more time and effort where it will yield the higher return, i.e. in the bottom right quadrant.

  A good example of firms in the bottom left quadrant could be (say) suppliers of office cleaning services. Such businesses should go for a Service Level Agreement (SLA) and, say, a five year contract reviewed every two years. If accepted, the customer's procurement function can now let you get on with supplying the service and be free to concentrate its efforts on the relatively big game.
- For the supplier, the 'killing ground' is that bottom right quadrant. Here the buyers can afford to walk away – at least for a time – and that provides them with the ultimate negotiating leverage. In this quadrant the buyer's best strategy will be to turn the quadrant into a commodity market and to buy from the supplier with the best value at the lowest price. Suppliers in this quadrant must seek to add the value that will move them into the top right quadrant – which is not an easy thing to do. It requires that the supplier becomes intimately familiar with the buyer's business (*in so far as it is affected by their products*), understands what 'value' means to their customer(s) and is able to communicate this effectively to the decision-makers (*at best in financial terms*).

So, at this point the supplier will have to start thinking of what values can be added, that are attractive to the customer, and ideally of low incremental cost. (*What we refer to as 'gold-dust' in the final chapter, Negotiation.*) To do this the supplier will have to get beyond the customer's procurement department. Almost invariably people in procurement are motivated, targeted and given incentives on the amount of money they can save their firm, which means that they are invariably personally motivated by the cost of acquisition. The up-shot of this is that the value additions which may appeal to the relevant DMU, will often not appeal to procurement.

In all firms, beyond procurement are people and concerns which are referred to as the Decision Making Unit (DMU)[vi]. The people in the DMU who are of most importance to us are the 'specifier' (*who is concerned with technical fitness for purpose*) and the decision-maker who most probably owns the budget. Occupiers of this last role can often be persuaded that 'lifetime value', i.e. the costs of ownership, is more important than the cost of acquisition (*i.e. the 'why the poor pay more' syndrome again*).

The best tool for this job is the Levitt construct (see overleaf) with inputs from good quality marketing research.

The total product concept

It is very useful to classify the features and benefits of any one product[10] along the lines suggested by the following model proposed by Theodore Levitt[vii]. This model is known by various names and is interpreted in as many different ways. However, for our purposes the author offers the following which his experience has found most useful.

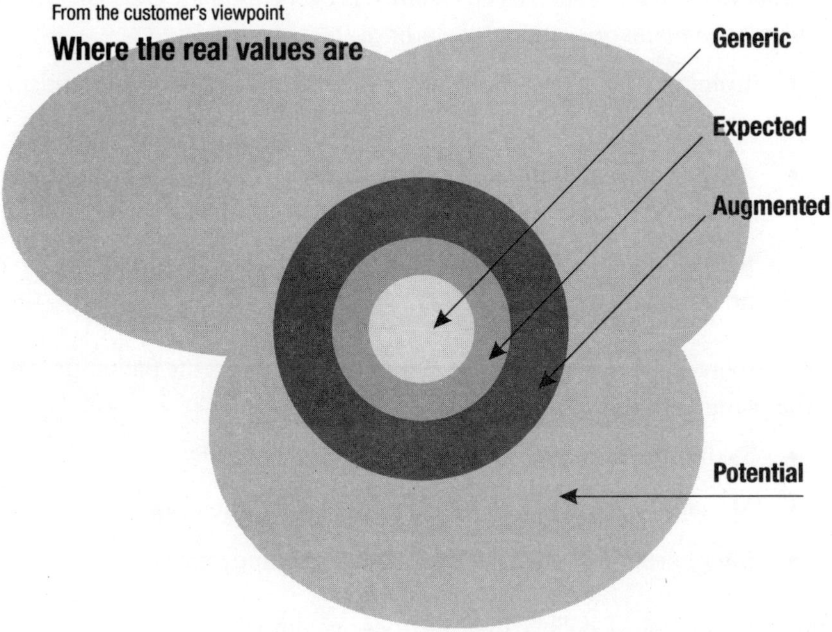

FIGURE 5.7: THE LEVITT CONSTRUCT

In this model the product can usefully be considered to consist of three layers, each founded on those closer to the middle. The product's future is the reservoir of ideas (i.e. the potential) which surrounds all three. This has no boundary, it is limited only by the company's collective imagination.

In the practice of value-based pricing we should aim to enhance our customer's augmented product, via the use of our own.

To describe, illustrate and reveal the relevance of each part of the product in turn:

'GENERIC' OR CORE

This is the heart and the foundation of the product. The generic is both internal to the company and to the product itself. It consists of all those things a company must do in order to get the product to offer the features that will yield the benefits/value additions required.

For goods such as a car, it could include the zinc galvanization of the under body, both zinc coated metal and the process that deposits the zinc. This 'galvanization' is a feature which confers less rust, longer body-shell life and thus the benefit of the vehicle maintaining its value longer.

For a service business such as an airline it is everything the company must do to get the plane operational including:

- Training all the crew – both air crew, cabin crew, airside and landside crew etc.
- At the end of a flight, and before the next – emptying all the tanks that need to be emptied, and filling all those that should be full.
- Servicing the engines regularly, ensuring the landing gear tyres have no bald patches etc.

It also involves the operational process necessary to get the passengers on to the plane with their luggage:

- Taking the bookings
- Managing the check-in for passengers and their luggage
- Shepherding them on to the plane at the appropriate time etc.

Some commentators believe that the generic comprises more than 70% of everything that the company does to bring about the product. And yet, done well, the generic is often invisible to the customer. The same commentators say that it directly contributes less than 11% of the satisfactions that a customer derives from the product – mainly because whatever skills and processes are involved they are beyond the customers' willingness or skills to evaluate. Because of this the generic is, and should be, so much in the background that customers take it for granted. Yet the quality of the generic is vital. It stays in the background only so long as things go well. When things go wrong, even though that mishap may be trivial, it can have a dramatic impact on the customer's perception of the quality of the total product.

As a former airline CEO[viii] once said, '...if the seat tray in front of the passenger is dirty with coffee stains from several flights ago, and is wobbly because some screws are missing, they can be excused for believing that this is the way we service our engines.'

Without a well founded generic no 'total' product can be built.

'EXPECTED' (AKA HYGIENE FACTOR, OR CULL TEST)

Customers feel qualified to judge this aspect. Any absence of factors which go to make up the expected for them, can have a direct impact on their ability to enjoy the basic benefits from the product. For a car it could be the quality of the ride, the in-car entertainment, a large enough boot space, an automatic transmission etc. For the airline: it could be the times of the scheduled flights to the desired destination. Does the airline go direct or will passengers have to change flights at a hub, the speed of check-in, the reliability of the baggage handling etc.

Sometimes the 'expected' is referred to as either a 'hygiene factor' (a term borrowed from Hertzberg's explanation of motivation[ix]) or a cull test, in that the absence of the right factors here will ensure that the company is not short-listed, it will not be invited to tender; or, current customers will leave if factors formerly present, are no longer provided.

'AUGMENTED' (OR COMPETITIVE DIFFERENTIAL ADVANTAGE [CDA])

Sometimes referred to as the 'product surround' this aspect of the product is 'motivational' (from Hertzberg again) in that it can cause customers to switch their business to this company.

The contents of this part of the product should provide benefits which uniquely satisfy customers, and do this better than the competitors products, and do this in the perception of the customer – not just the marketer. The items that comprise the 'augmented product' should be designed to address the customers' 'mission critical' issues.

Therefore, the benefits offered here must be targeted at, and be specific to the intended customer. The acronym K.I.S.S (*Keep It Simple Stupid*) is appropriate, because the seller must focus their proposition on the key value (*or values*) which are being promoted to support their price.

Examples of augmented factors are:

For the motor car

- Guaranteed buy-back at a guaranteed price.
- Air conditioning.
- It confers status in the driver's community.
- Side impact bars for safety – etc.

For the airline

- Limousine collection and delivery to the airport of departure and delivery to the destination at the other end.
- Larger, more comfortable seats on long-haul flights.

- Power points for notebook computers in business class.
- Seat-back video screens etc.

The lists can go on – but note how each facet is easy to copy, one auto-manufacturer does it, and soon the rest will follow, it is the same with the airline examples. If any innovation gives one company an advantage, the others in the market would be negligent not to follow suit, or to try and leapfrog with a different innovation. And thus yesterday's augmentation can quickly become an expected, a standard, a cull test, a hygiene item tomorrow.

The potential product (or reservoir of ideas)

In an increasingly competitive world, as yesterday's 'value added' differential rapidly becomes today's expected, it is critical for both ourselves and our customers to stay one step ahead of the competition. The wise supplier, therefore, will constantly be collecting and evaluating ideas as to how to differentiate his/her product from all the sources available. Including the use of formal marketing research.

It is the mark of a good entrepreneur that they are not too proud to borrow ideas from others. Ideas can be had wherever one looks, keep cuttings, make notes (*Somerset Maugan's note books went for a fortune at auction, not just for the collector's value, but for the wealth of plot ideas*) no one ever knows when an idea will come in useful. However, it is the sign of a good marketer that they don't try to transpose these ideas into their own market, it may not be right in its raw state, it may require translation.

To illustrate this:

The author once consulted for a major department store in Plymouth. It was about the time that the phrase 'have a nice day' was first crossing the Atlantic. The client wished the floor staff of several stores to adopt the saying to see how well it would work in the UK. Typically customers were cynical, and the occasional few were openly derogatory – '...and what's it to you!' was one vehement remark which caused upset.

One evening the author discussed this with a taxi driver. When the author finished his journey, the taxi driver wished the author a safe journey, said that he hoped to see him again soon, and asked the author to give the taxi driver's regards to Plymouth.

Before handing the author the receipt for his fare, the taxi driver asked to be told what he had just said – after a short discussion in which the author was at a loss to answer to the taxi driver's satisfaction, the taxi driver declared that he was saying the equivalent of 'have a nice day' in English-English, as apposed to American-English, and by golly he was!

This makes the point beautifully – the supplier should never just transpose an idea into his/her market, they should know their market sufficiently to be able to translate the idea (i.e. into 'English-English' or whatever your language).

The ideal value based strategy therefore must be to put in place a continuous programme expressly for the generation, evaluation and 'banking' of ideas.

Marketers should read widely, particularly the business and trade press (*but should not be confined to them*). In consumer markets, there is little that provides better results than regular focus group discussions with customers and consumers.

The following two examples of potential ideas for B2C markets come from many years of running focus group discussions with customers of taxi companies and patients of medical practices. Some of these ideas are:

For taxi companies

- Payment by credit card (*now very common in the USA, in some places it is an 'expected' – a true cull test. Airline passengers will frequently not use cabs that don't accept credit cards*).
- Loyalty schemes for regulars (*air miles/taxi miles, in some cases*).
- Choice of music for longer journeys.
- A rack of today's papers close to the passenger.
- Cell-phone for passenger use, paid for with the fare or by credit card.
- Lady drivers for lady passengers, particularly after dark etc.

For a medical practice

- Refreshments in the waiting room, tea, coffee etc. (*A practice in north Somerset serves wine with evening meals according to the Times 11 November 1996.*)

- Very early (*6am*) and very late (*9pm*) surgeries to serve those who commute to work.
- A creche for the patient's children.
- Public telephone facilities (*not everyone has a mobile*).
- The doctor comes to the waiting room to greet patients.
- Consulting rooms on mainline rail terminuses, etc.

Ideas so gathered should be evaluated, and if they prove they have potential, they should be stored in readiness for the day that the competitor either copies our current value added scheme, or betters it. When that happens, the appropriate new idea should be brought into action with ultimate speed, so as to ensure that the competition has little chance to gain a lead by exploiting their (*temporary*) parity or advantage.

Ideas in the category 'potential' should be stored in such a way that they are regularly, and not too infrequently, dusted off and updated. There is usually not enough time to do this when their presence in the marketplace is suddenly required.

The total product concept has enormous beneficial impact on the potential profitability of the product. Factors that 'augment' the product form the basis for much of the good practice in value-based pricing.

Exercise 5.2

Deconstruct the product that you used for the Landscape Grid in Exercise 5. Say what you believe to be the relevant facets of:

- **The generic product,** i.e. the necessary +70% that makes up the generic part of the product which customers don't care about until it goes wrong.
- **The expected product,** i.e. the minimum the product must have to be acceptable – those aspects which the customers feel capable to judge you by.
- **The augmented product,** what does actually give you a competitive advantage? What will make customers come to you, stay with you, wait for you, and pay more for your product?

Now brainstorm to discover all the ways, no matter how fanciful, whereby you can provide a competitive advantage/value addition for your customers in the future, in other words build a list of the factors that could comprise **the potential product**.

Some ways to add value for the customer

Earlier in this chapter we said that there were essentially only three areas where we could add value, reduce the customers' costs, improve their prices (to their market) and enhance the aesthetics of our product. The first and last of these can apply to both business and consumer customers. The second is (almost) exclusively business to business.

As simple as this sounds, the application of any of the above can be quite complex. The following will hopefully provide the reader with some starting points and stimulus to thinking when looking for values that will at least stem the erosion of price, and/or improve their price point to their customers.

Just a quick reminder to bear in mind when reading what immediately follows – a product is a bundle of benefits enjoyed by the consumer/customer, and can be either a tangible good (*e.g. a motor vehicle tyre*) or a service, (*i.e. fitting that tyre*), or a combination of these (*Quick-Fit who survey, recommend and replace your worn-out tyres while you wait*).

For their businesses customers Quick-Fit also provide a service whereby they will regularly visit your vehicle park and survey the tyres on your fleet, thus keeping your fleet safe and legal. They will also come to your rescue to replace damaged tyres in the field.

The addition of service to add value is the most favoured stratagem when appropriate. Some authors estimate that the service element is applied in circa 75% of all successful Value Based pricing situations.

So the two major classes of ways that services can be used to add value are:

1. Direct value from services

Phase of the sale	Can make a charge: Service expressed as, for example:
Before	Training, Audit, Consultancy, Analysis, Funding
During	Training, Hotline, Stock Management *(e.g. forms, wine and tyres)*
After	Insurance, Maintenance, Training, Upgrades, Applications, Warranty.

NB: We can make a charge for these services, but many firms fail to make even a nominal charge. Later when the values are being totalled, or eventually the firm has to make even a nominal charge (*which is better than nothing*) **we will meet customer resistance**.

A good example of this was when under the Thatcher government, in the late 1980s; farmers were told that they would henceforth have to pay for the advice, re animal husbandry provided by the Officers' of the Meat & Livestock Commission (MLC). (*Which advice had normally been given free since the Second World War*). Farmers refused to shoulder this extra cost, MLC officers called less often, and in some cases not at all. And about that time BSE (i.e. Mad Cow Disease) became endemic, with tragic consequences for nearly all concerned[x].

Additionally, in this group of approaches it is important to remember that if we add value AND DON'T CHARGE FOR IT RIGHT AT THE START we may never be able to.

EXAMPLES FROM 'FORMS, WINE AND TYRES:'

FORMS

In the decade 1985 to 1995 the financial services industry went through a major metamorphosis, part of which was the so called 'big bang'. One of the author's clients, to whom we provided market research and consultancy was a paper converter based in North Somerset. Up to 'big bang' this firm's business had been supplying pre-printed forms to many types of large firm. These pre-printed forms for the Financial Services Industry ranged from cheques to balance statements. 'Big bang' created a great deal of competition between the various financial services where little or none had existed before. Competition caused an internal focus on costs which our client saw as a huge opportunity. Initially they held the stocks of forms themselves and supplied them to the clients on a just-in-time basis so doing for HSBC what Lanes had done for Body Shop, re. the inventory carrying costs. Eventually our client installed printers in their customer's premises so the customer's people could print completed documents on demand (*format and content printed at the same time*) from the plain paper, and via clever programming etc. customers did not pay for anything until the form was in the mail to the bank's customer. Needless to say, the converter not only kept their customers, but made more profit as they could now negotiate to enjoy a share of the savings they had enabled their clients to enjoy.

WINE

Until a short while ago a wholesaler owned by a co-operative of Italian wine producers sold wine to their restaurant customers like any other wholesaler. Dissatisfied with their margins they decided to go up-market in terms of the restaurants they supplied, and in so doing ran head-on into the incumbent wine suppliers. To avoid a price war they chose a strategy of value-based pricing.

They did their research and discovered that at that time most of the upper bracket restaurants in the major European cities were each holding an average of some half a million Euros' (c.$350,000.00) worth of wine **at wholesale prices**! And for these top bracket restaurants, times were getting tough.

The co-ops' answer:

They provided their top echelon customers with a service that managed the restaurants' wine cellars for them. At the start of the programme, when a new restaurant joined the scheme, the co-op bought-back or otherwise purchased all of the wine in that customer's cellar, thus freeing-up a large amount of the customer's capital, and/or reducing their overdraft. The co-op managed the customer's wine cellar physically (*e.g. husbanding the wine in the cellar at optimal temperature and humidity etc, keeping it stocked with a similar range, but a lot less of each vintage – i.e. the restaurant did not have to buy in bulk any longer*), and financially so that the restaurant did not pay for the wine until the week after it had been sold – but then at a much narrower margin that had formerly been the case. Thus they shared the cost savings between the two.

TYRES

In the early 1970s Michelin were innovating the 'radial tyre' and in the process causing a paradigm shift throughout Europe. Their tyre was superior in terms of safety and wear compared to anything else available on the market, both for personal motorists and haulage fleets. The 'cost per tyre mile' (*i.e. the cost of ownership*) was so much lower than any other producer's product that they could charge more than twice their competitor's price for a similarly sized tyre and the customers still thought that they had a bargain. On top of all this, because more of the tyre was in contact with the road at any given time (*versus the competition*), the tyre was safer and thus fleet operators could get reduced motor insurance premiums.

Yet, even in the face of this superior product, some tyre companies were still able to win business away from Michelin WITHOUT having to reduce their prices. An example of this was Goodyear Tyre Company of the UK.

At that time, a major motorway (the M5) was being extended from Bristol to Plymouth. There were 15 separate contractors working on this motorway carving the earth into the shape that would eventually form the foundation of the roadway paving, and Goodyear supplied more than half of these contractors at full price.

The Goodyear team had realized that the way a civil engineering contractor of this type perceived their costs was not the initial purchase price of the tyre, but the productivity of that tyre over its life. They could get more tons of earth moved per pence of that tyre's cost if they fitted the tyres on the vehicle at the construction site, rather than fitting them at the factory, and then driving that vehicle down to where the earth was being moved (c. 100+ miles). (*If this were done at 30/40 mph, without stops for cooling, a great deal of the tyre's life would be expended in that drive.*)

This strategy was facilitated by a small crew of tyre engineers from Goodyear. They regularly visited their customer's construction sites, audited the tyres, and trained the drivers of the earth moving equipment how to be more economical with the tyres that were on their vehicles.

No other tyre manufacture did any of this, and one even fitted the tyres on their customer's earth movers at Dover on a Saturday, and then on the Sunday, sent the driver off across the south of England (*c.130 miles and no motorway*) accompanied by a small van with tools in case of breakdown, and with instructions for them both to be back at Dover for the last sailing back to Europe that evening. Result: great tyre – but at least half of its life had gone before it did any productive work.

Finally, re the above analysis – note how often training appears. It is a superb way to add value for your clients, and has the additional benefit of winning converts within their teams who will advocate your product in times to come.

2. Indirect value from service

	Usually no charge:
Phase of the sale	**Service expressed as, for example:**
Before	Demonstration, Speed of Reaction, Case Study, Reference Sites, Applications, Know-how etc.
During	Progress Reporting; Testing.
After	Confirmation, Trend Analysis, Reminders, New Ideas, New Products, Guaranteed Buy-back.

This is strategically the most important area

Of the above, several deserve more detail:

BEFORE

Speed of reaction can be vital; it is one of the 'flavours of time' in the marketing and delivery of any service. Customers will be losing money from the time their product develops the fault to the time it is 'back-up and running', thus time is money and although one can infrequently charge extra for this facet, careful highlighting of this value should assist preventing price erosion (*at least in the value customer and the partner, re SPG's Super Segments*). Reference sites: there is nothing so powerful than a satisfied customer telling your prospects how wonderful you are – choose your reference sites with care, handle them with lots of TLC and you will be rewarded ten-fold for your troubles.

DURING

Silence is the antithesis of time's 'speed of reaction'. Keep the customer in the picture good and bad. However, remember Machiavelli's advice – to paraphrase it 'Tell people all of the bad news at once – get it over with quickly and in one dose. BUT for good news, spread it a bit at a time, so each item may be savoured separately, and thus make good news appear to be greater than it would otherwise.'

AFTER

Never walk away from a customer just because you perceive that there is nothing more that you can sell them at this time. Not only are you foregoing the potential benefits of having an advocate (*those who will tell up to five prospects of their satisfaction with you*) or a partner (*those who will constructively show you how you can improve your offering*) but when new personnel who you don't know appear on the scene, they will form their own allegiances – perhaps even with new suppliers.

Today, via customers being able to download helpful material from your website, and the use of industry newsletters and conferences there is no excuse for becoming estranged from any customer.

Researching price

VERY FEW FIRMS DO SERIOUS PRICE RESEARCH:

Surprisingly few companies use pricing research effectively. A survey[xi] found that 88% of companies did little or no serious pricing research. Only 8% of companies could be classified as conducting pricing research professionally in support of the development of an effective pricing strategy. This is corroborated by a McKinsey & Company pricing benchmark study that estimated that only circa 15% of companies do serious research of pricing.

Below we summarize the currently available techniques, tools and approaches for researching price.

Pricing research analysis:

Intention based	Direct questioning
	Gabor-Granger buy response question
	Price sensitivity meter (PSM)
	Conjoint analysis
	Discrete choice modelling (DCM)
Purchase based	Historical sales data
	Panel data
	Store scanner data
	Purchase laboratory experiments
	In-store experiments

We will highlight each of the above in turn.

Intention based research

This approach aims to uncover buyers' intentions. It attempts to gather meaningful customer input in the context of a competitive market. Customer research on prices is notoriously difficult to interpret and sometimes unreliable.

For example, setting Internet prices, customers claim to buy on-line for the lower prices[xii]. Yet their behaviour belies this. McKinsey & Company showed that 89% of on-line book buyers bought from the first site visited. Similarly with 84% of toy buyers and 81% of music buyers. In separate research, fewer than 10% of Internet purchasers turned out to be deliberate bargain hunters. **Customers may say one thing but often do another.**

DIRECT QUESTIONING

When asked, "How much would you pay for this?" customers seem unable to answer honestly. The study 'The price is right (or is it?)[xiii]', states: that when hearing such a question, many respondents immediately shift into bargaining mode and produce opening offers that don't reflect what their real behaviour would be.' Customers seem to try to encourage price cuts, or may simply be unable to admit to reasons for paying more than the minimum price. It is therefore not wise to develop a pricing strategy based on reactions to customers playing off one supplier against another.

BUY RESPONSE QUESTION

A simple but more reliable direct question is the 'buy response question'. This is known as the Gabor-Granger technique[xiv]. The method is to describe or demonstrate a product with its features, mentioning the price in context.

Gabor-Granger tests are simple, defensible and widely used to predict demand at different price levels – they are sometimes called 'purchase probability curves'. These can also be used to forecast optimum revenues. One would expect that the lowest priced product would have highest market share, unless the offering is priced so low that the customer questions its quality. The customer is asked, 'Would you buy it?'

It is important that the respondent's attention is not drawn specifically to the price tag.

It is also possible to present a range of competitor products and to pose the question 'Which, if any, would you buy?' Thus the price should be presented unobtrusively, i.e. as just one of the features of the product.

This tool tests different price options to gauge price sensitivity. Obviously, if a single respondent were presented with a second option of an identical package apart from a price change – then respondents would probably realize that price is the issue and thus will be sensitized to price and revert to their bargaining mode. Sequential tests with the same respondents may be appealing in terms of reducing research costs, but they actually destroy meaning. Therefore monadic tests are used, i.e. each respondent is asked **once only**. Prices vary between different respondents in the overall sample. Respondents are unaware that others are being shown different prices or that price is the object of the survey.

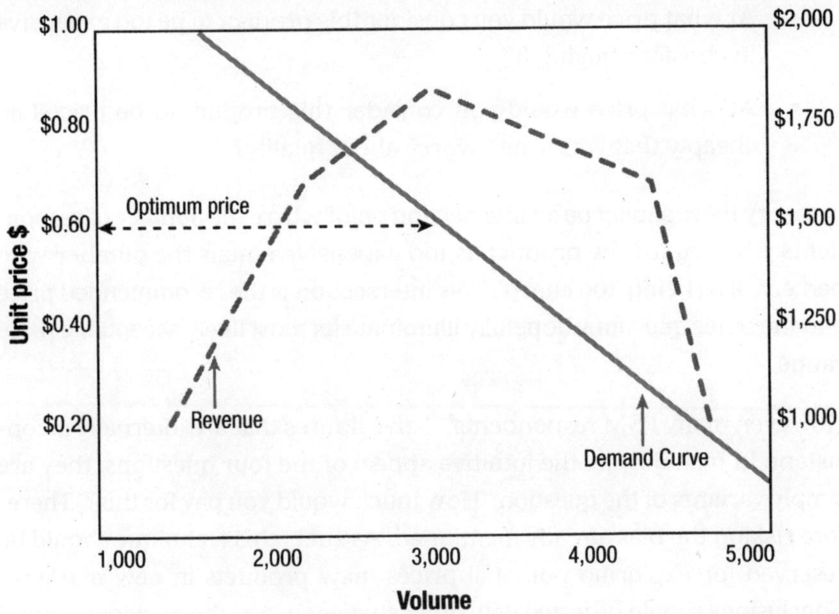

FIGURE 5.8: THE GABOR-GRANGER PRICE/VOLUME CURVE

However, as in any research, accuracy is a function of the sample size. In order to give a reasonable level of confidence for each price step, a sample size of more than 200 should be used. Larger than normal sample sizes are needed to provide statistical accuracy, especially where price changes are as small as 5-10%. Cell sizes[xv] of less than 100 lead to large sampling errors and even reversals of the expected price-volume relationship. The recommended techniques to increase accuracy are to use:

- larger samples,
- a smaller number of price steps tested, and
- bigger differences between the chosen prices.

PRICE SENSITIVITY METER (PSM)

The van Westendorp price sensitivity meter (PSM) is a more sophisticated version of Gabor-Granger[xvi]. It is most often used for new products where there is no obvious value benchmark or competitor equivalent. It describes or demonstrates the product as before and then poses four questions:

- At what price would you consider this product to represent good value?
- At what price would you say this item is getting expensive but you would still consider buying it?

- At what price would you consider this product to be too expensive to consider buying it?
- At what price would you consider this product to be priced so cheaply that you would worry about quality?

In theory there should be an intersection point where the number of respondents who regard the product as too expensive equals the number who perceive it as being 'too cheap'. This intersection is the recommended price and the other questions hopefully illuminate its most likely acceptable price range.

However, many PSM respondents[xvii] give figures that are internally inconsistent. In fact, despite the intuitive appeal of the four questions, they are simply variants of the question, 'How much would you pay for this?' Therefore risking the bias already mentioned. As such, this technique should be reserved for exploring potential prices 'new products in new markets'. Conclusions should be tested with other studies such as the monadic method or conjoint/trade-off analysis.

CONJOINT ANALYSIS

Trade-off or conjoint analysis is a statistical technique[xviii] which reflects how our brains make decisions.

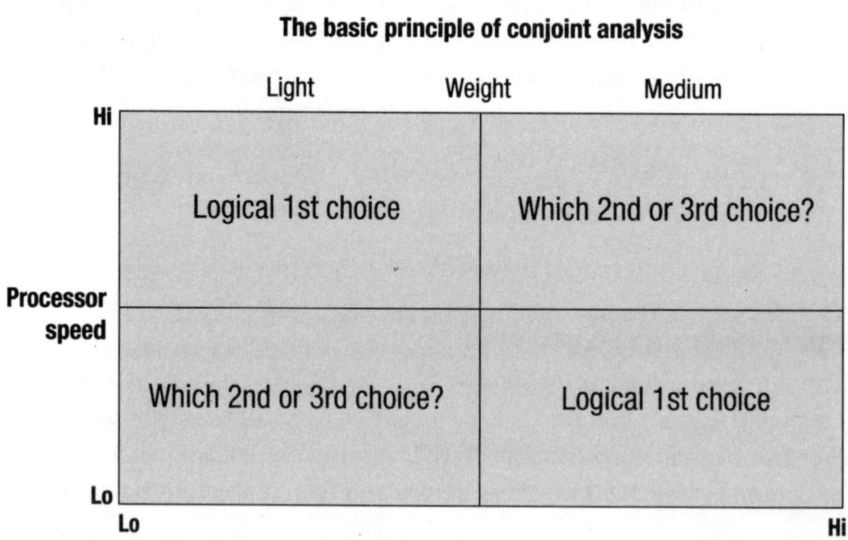

FIGURE 5.9: THE PRINCIPLES OF CONJOINT/TRADE-OFF ANALYSIS

The technique compels respondents to make either/or choices and to do this via ranking benefits and combinations of features against different price points.

The above example contrasts the microchip processing speed at two levels, with two different weights of laptop. It could similarly be done for style and price.

In the above matrix respondents are asked which will be their first choice, and which their last. Then they are required to choose which will be the second and third choices. They will do this by ranking their first choice as the highest value.

In simple terms, the obvious normal first choice is the highest speed at the lightest weight and the last choice the medium weight at the lowest speed – but after that which comes second and which comes third will start to indicate how these customers trade off speed against weight.

For an illustration of the principle of how a complex data capture tool (*i.e. questionnaire*) can be structured, see the data capture form for mobile telephone handsets at the end of this chapter. The form is designed to assess a range of brands, combined with a range of functionalities, warranties and prices.

Another example is the trade-off customers sometimes make to buy motor fuel. How much lower must the price of fuel on the other side of the road be, in order to compensate for the inconvenience of crossing the carriageway? Again respondents are invited to choose between different paired offers (*as above*).

The offers consist of various attributes and for each attribute a number of levels. For example, one attribute of a laptop computer might be portability and the levels might be two (*or more*) specified weights.

By giving a significant number of choices to a representative sample (*i.e. +200 respondents per price point so as to be statistically significant*), it is possible to develop a robust model of the price that people are prepared to pay for any potential combinations of benefits. Customers' preferences for different offers are ranked and then decomposed in order to determine each person's inferred perceived value for each element of the benefit package. Respondents' choices show the trade-offs they would make and express the relative importance of each attribute in numerical terms.

Conjoint analysis can be administered cost effectively on-line once the sample has been qualified by telephone recruitment. Dobney, the Bath (UK) based market research agency, has devised a simple illustration of how an on-line conjoint analysis can refine the understanding of priorities, see 'Conjoint analysis in action' on their web site: **www.dobney.com**.

In *Marketing Management,* Philip Kotler cites how Courtyard by Marriott the mid-market hotel.brand, developed its value proposition through the use of a study involving conjoint analysis that determined which were the most appealing and profitable combinations of benefits for the new hotel offering.

There is a recognized bias in conjoint analysis: it tends to imply a lower price sensitivity than occurs in reality. Perhaps hypothetical product images on screen accompanied by a list of features in words are insufficient and, in this context, the price begins to act as a subliminal indicator of quality such that people may feel that at the higher price the product is somehow better – the concept of 'you only get what you pay for' – will skew their responses in a way that would probably not be reflected if they were comparing products physically in store.

However, conjoint analysis can have the opposite effect when non-price factors are at issue and price itself is less important. For example, in a market for safety equipment, where brand reputation can be critical, the artificiality of results produced by conjoint analysis may imply greater price sensitivity than is the case. In the market for pharmaceuticals doctors tend to be more concerned with clinical effectiveness and the side effects than with price. However, this may not be reflected in the conjoint studies.

So called 'focus group discussions' are the most important way of identifying the attributes that can be used in conjoint analysis. They may also suggest the options and levels that need to be selected. However, the group's dynamics and other factors mean that reactions to prices in focus groups may be misleading.

In-depth interviews with individual consumers or B2B customers (*with members of the DMU*) can help draw out how users perceive the product and its useful value to them.

These interviews try to discover which product benefits are critical. In a business-to-business (B2B) context, researchers may infer the monetary value of a good or service – how it supports revenue earning for the customer or cuts their costs – without asking direct questions. In-depth interviews are especially relevant in teasing out psychological or emotional benefits that a customer may consider significant.

DISCRETE CHOICE MODELLING (DCM)

This is a refinement of conjoint analysis where the offers are presented as competing products from named brands with elaborated specifications and performance details described. Ideally, respondents are able to examine and handle sample products. This addresses the 'hypothetical' concern with conjoint analysis.

Typically, three competing brands will be offered instead of the paired trade-off, and specifications and benefits would mirror the market situation. Once the product options are clearly understood the respondents select one of the three priced packages shown on screen. At this point the DCM software generates a slightly different set of choices, such as a longer warranty for one brand. The respondent chooses from the new set. If the choice has remained the same, the software creates another option, perhaps lowering a price of one of the other brands. If the choice has now changed the software tests this new choice with further variants. Overall 12 to 15 choices may be made. Taken as a whole, these choices contribute to a better understanding of the customer's value map and may indicate opportunities to increase prices or raise specifications to command a higher price in the market.

However, the reservation that DCM would show a higher sensitivity to price since it is evidently about price is not borne out in practice. The reason may be linked to the fact that very specific products are presented in a context mirroring reality.

DANGERS OF PRICE QUESTIONS

Probing intentions and preferences around price can be misleading. All the approaches and techniques mentioned carry with them the risk that indicated behaviour may not occur in practice. Any survey about price has a chance that respondents will not reflect their normal behaviour in an artificial environment. They may exaggerate the importance of price when the researcher focuses his or her attention on this element, or may be distracted by numerous appealing features which may under represent the role that price may have in making real decisions. The most reliable findings come when people are making normal decisions in a familiar environment. If it is possible to use actual behaviour as the guide then we must do so.

Purchase-based data

HISTORICAL SALES DATA

Internal sales records are often readily available. Many organizations have comprehensive records of purchases by individual customers from which responses to price increases or promotional discounts can be implied. The costs of computer processing, together with the costs of data inference and modelling are continuing to fall, as is the price of the software packages available to help. Studying the changing behaviour of buyers which results from price increases can lead to insights about the timing of price hikes. For example, where products are clearly seasonal, annual price increases can be moved to the start of the peak selling period in order to stimulate sales in the slack period and capture value as demand rises.

However, interpretation needs care. Sales to wholesalers or intermediaries may include fluctuations in the size of their stocks and fail to reflect end-user patterns. Trends may relate to non-price factors. There can be responses to external occurrences, such as unusual weather patterns or political, economic, social or religious events. For examples of the latter consider the European consumption of sweets and chocolates in the first quarter of any year. The timing of Lent, the Christian festival, is according to the phases of the moon. So the act of people giving-up such pleasures for Lent will occur at different times of the year – similarly with Ramadan and Eide, which are Muslim festivals the dates of which also move according to the phases of the moon. That is to say, past sales data MUST be discounted by the effects of such events.

Market factors can also distort results. This makes interpretation difficult. Some examples of such disruptions to the market are:

- New product launches and customer anticipation of future launches.
- Changes in advertising weights or campaign messages by the brand studied or by competitor brands.
- Product promotions by the brand studied or competitor brands.
- Stock shortages or delivery problems by competitors.

Retail sales data from research organizations, such as AC Nielsen, can help to reconcile some of these factors. However, historical sales reflect many influences on people's purchase behaviour of which price is only one.

PANEL DATA

In consumer markets with multiple products and frequent transactions, panels of buyers can provide solid data. A number of research agencies, again, for example, AC Nielsen recruit and maintain consumer panels whose members record their actual purchases. Worldwide Consumer Panel Services cover 18 countries around the world, capturing actual consumer purchase information for almost 125,000 households. This purchase information shows the actual items bought, price paid and any coupons used or discounts taken. Market share changes can also be tracked against relative prices of competing brands. It is also possible, subject to sample size, to correlate price sensitivity with the consumer's age, sex, socio-economic group, occupation, education et al.

Of course the quality of the data depends on how accurately the panel represents the market. Recruiting typical consumers may not be easy; those joining panels may not be typical because the sample may be more interested in shopping, product comparisons and prices than the overall market is. Buyers who are time-poor are less price-sensitive – they don't have the time to make price comparisons. But, by their very nature, panels tend to attract time-rich consumers. This drawback is being addressed by innovative techniques that simplify the obligations of panel membership. For example, consumers no longer need to keep purchase diaries. Current technology allows consumers to buy with a special credit card or have their purchases scanned in store.

STORE SCANNER DATA

Several supermarket chains may, from time to time, make available to their suppliers the results from store scanners (see Tesco mentioned below).

PURCHASE LABORATORY EXPERIMENTS

This technique is used to investigate what the market will bear. Using DHL for a business-to-business example[xix] and the research conducted for DHL by the Texas-based pricing consultancy Zilliant. Zilliant's skill is to measure what the market will bear, rather than trying to get the price right mathematically, Zilliant looks for the **right price**. The software runs numerous experiments, testing slightly changed prices on real customers. They measure the response of cells of customers. Tests cover prices for all weights of package across many different markets. The software specifically measures customers who enquired after a price and then did not use the service, i.e. **the prices failed**. These failures indicate the price ceiling. Lower prices calibrated the potential for volume increase. The results of the above study indicated that DHL's strong international brand meant that it did not need to match its lower-priced rivals such as UPS and FedEx. Hundreds of prices were changed. Some of which were lowered slightly, whilst still maintaining a premium over competitors, and DHL still gained volume, revenue and profit.

The ratio of customers who check for a price and then fail to buy is a valid measure of pricing effectiveness used by the smarter Internet businesses. Software can track the number of customers who have viewed a product and/or investigated specifications on-screen. It can also measure the proportion of these who proceed to book an order. If the 'look to book' ratio rises then prices may be too high. Conversely, **if all those who look** also proceed to book orders, then **the price may be too low**.

IN-STORE EXPERIMENTS (VIA THE USE OF CLUBCARDS)
Retailers are able to test different prices and price relationships in different stores to determine the levels that optimize sales. A high proportion of the customers of the UK-based supermarket, Tesco, hold Clubcards. These use a customer reward mechanism to encourage the card being swiped when making a purchase from one of their stores. This enables the company to monitor every single in-store purchase these customers make. So that with this tracking system, Tesco can test new prices on real customers and measure responses precisely. Thus they use collective customer responses to indicate which are the 'right' prices.

Pricing research – the bottom line

The conclusion to draw is that pricing research is fraught with the twin perils of exaggeration and under-estimation. People, in B2C and B2B markets find it almost impossible to be dispassionate about prices. Expert advice from pricing consultancies may be necessary. Managers must always remember that research on intentions is only a support or challenge to executive judgement. The best test of what customers will pay is to run live experiments and monitor the results closely (*but this luxury is mainly confined to consumer markets*).

Pricing questions for your business:

- Is your business leaving value on the table? Are some of your products under-priced?

- Do you gauge price analytically with statistically significant samples, or are your pricing decisions based on the views of vocal customers and/or your sales team?
- Would conjoint analysis help you to price new lines more professionally?
- How can/could/should your business test new prices on real customers?

Selling the 'value-add' to the customer

People can be forgiven for believing that the aspect of the 'value triad', of reducing the customer's costs, are the sole perogative of B2B VBP, but as we have seen, this is not so. The costs of ownership are just as much an imperitive, whether we are talking about the productivity of earth-moving tyres, or the shoes of children of the families of middle income professionals.

So we will need a way of calculating and communicating these values to customers. The only real difference is that the B2B customer can be expected to be more 'professional' in their choice and evaluation of data – after all, the assumption is they are profit and/or cost responsible.

Two tools are commonly suggested to calculate and communicate the hard numbers behind value: they are discounted cash-flow (DCF)[xx] based, and payback period.

The first of the above itself comes in three forms:

1. Net terminal value (**NTV**),
2. Net present value (**NPV**), and
3. Internal rate of return (**IRR**).

All three of the above are ways of expressing the time value of money.

The first one asks: 'If I make an investment now, given the cash flows this will generate, and the expected cost of capital, will I earn more money from it, over its lifetime, than if I put that cash in the bank?'

The second one asks: 'How much would I have to pay now to get those income streams in the future, i.e. over the expected life of the project?'

And

Thirdly: The (investing) organization has a hurdle, in terms of the rate of return on investment required before any project can be considered a viable proposition, and thus it asks if the contemplated project will exceed that hurdle.

The calculation looks something like the following:

$$NPV = \left[\frac{R_1}{(1+k)^1} + \frac{R_2}{(1+k)^2} + \dots\dots\dots + \frac{R_N}{(1+k)^N} \right] - C$$

And is frequently expressed in its abreviated form:

$$\text{i.e. } NPV = \sum_{t=1}^{N} \frac{R_1}{(1+k)^t} - C$$

Where:

- **'R'** represents the net cash flows, of the project;
- **'K'** is the marginal cost of capital;
- **'C'** is the initial cost of the project (i.e. the investment in your higher price for example); and
- **'N'** is the projects expected life.

Net Terminal Value is to all intents the same expression but solved for the terminal value.

The calculation for **IRR** (i.e. Internal Rate of Return) looks something like this:

$$\sum_{t=1}^{N} \frac{R_1}{(1+k)^t} - C = 0$$

In this case, everything is known except for **'R'** so the task is to solve the expression for **'R'**.

The above is all well and good, but many people are a bit cynical about using these tools today. Firstly, they can be 'fiddled'! For example, the quality of the calculation depends on the veracity of the data entered, and people do fiddle the data from time to time.

Tom Peters has said in *Managing in Chaos*[xxi] , 'If the threshold for investment is an IIR of 11% it is amazing how often proposals work out to have that value' (*or words to that effect*).

Secondly, many customers for SME's don't trust this approach, either because they are not that sophisticated and/or they are cynical (*often with good reason*) about how far they can predict the future. These people would much rather be confronted with a more straightforward expression of value where the timeframe can provide more confidence. This approach is the so called 'payback period' calculation.

This calculation aims to express the value of the investment (*i.e. your higher price*), in terms of how long it will take to payback, i.e. be fully recovered.

The situation may go something along the lines of the following table – assessing two projects 'A' and 'B' as shown below:

For projects A ' and 'B' where both investments are $1,000.00		
Net expected cashflows .. After taxes, but plus depreciation		
Year	Project 'A'	Project 'B'
1	$500	$100
2	$400	$200
3	$300	$300
4	$100	$400
5		$500
6		$600

So, if you were a customer, and the options were as above, which one would you prefer, i.e. which of the two projects with the same price premium of $1000.00, would you choose?

There is no simple answer. Project 'A' may well appeal to the very 'risk-averse' because this project recovers its costs somewhere in year three, they would probably be happier with the quicker payback period. Whereas Project 'B' would appeal more to those who are not so risk averse, because it makes up for the longer payback period (end year 4) by apparently continuing to grow – perhaps even after year 6.

Some approaches to discover ways to add value for your customers

Impact on our customer's cost structure?

Key questions to address are:

- Does our product (*good and/or service*) reduce or increase the customer's cost structure, and if so, by how much?
- What input does the product reduce or eliminate?

- What capital or operating costs does the customer incur in order to use our product?
  - *For example, the need to purchase new hardware in order to run a new software product*
- What is the customers' total cost of acquisition?
- What is their total cost of ownership?
- Can either of these be improved by us?
- If so, how?

Impact on our (i.e. the supplier's) **cost structure?**

- Does serving the customer have an impact on our (i.e. the supplier's) cost structure?

For example:

- Reduction in shipping costs to centrally located warehouses vs. shipment to remote locations.
- Lower packaging costs (*bulk vs. packaged delivery*).
- Volume shipments (*full truckloads vs. less than truckload quantities*).
- Can any of our savings be passed on to our customers **without lowering our prices?**

Impact on customer's non-operating costs

(i.e. what is their downside risk?)

- What are the incremental expenses or risks associated with the customer's purchase of our product/s? Examples could include their:
- Employee training costs
- Environmental risk or expense
- Corporate image.

Impact on our customer's profitability

- What impact does the product have on the customer's sales revenues and profits?
- Does it enhance the customer's position in the marketplace versus their competitor's?

- If so, then by how much? What is the extra monetary value contributed?
- Does the customer have exclusive use of the product?

Exhibit: Simplified example of a conjoint analysis 'data capture'

Brand preference study re. mobile phone handsets

Here are 16 descriptions of mobile phones. Rank these products from most preferred (indicated by a score of 16 to a least preferred – score of 1). Enter these 16 ranks in the spaces to the left of the each product description. Please do your best to make sure these ranks accurately reflect your preferences for these 16 product alternatives.

A.___ Nokia, 1 year warranty, EUR 190, 10 additional features.

B.___ Siemens, 5 year warranty, EUR 190, 3 additional features.

C.___ Motorola, 5 year warranty, EUR 220, 10 additional features.

D.___ Ericsson, 1 year warranty, EUR 250, 10 additional features.

E.___ Siemens, 1 year warranty, EUR 250, 3 additional features.

F.___ Siemens, 1 year warranty, EUR 220, 10 additional features.

G.___ Nokia, 1 year warranty, EUR 280, 3 additional features.

H.___ Motorola, 1 year warranty, EUR 280, 10 additional features.

I.___ Motorola, 1 year warranty, EUR 190, 10 additional features.

J.___ Ericsson, 1 year warranty, EUR220, 10 additional features.

K.___ Siemens, 5 year warranty, EUR 280, 10 additional features.

L.___ Nokia, 5 year warranty, EUR 220, 3 additional features.

M.___ Motorola, 5 year warranty, EUR 250, 3 additional features.

N.___ Ericsson, 5 year warranty, EUR 190, 3 additional features.

O.___ Ericsson, 5 year warranty, EUR 280, 10 additional features.

P.___ Nokia, 5 year warranty, EUR 250, 10 additional features.

Scoring sheet for conjoint analysis

Attribute	Enter your rank for	Average rank
Brand		
Nokia	A. G. L. P.	
Siemens	B. E. F. K.	
Motorola	C. H. I. M.	
Ericsson	D. J. N. O.	
Warranty		
1 year	A. D. E. F. G. H. I. J.	
5 years	B. C. K. L. M. N. O. P.	
Price		
EUR 190	A. B. I. N.	
EUR 220	C. F. J. L.	
EUR 250	D. E. M. P.	
EUR 280	G. H. K. O.	
Features		
3 features	B. E. G. L. M. N.	
10 features	A. C. D. F. H. I. J. K. O. P.	

(See '*Conjoint Analysis: Peering Behind the Jargon*' Joel N. Axelrod & Norman Frendberg.)

References

i As published in the Video Programme 'Management Imagination' by Tom Peters with the *Financial Times* and the BBC – 1992.

ii The reader is recommended to view the original publication by Tom Peters. We have only mentioned the main thrust of the relationship above, but the structure and the contents of the agreement are worth studying for any type of Business to Business enterprise, and has lessons for any type of business, let alone transportation.

iii Greenwood Press, of Oxford, UK. Editor Gregory G. Squires.

iv There are said to be some five elements to the marketing mix for goods i.e.:

P1 = Positioning (in fact Segmentation + Targeting + Positioning) see '*According To Kotler*' published by the American Management Association (AMA).

P2 = The product which is no more than the bundles of benefits/values it delivers.

P3 = Distribution, i.e. the route to market for the product – value chains etc.

P4 = Promotion, the way we bring our product to the customer's notice, and build its 'image'.

P5 = Price, i.e. how we harvest all the values from the above in terms of payment from the customer. See '*Mastering Marketing*' 2nd edition by this Author and this Publisher.

For Services the mix as above is extended by the addition of five more elements of the mix:

P6 = Physical evidence – because services are intangible

P7 = People (HR policy etc.) are at the heart of all services

P8 = Process, because at the heart of a service is what is known as the 'moments of truth', i.e. that point in time when it is delivered and process describes how these episodes should be conducted

P9 = Time, this factor is the objective aspect of a service, all else is subjective, and it comes in 5 flavours, Punctuality, Availability, Duration, Speed of Response, Speed of Innovation.

P10 = 'Resource Management' or the 'Capacity Constraint'. How the business intends to manage its resources so that it has enough to cater for peak demand, without having too much financial burden when the market is slack.

For more information on this refer to *'Marketing your Service Business'* by this Author and this Publisher.

v After Professor Malcolm MacDonald of Cranfield University, as referred to in *Key Account Management*

vi Refer to *'Mastering Marketing'* 2nd edition 2006, by this Author and Publisher.

vii The Differentiation of Anything HBR 10807.

viii Mr Van Tripp, the founding CEO of Pan American Airlines.

ix Ref for Hertzberg from 'Management' etc.

x Although the Author's father was a farmer, he claims no insight into any cause and effect between the UK farming community's refusal to pay for MLC officers advice, and the outbreaks of BSE.

xi Quoted by Kent B. Monroe and Jennifer L. Cox, writing in *'Marketing Management'* (September 2001).

xii According to Baker, Marn and Zawada (2001).

xiii David W. Lyon's award-winning article 'The price is right (or is it?)' (2002).

xiv After the two economists who invented it in the 1960s.

xv According to David W. Lyon.

xvi A technique, devised by the Dutch psychologist Peter van Westendorp in the 1970s.

xvii According to David W. Lyon.

xviii Developed by Luce, a mathematical psychologist, and Tukey, a statistician. See also *'Conjoint Analysis – Peering behind the Jargon'* Axelrod & Frendberg.

xix Writing in Fast Company, Charles Fishman (2003) relates the price research of DHL the global air express transportation company.

xx For more detail see *'Managerial Finance'* by Eugene F. Brigham & James L. Pappas

xxi *'Thriving on Chaos'* by Tom Peters, Published 1988, Macmillan London Ltd.

SIX

PRICING TACTICS

Dealing with the day to day pressures on price

PRICING TACTICS – dealing with the day to day pressures on price

"No one should ever write a strategy which he has not the tactical ability to deliver." **General von Molké**

Synopsis

This chapter brings together in one place as many of the pricing tactics that we can use when managing our prices in the field. Albeit that some tactics have been left to more appropriate chapters due to their intimate association with specific pricing situations. For example, there are a whole range of paradigms (tactics) associated with negotiation that have been deliberately located in Chapter 8.

The dangers of discounting

All the good work we have done thus far in analyzing our market, targeting the customers we wish to address, selecting a pricing strategy for them and promoting the same, can often be wasted via a lack of discipline and/or poor understanding exhibited by those in direct contact with customers. This last link in the chain, be that by phone, in retail outlets or in the field, is often the one most poorly equipped, trained and informed in how to implement our desired pricing policies. In addition, these customer facing people are usually motivated (*if at all*) by bonuses rewarding the volume of their sales, not their value (*and hardly ever the profit or profitability of the deal*). This is a vital sales management issue!

In order to fully and profitably implement pricing strategies and policies in the field, Sales directors and their managers must inform, train and motivate their people who form this critical link in the pricing chain. Their teams should know:

- Of the dangers of poor discounting practice, and
- How best to discount, if discount they must!

Exercise 7.1.

The following is a very useful exercise for both you and your teams.

Taking the following P&L ratios:

A small business produces and sells items from a 'shop-house'.

Item sale price	$1.00 each
Factory value added	
Materials	$0.30 Per item
Labour	$0.30 Ditto
Daily overhead*	$30.00 Per day

Assuming this sale is/will be the only one today, calculate, the profit on:

- A sale of 100 – with no discount,
- A sale of 100 – with a 10% discount
  - with no extra volume,
  - with 10% extra volume,
- What volume at 10% discount will re-establish the original profit?

To check your results, refer to Appendix 1, Exercise 7.1 for the answers.

There are essentially two approaches: the first, a mental arithmetic approach, is explained in Appendix 1, under Exercise 7.1; the second method follows.

The second way of doing the above calculation to find how much extra volume is required to restore the net profit earned can be addressed via two tools.

The first is a graphic tool – a small picture of which is shown below:

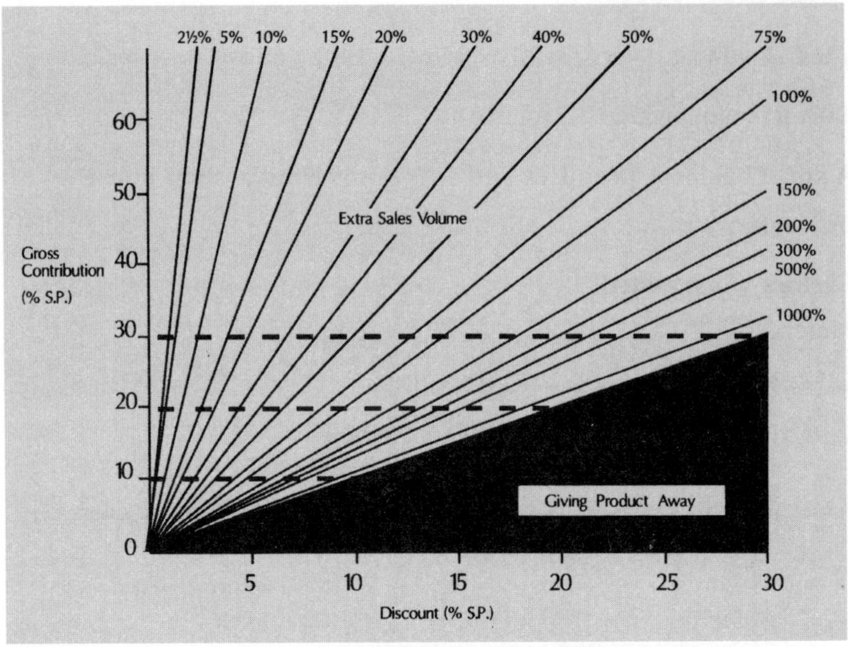

FIGURE 6.1: GRAPHIC DISCOUNT/VOLUME CALCULATOR[i]

First to explain the tool itself:

1. The divisions on the vertical scale show the contribution margin (*or gross profit margin*).
2. The horizontal scale is the discount being requested.
3. The radiating lines are known as the 'lines of constant profit' at the end of which are the amounts required just for the net profit to stand still in the face of any given discount.
4. The large black triangle resting on the horizontal axis shows the area where it is totally impossible for an increase in volume to recover the situation.

To calculate the volume required to restore the original net profit to the bottom line (*for a given discount*).

Using the discount situation as on the previous page:

- **First** lay a straight edge across the page at the gross contribution point (*at right angles to the vertical axis*) – in this case the 40% point.

- **Secondly** extend a vertical straight edge from the discount being requested – in this case 10%. Estimate, from where these two straight edges intersect, approximately where this intersection lies between the lines of constant profit.

In this case this point lies just short of halfway between 30% and 40% at say about 34%, ask for 35% extra volume and you will be on the safe side.

The second tool is a table as follows:

Price Reduction	Gross margin							
	5%	10%	15%	20%	25%	30%	35%	40%
1%	25.0	11.1	7.1	5.3	4.2	3.4	2.9	2.6
2%	66.6	25.0	15.4	11.1	8.7	7.1	6.1	5.3
3%	150.0	42.8	25.0	17.6	13.6	11.1	9.4	8.1
4%	400.0	66.0	36.4	25.0	19.0	15.4	12.9	11.1
5%	-	100.0	50.0	33.3	25.0	20.0	16.9	14.3
6%	-	150.0	66.7	42.9	31.6	25.0	20.7	17.6
7%	-	233.3	87.5	53.5	38.9	30.4	25.0	21.2
8%	-	400.0	114.3	66.7	47.1	36.4	29.6	25.0
9%	-	1000.0	150.0	81.8	56.3	42.9	34.6	29.0
10%	-	-	200.0	100.0	66.7	50.0	40.0	33.3
11%	-	-	275.0	122.2	78.6	57.9	45.8	37.9
12%	-	-	400.0	150.0	92.0	66.7	52.2	42.9
13%	-	-	850.0	185.7	109.3	76.5	59.1	48.1
14%	-	-	1400.0	233.3	127.3	87.5	66.7	53.8
15%	-	-	-	300.0	150.0	100.0	75.0	60.0
16%	-	-	-	400.0	177.8	114.3	84.2	66.7
17%	-	-	-	566.7	212.5	130.8	94.4	73.9
18%	-	-	-	900.0	257.1	150.0	105.9	81.8
19%	-	-	-	1900.0	316.7	172.7	118.8	90.5
20%	-	-	-	-	400.0	200.0	133.3	100.0
21%	-	-	-	-	525.0	233.3	150.0	110.5
22%	-	-	-	-	733.3	725.0	169.2	122.2
23%	-	-	-	-	1115.0	328.6	191.7	135.3
24%	-	-	-	-	2400.0	400.0	218.2	150.0
25%	-	-	-	-	-	500.0	250.0	160.7

FIGURE 6.2: TABULAR METHOD OF CALCULATING VOLUMES REQUIRED TO COMPENSATE FOR REQUESTED DISCOUNTS, JUST FOR THE NET PROFIT TO STAND STILL

From the above we can see agreement with the black areas on the foregoing graphic Figure 6.1, i.e. there are situations where no volume will compensate for the discount required. Check out these two and you will see that they agree, the only difference being that the graphic provides more fineness, though the table is more absolute/accurate.

So what are the rules for discounting that if adopted will help to reduce the otherwise erosion of profits?

1. DON'T PUBLISH DISCOUNTS

By this we mean don't have them printed or put into any form that can fall into the hands of your customers, and from there to your competitors! If they do, they will be used against you. Customers will demand, may even just take, the discounts they decide, not the ones you believe they have earned.

2. NEGOTIATE DISCOUNTS INDIVIDUALLY

You should negotiate discounts so that different customers will get different discounts, depending on your aims, your objectives and assessment of how much money is 'on the table'.

3. VARY THE TERMS A LOT

The intention here is to ensure that one customer should find it difficult to emulate the conditions under which another customer had obtained their discount. Customers do talk, especially at the procurement end of the organization. Here there is no advantage in secrecy, and much to be gained by working together with other buyers.

4. PUT A TIME LIMIT ON EVERY DEAL

Your costs change over time, more often upward than down, and you cannot afford to honour deals which were left dormant for several years or so. The Author once obtained a quote for a loft extension to the house his family lived in. The planned extension, for one reason or another, was not commissioned for some three years. When the Author finally decided to proceed, the Builder insisted that he would have to re-quote. On the one hand the author admired the professionalism of the builder, but on the other hand was miffed that now he had to find more money to get the required work done. Be like that builder, don't accept old prices, re-tender whenever possible.

5. RENEGOTIATE EVERY LAPSED DEAL

And that is what the builder cited above actually did. He realized that this time the project also included a downstairs toilet, and front-of-house paved parking for the family cars. He bundled all of that into the deal as a way of ameliorating the price rise he would have to impose on the loft extension. It worked and we were very happy with the outcome – and what we were now able to afford for him to do.

6. NEVER LET DISCOUNTS BECOME ROOTED IN YOUR PRICE LIST/STRUCTURE

There is a saying in England that 'old habits die hard', if customers keep getting the same deal, 'year in and year out', they will come to believe that the deal is their's as a right. Indeed, the buyer may well consider that the discounted amount is the actual price and behave accordingly.

It is a fact of life that people do not stay in their current jobs for ever, they move on, they leave their employer for another or they can get promoted within their firm – and one way or another there will be a new face in that position with a new agenda. This new face will examine all the past invoices, credit notes and deals done between the supplier and the customer. They are looking for evidence which will indicate past behaviour, re discount or other incentives between the two firms. And, if they find such 'evidence' they will use it as a negotiating lever, saying, "this is the discount you normally give". The selling firm must always be on their guard to ensure that, whenever possible, discounts are not shown on the invoice but are provided. If provided they must be via a 'credit note' clearly stating what this is for.

7. IF IN ANY DOUBT – SET PRICES HIGH AND GIVE LARGE DISCOUNTS

The size of discounts obtained sometimes seems to be regarded as a virility symbol by certain buyers. So play to this foible. Many years ago the Author did much business in a developing country. He obtained this business via a local person who had at one time been a manager in a client company, but had now gone into freelance training himself. This local acted in the role of an agent with exclusive rights to the Author's services – or so he boasted. Additionally he quoted the Author's time at an outrageous daily fee but assured his clients that because he gave the Author so much business, he and only he, could get at least 33% off that daily fee level. It worked and for many years the income from that ruse was well appreciated. Oh and by the way, this price also gave the agent a good margin for his troubles.

8. KEEP THE SITUATION FLEXIBLE FOR YOURSELF AS LONG AS POSSIBLE

Don't be too quick to agree. Resist the temptation to do a deal at the first sign of the business. Indicate interest – **Yes but!** before you say 'yes' to the customer, first find-out how much money is on the table. Talk through all the options with the customer, 'test the waters' see how eager s/he is to deal; see what the real chances are that they are willing to walk away (*more of this in Chapter 8*).

Pricing in a Declining Market

1. LOW PRICE WILL NOT COMPENSATE FOR PRODUCT DEFICIENCIES OR POOR SERVICE

If your product is having to contest the declining market with superior, more up-to-date products, a lower price will not be seen by the remaining buyers as being a good deal – it will only confirm the suspicion that your product is inferior.

For several years, up to and after the turn of this century, so called low cost airlines have been taking traffic away from the British railway companies, particularly on the long distance routes from London to the North (to places such as Newcastle, Manchester, Glasgow and Edinburgh). These rail operators have tried almost every price trick in the book to lure passengers back. But the quality of the travel experience is dire and lasts longer than the flight. Whereas on the continent of Europe, particularly France, the high speed trains more or less 'rule the roost'. Travel from the centre of Paris to the centre of Marseilles can be done in under four hours, in comfort, with the ability to stretch one's legs, work on your laptop and spend a few breaks in the bar. The TGV[ii] is booming in spite of the fact that, for the normal ticket, it is more expensive than the flight, though a lot less hassle.

2. IN B2B AND B2C LOW PRICE ONLY WORKS IF PASSED ON TO THE END CUSTOMERS

In business to business the end customer could well be part of the value chain and the product gets used-up at a point before the final product gets to the consumer. Good examples would be cutting oil, shrink wrap film, transport and logistics and sales training or management consultancy (to any links in the chain). In business to consumer markets, it is the consumer who very much drives the value chain. However, for an incentive to work, it must get to the end customer, be that an intermediary, or consumer. They will then 'pull' the product through the value chain.

Without this pull any incentive, including a price cut, will fail to produce any improvement in sales. The most frequent cause of any failure of such an incentive is that it ends up not where it can do the most good, but in the pockets of the various intermediaries that lie between you and the intended recipient, the customer or consumer.

3. FULL PIPELINES WILL CLEAR THEMSELVES

Rather than 'pushing' the product down through the value chain (*i.e. the pipeline*) via incentives of one sort or another, which, as we have said above, are more likely to end up in the back pockets of the intermediaries who do little if anything to influence the 'flow', it is far more cost effective to allow the market's natural forces to do their work. As long as the market is not in the decline stage of the PLC the pipeline will clear of its own violation, in its own time. Consider that intermediaries have the best incentive of all to help the flow, it is their money which is tied-up in their stock of your product. By and large money lying idle earns no return!

4. LOW PRICE WILL NOT CAUSE AN UPTURN IN A DECLINING PLC

The product life cycle goes from saturation to decline because customers discover and then migrate to products, goods or services which better satisfy their needs. The telegram gave way to the telex when those machines became more affordable. In turn they gave way to the fax machine, more affordable still, plus the benefits of a real branded facsimile complete with letterhead. Then email took over, more speed, more variations in how they're sent and received etc. What next? Voice over Internet perhaps, and when? Those are the $64,000 questions – but in time emails will be replaced, the author is certain of it, and if he did know what would replace the email, he would not tell you, he would make his fortune first!

KEY QUESTION

"What will be the long term implication of any price change you make now?"

In a declining market there are seven things that we must never do, they are:

1. **Not to: Confuse rumours with reality.** It is amazing how many times customers try to start a price war between their suppliers – historically this is the major reason they break-out.

2. **Not to: Confuse sales decreases with market share decreases.** For a whole number of reasons, markets can get depressed, such as: reduced consumer spending power as a result of:
   - The general economy suffering a down-turn.
   - Tax increases or increased utility prices etc.
   - Consumer loss of confidence causing increased savings et al.
3. **Not to: Blame price alone for sales decline.** It could be the start of the decline stage in the product life cycle etc. OR any of the reasons in item 2 above.
4. **Not to: Concentrate on some prices to the exclusion of others.** As we saw in Chapter 4, whether we like it or not, customers may well view our product range as being in the form of price lining. If we change the price of one item of the range, and not the rest, we will create confusion in the mind of the buyer, and perhaps devalue the entire range, not just the product whose price we change.
5. **Not to: Wait for the crisis to resolve itself.** On the one hand don't panic, but on the other hand, make decisions without undue delay. The person in charge of pricing must take decisive action to retain the initiative and avoid being caught-up by, and becoming the victim of, events.
6. **Not to: Drop prices before it is necessary.** Reducing price is often a one way street. Reducing price takes no talent at all – its very easy to do. The skill comes in putting the price back-up again, so think before you leap.
7. **Not to: Believe that you offer the right price for all time.** Markets are dynamic, living, breathing things. Yesterdays prices, like yesterdays products soon outlive their usefulness. Referring to the price landscape we discussed in Chapter 5, overtime, the price of most products will tend to move to the left, i.e. decline via natural forces. Whilst at the same time value moves upward in a similar way. So, in spite of everything said above, if your analysis indicates this is what is happening to your products and their markets, then go with the flow – not even King Canute could turn back the tide.

The central rules in tough times are

- **Preserve your gross profit – your commercial life depends on it.** To do this, you must manage your costs like crazy – All the evidence shows that, especially when times are tough, firms that preserve their gross profit are more likely to survive the down turn than those who do not. So think of how to turn as much of your fixed costs as possible into variable costs via such strategies as BPO[iii] (*Business Process Outsourcing*).

Consider:

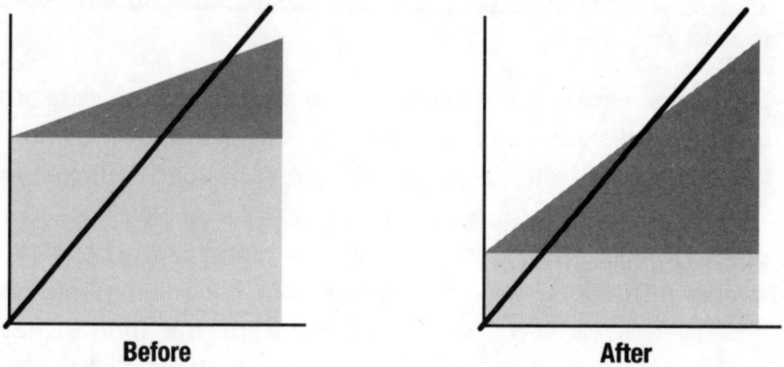

FIGURE 6.3: THE EFFECT OF TURNING FIXED COSTS INTO VARIABLE COSTS

In Figure 6.3 above, we see two simplified graphical break-even analyses. The 'Before' diagram shows the situation where the business has a very high level of overhead compared to its variable costs. The 'After' diagram shows the same firm (lets say) but where much of the overhead functions of the business have been turned into variable costs via business process outsourcing[iii].

In the first case (Before):

- The fixed cost to variable cost ratio is very high – and as a consequence:
- Break-even will be relatively late.
- The cone of loss (i.e. prior to break-even) or the cone of profit (i.e. after break-even) are both large, i.e. in this situation you either win big or you lose big.

Therefore the firm is forced to **go for volume**. A good example of this is a passenger airline. The variable costs of one extra passenger at break-even are very small, this incremental cost mainly consists of only the extra fuel to carry that extra weight; the food is already loaded, no extra cabin staff are required etc. But the revenue supplied for one extra passenger, particularly if they are in business or first class seating, is large and nearly all profit. Likewise the loss is large if, before break-even, any passengers fail to show up for the flight.

The imperative to seek volume is why the airlines have special PEX rates especially for economy or coach class. The earlier the passenger books, the lower the price for their seats. As soon as all the seats in economy/coach are sold, the airline knows that it is at, or very close to, break-even and they can now go for value.

However, a problem for the airline is the numbers of business class passengers who will not show-up on the day. A business class ticket is normally fully flexible, it is fully refundable and it is almost as good as money, so it is fairly normal for a few business class passengers who have booked not to turn-up for the flight. These no-shows represent a considerable loss of revenue for the airline. Thus it is vital that the losses from those flights which do not break-even are recovered from the profit of the flights that do. This explains the admitted large amounts of over-booking practised by airlines, on their successful routes just to re-coup the losses made by the half empty flights on their not so successful routes[1]. Overbooking is often accompanied by the practice of 'bouncing'. This is where some of the economy class passengers are taken off the flight (*sometimes with incentives*) to make way for the urgent business class passengers who may occasionally turn up in more numbers than there are seats on the plane.

In the second case (After):

- The fixed cost to variable cost ratio is **low** – and as a consequence:
- Break-even will be relatively **early**.
- The cone of loss (i.e. prior to break-even) or the cone of profit (i.e. after break-even) are both **very small**, i.e. in this situation the firms winnings or losses will be comparatively small. So here the imperative is **to go for value.**

Airlines almost pioneered the BPO approach to address that part of their overhead which is not central to their identity or an exclusive business skill. In the United Kingdom's major airport, Heathrow, no airlines do their own catering any more – it is all outsourced as are the ground staff functions, such as passenger check-in.

Scandinavian Airlines Systems (SAS) now provide many other airlines in the Star Alliance group with all their passenger ground-handling needs. If done well, this means that SAS will probably be making money on what otherwise would be a costly overhead at Heathrow.

BPO is not just outsourcing your business call centre to India.

- **Focus closely on your customers AND get closest to them (i.e. strengthen the relationship).** This imperative is mainly for business to business and for major accounts. Too few organizations get really close to their key customers. Often the contacts do not go beyond the customer's procurement department. Tough times mean that we have to have close contacts with the so called 'dominant coalition' within the decision making unit – but space does not allow a detailed discussion of this aspect of business in this book.
- **Provide better value than your competitors (in the customer's perception).** It is critical to know what drives your customers to buy from you versus the competition. We addressed this issue in more depth in Chapter 5. These values must be seen as being worth more than those on offer from the competition, which means that the process of identification, fulfilment and communication must be a constant process.
- **Use price as a dynamic element of the mix.** For the conventional marketing mix (as amended by Phillip Kotler[iv] where pricing is said to be P5), it is the *raison d'etre* of the other four elements, in that their whole purpose is to command a better price in the marketplace. It also has a dynamic influence on the effectiveness of the other four elements. Price is the single largest influence on customer's perception of quality AND it can also act as a valve to influence demand. In many cases the higher the price, the lower the demand, and vice versa (*a notable exception to this rule being perfume*).
- **Remember that it is possible to sell too much for too little, you must beware of re-entry.** Complementing the last part of the above, i.e. price as a valve on demand, please refer to Chapter 3 where the demand curve has been factored into the break-even analysis and we can see that in some cases as the price lowers the volumes demanded re-crosses the total cost curve, and from that point on the product is being sold at a loss. Refer also to the graphic and the tabular calculator at the beginning of this chapter where again

it will be seen that there are situations where no amount of volume will compensate for the discount demanded.

- **Obey the rules for using marginal pricing which now follow:**[v]

Never do it:

- **If it sets a precedent for the long run**. It is amazing how often a special deal done for your customer out of the goodness of your heart, to help them out of a spot of trouble, can come back to haunt you time and again. If there is any suspicion that this can happen, then either don't give the discount, or do it by credit note, as mentioned above.
- **If you can't stop the news spreading.** As we have discussed, customers do talk to each other – it's in their interest to do so. Thus you must carefully choose with whom you deal. Can they keep their lips sealed, or are they 'blabber mouths'?
- **If it commits you to extra capital expenditure.** Not only are you running the risk of not covering your overheads by the end of the financial year, but if you are also having to incur extra capital costs, such as inventory carrying costs, or the purchase of new machinery. Don't do it.
- **If it uses precious resources needed elsewhere.** So just as in the previous case, why incur two costs where you already have one.
- **If it costs cash flow by giving credit.** Boy! A marginal price, AND credit! But then there are more and more buyers who would also like to drink your blood given half the chance.
- **If it undermines you or your people in the market.** It could well be that in some parts of the market your people are not giving such concessions AND are still getting the business – if the word that your company is a soft touch spreads to their customers – they will be under enormous pressure to give the same deals as the weaker members of the team have agreed with their customers. To do so now will devalue the whole of your market.

SO in the light of the above you can prevent much of this happening if you take care NEVER to delegate discretion on marginal pricing down the line – keep it as your sole prerogative.

However, if you are going to sell a product via marginal pricing what rules of thumb should you now take care to observe?

If you MUST do the deal, then:

- **'Dump' the product well away from your usual market.** So as to try to stop the word spreading.
- **Keep the competition on their back foot in their own patch.** If you are going to use marginal pricing, for whatever reason, make it work twice for you – not only to turn your stock into cash (even at a slim margin), but also to discommode your competition where it will hurt them most. If you are unable to do this without being identified by the competition as the protagonist – beware you don't start a price war!!
- **Clear excess stock/capacity.** As per the above, liquidate that money tied up in stock, it's not even generating interest.
- **Cash up front.** As previously mentioned, such prices should at least earn you cash flow.
- **Keep it to a 'one-off' basis.** Many years ago the Author ran his own marketing research business. In this type of operation the workload is never at a predictable and even level. The volatility of workload particularly applied to the administration team. Some weeks we were having to work almost 18 hours a day for 6 days at a time, other weeks, when the projects were in the field, the admin office was like a morgue it was so quiet. We could not outsource our peaks because the work required training and experience that temps would not usually have. So we turned the admin office into a separate business, which in addition to supplying services to our marketing research team, also provided administration services to other local small businesses, and to students for their dissertations at the local university.

  The small businesses were charged prices designed to make a 'contribution' over and above the hourly rate of the person delivering them. Students were charged at a rate designed just to pay the hourly rate of the person who word-processed the dissertation. Our office manager ensured that local businesses would not be able to pursue the rates given to students as their deal did not guarantee to meet any deadlines.

- **Ensure only one person has the discretion.** In a small business, or a division of a larger one, if you have profit responsibility: that person is YOU and you alone!

And even then ONLY DO IT AFTER YOU HAVE REACHED FULL-COST BREAK-EVEN NOT BEFORE!!

Pricing new products

There are two classes of new products:

1. New products in existing markets – either that you launched yourself or where you were not the first to market.
2. New products in totally new markets where you are the market-maker.

Dealing with the first of these two:

NEW PRODUCTS IN AN EXISTING MARKET

i **Establish the perceived value of competitive products** (*benchmarking*)

- You must know what you are up against.
- What are the price-value points? (*Use the price/value landscape tool as per Chapter 6*).

ii **Do a full competitive analysis of existing players in the market**

- Who is the market leader and why?
- Where is the main volume of business?
- Where are most of the competition?
- Are there gaps in the market for you to enter and not upset any indigenous players?
- (*You can always upset them later on when you have an established base from which to attack their business, but not in the early days when you are vulnerable.*)

iii **Use your list price as a communication channel to the market-place** (*e.g. line pricing*). Remember, your list price sets the expectations, but after that need bear no resemblance to reality.

iv **Use promotion pricing to induce trial**. The key skill is having to handle a strategy whereby after the promotion, prices can return to the desired level. Anyone can drop the price, but it takes a skilled practitioner to be able to put prices back up afterwards. (*Consider the 'Thracian Wine' model discussed in Chapter 5 or the Amstrad strategy discussed below.*)

v **Once established, use penetration pricing to gain share**. In late 1987, long before the Michael Dell operation was present in Europe. Alan Sugar launched Amstrad Computers in the British market.

Up to that time the market leader was IBM, and the starting price for their basic desktop PC which had only two floppy 5½ inch disks and a monochrome screen, was £2,000.00 (*c.€3,300 if there had been Euros then*).

The entry level model Amstrad 1512 was almost exactly the same configuration as the basic IBM PC but was priced at £512 (*plus VAT*).

During the following year (1988), Amstrad 1512's revolutionized the PC market, reputedly selling more than the whole of the market for PC type computers in 1987, but probably making no money for Alan Sugar in the process – so why do it?

vi **Use product upgrades to regain any lost profitability**. That's exactly what Alan Sugar did in 1988 – this time, having made his name, he launched the Amstrad 1640. It had a full colour screen a 3¼inch floppy disk and a hard drive, it sold for £1,640 (*c. €2,640*) (*again plus VAT*).

The only reason that Amstrads are not still around is probably that the Sugar/Amstrad business model, which lasted until well into the 1990's could not match the very sophisticated Dell model of not making anything until it was already sold and paid for.

New product pricing in a new market

1. **Study the value systems of your potential customers.** What does value mean to them? What current or potential product factors/ features/advantages/benefits etc. will they respond to. Remember there are three different types of innovation (*see Chapter 2, the Technology Adoption Curve*). The more an innovation is toward the dynamic discontinuous type, the harder it will be for the target group customer to relate – by definition they have no point of reference.

   Thus the person in charge of pricing will have to use reference to Maslows price/value landscape matrix, the Levitt construct, the conjoint analysis tool and plan how the product will be taken across the 'chasm' and into the 'bowling alley' beyond.

2. **Seek the value of comparable products (*goods/services*) OR the value or the penalty of not having the product at all.** What did your target group of customers use before your 'product' was available? This will give you a starting point. Then examine the extra advantages, some functional (*e.g. speed, ease of use, etc.*), some psychological (*e.g. status, fashion et al*), and plot these on the price/ value landscape matrix.

3. **Identify potential entrants and conduct a complete competitive analysis of them.** If your product launch is a success, you can expect the competition to try to move in on your new market, study them carefully and have your riposte fully thought-through and ready to go.

4. **Price high at first (*skimming*).** As we have discussed under Pricing Strategies, the Sony model of price skimming is the strategy of choice unless your firm has complete control over its shareholders, in which case barrier pricing is preferred.

   The first strategy is designed to:

   i Recoup the costs of development including the initial marketing at launch, and

   ii Establish the optimal price point, and

   iii Establish the probable volumes demanded so that the size of the production facility required can be decided and funded without either having a costly excess of production, or leaving too much of the market unsatisfied and therefore open to your competition.

5. **Before competitors enter, drop the price to defend your position in the market.** Here we must have a very good industrial market intelligence operation – as has Sony.

   Refer to Chapter 4, where the Author has outlined his desire to have a Sony digital camera. Then just before he had resolved to buy the Sony camera, Fuji launched its three mega pixel 'FinePix' with a price obviously designed to undercut the former price point of the Sony CyberShot. Don't believe that it was just good fortune, Sony had learned of Fuji's intention, and had moved to pre-empt this move. Brilliant!

   Lesson: too early and you risk 'leaving money on the table' – too late and it looks like you are weak. Either way you will be the loser.

6. **Price test.** For many reasons it is not always possible to launch the product in different markets at different prices today. We are often in global markets and such behaviour invites so called 'grey imports' from the low price markets to the higher priced markets (*see Dual and multiple pricing in Chapter 4*). But if you can differentially price during testing the market, the different take-up at different price points will provide very valuable insights into how your market will most probably behave when fully launched.

7. **Stay unbundled until you understand the market.** As we will see below, in new markets with totally new products, especially when they are either dynamic or dynamically discontinuous innovations, bundling just confuses the issue. There is the danger that we don't exactly know what it is the customer is buying.

The PLC and bundle vs. break

- **Introduction/growth** = break the offering into separate factors. Early in the product life cycle bundled items are seen by customers as being confusing and poor value. In addition, this extra cost etc. will put you at a competitive disadvantage!

- **Maturity** = involve much bundling to add value (*e.g.. PC's with soft/hardware*). The vendor should always be able to get discounts for volume, thus it is often a great way to add value for the customer at a cost well below what he/she would normally have to pay.

In short: bundle when you need to: – Upgrade the sale
– Avoid cherry picking
– Gain a CDA

Pricing a tender

Strategies for the invitation to tender

The question that must be asked is, 'Do you really want the work now or not?' Maybe your organization is up-to-it-eyes in work at the moment and into the foreseeable future – in which case the question to address is 'Can we afford not to tender?' If you don't tender you may not be asked again and at some future date you may need the work.

If your firm does not need the work then price high, but not too high that you don't get invited again, but high enough that if, heaven forbid, you do win the tender you can afford to put some of your current business on the back burner. We should all be so lucky!

However, if you do want the work now, if possible aim to:

GET INVOLVED IN SPECIFICATION DESIGN

The ideal tender strategy is to get involved in the design of the specifications long before it goes to tender, if your market's business culture permits. (*This is very hard to do if you are in, say, a business of working for government departments or public services.*)

This means that ideally your sales and marketing functions must be very proactive. They should always be looking to get involved with current and future customers to the extent that they are seen by them as being a resource. The trick now is to assist the customer in the design of the tender specifications in such a way as to ensure that it favours your firm's capacity and capabilities whilst at the same time it puts your competitors at a disadvantage.

A good example of this tactic, was to be found in a British firm that produced food wrapping film, lets call them BritFilm. This firm had a huge R&D budget of which less than a quarter was spent inside the firm; the rest was spent assisting the R&D functions of firms that made the machinery that was used by supermarkets to wrap fresh foodstuffs prior to displaying them on their shelves.

Even in those days, the buying departments of supermarkets were very professional, some would say predatory. So when they upgraded their wrapping machines, they would go out to tender for the supply of food wrapping film. Guess whose film was the only one that would fit these new machines? And was the film cheap? Why should it be? BritFilm was the only one that could supply to these new specifications.

Of course the competitors quickly reverse engineered BritFilm's new product and soon caught-up with their specifications, but by then BritFilm had recouped its R&D and made a handsome profit. Thereafter BritFilm could afford to be competitive until the next generation of food wrapping machines came on to the market. This is price skimming applied to a tender driven market.

This story is by no means unique, in fact, it is fair to say that if you are not doing a BritFilm then by the time you receive the invitation to tender you have probably already lost. Your bid is most often just being used to make up the numbers so that the buyers can say, in all honesty, that they went out to tender and got the required three (or more) bids. Plus it always builds pressure on the incumbent supplier not to think that they have the business all their own way.

LOOK FOR ADVANTAGES

In order to be profitable in the long term any tender must be based on value not the lowest price. Some fairly unsophisticated ways of doing this are:

1. **Reciprocal trade:** This is rarely something that can be done with Government departments, national or local, but it is a ploy that is often possible with other businesses. Take the example of a haulier working for a tyre producer.

   Long ago the Author worked in the sales and marketing team of an international tyre manufacturer. On one occasion our team landed a large contract to supply earth-moving tyres to several contractors engaged with the building of a major UK motorway thus we had the need to transport these very large tyres from our central depot to the construction sites where they were to be used. Because our margins were relatively slim (*we had put in a very low bid in view of the volumes required*) we decided to go out to tender ourselves.

The winning bid was not the lowest price, though it was competitive. What persuaded us to go for the winning haulier was that he guaranteed to re-fit all of his lorries (*and he had a fair sized fleet*) with our road tyres if he won the bid. The decision was not sentimental on our part, when we discounted the bid he had submitted by the profit we would make on the lorry tyres he would buy from us, the bid was the clear winner all round – what is today often known as a 'win-win' situation.

2. **Use of local people:** On another occasion, when many years later, the Author owned and ran his own marketing research company, his firm lost a bid to a relatively naive newcomer to the business.

   Again the winning bid was not the lowest one.

   The Author's firm had been asked to tender for the research necessary for a local government facility to begin operating. We had done much work for them previously and treated the tender process as a necessary formality. Our price was competitive, but higher than the norm to reflect the experience we had gained from previous work for the department, and thus the greater reliability of our research approach and analysis.

   The winning bid however, undertook to establish its offices within the clients' county boundary (*at that point they were operating out of temporary accommodation in the next county*) and to employ only interviewers who were resident therein – thus providing the adjudicating panel with the prospect of being seen to be favouring a local firm and local employment.

   The motto of these stories is that the extra value you provide does not have to be monetary, it can also be psychological. In the right circumstances it can be just as effective to appeal to motives other than obtaining the lowest price. If makes the clients' decision makers feel better about choosing supplier 'Y' over potential supplier 'X', if lets say it appeals to their public spirit. The decision-makers in this case probably saw a better chance of being re-elected in one of the bids versus the others.

3. **Look for areas outside the specification:** You should know your business better than your customer does, although nowadays customers are getting very savvy indeed in their own right. On occasion they hire consultants to help them draw up the technical bits of an invitation to tender.

   Nevertheless, things can be missed out that should have been included, and things that are included can be erroneous in some way or another.

   The motto is to inspect the tender specifications minutely for errors and when they are identified, use them to the maximum advantage. You must judge whether you bring these errors or omissions to the clients' attention early in the process, or you hold back on bringing attention to these errors until the very last moment. The hope is that only your tender can benefit from offering a solution to these faults. This assumes that your competitors have not spotted them, and are doing the same.

   Whatever your choice of action, you will only add value to your bid, thus resisting downward pressure on your price, if you can show how you will be able to deal with these errors or omissions in a way that is to the potential clients' advantage. There is another tactic which is a bit underhand – but we will leave this until the end of this section.

Whatever, whether it is 1, 2 or 3 from the above, or a combination of two, or all of these situations, your tender and everything you do prior to the selection must sell the added value aspects as hard as possible; stress benefit, benefit, benefit till you get your message home.

Forecasting the probability of an opponent's bid

In some markets where the amount of all the bids submitted are published, it is possible to set-up a bid forecasting system so that firms in that market can track their competitor's past behaviour and use it to calculate the probabilities of each possible price stance they may take in a given situation.

For any given (historical) tender bidding situation we don't know for certain what the competitor's costings are/were, however, we (should) know for certain what our estimates of costs were at that time and for that given bid.

So, assuming that the competitor is using the same costing procedures or something fairly close (*if they were not professional enough to do this they would not last long*) then we can create an historical record that will help us predict the probability of winning (or losing) against that given competitor at a given price to cost ratio.

Competitive oriented tender pricing (A)

A Model **E (B) = [B-C]** **[Pr (win)]**

$$\text{i.e. Expected value of our bid} = \left[\text{Sum bid} - \text{Cost of fulfilling contract}\right]\left[\text{Probability of winning at given price}\right]$$

Method

Using our cost records and past experience of competitive bids, we generate the following table.

Ratio of competitors bid to our cost estimate	Relative frequency of ratio in past	Probability that competitor's bid is > ratio
0.8	0.01	1.00
0.9	0.02	0.99
1.0	0.05	0.97
1.1	0.10	0.92
1.2	0.15	0.82
1.3	0.23	0.67
1.4	0.20	0.44
1.5	0.15	0.24
1.6	0.07	0.09
1.7	0.02	0.02
	1.00	

NB

This is one competitor bidding. If two or more, they can be treated separately or as a compound.

FIGURE 6.4: COMPETITOR BID HISTORY

Consider Figure 6.4 above. At the top of the figure the reader will see the algorithm at the heart of this process.

Essentially it is saying no more than the profit potential (expected value) is the money to be made if we win the contract, multiplied by the probability of winning the contract at a given tender price. Figure 6.4 above shows:

- **In the first column** the range of ratios (0.8 to 1.7 of the prices of their bids versus our costs) within which the given competitor has made bids in the past.
- **In the second column** we see the past behaviour of that given competitor being tracked. It sets out the frequency with which they have made their bid at the ratio given in the first column.
- **In the third column** it expresses the probability that the competitor's price will be equal to, or greater than (≥) the price we quote at that ratio of cost to profit (shown in the first column). So we see that if we bid at 80% (or less) of our estimation of the cost of doing the job we will win 100% of the time (*but who in their right minds would wish so to do*?).

If we bid at 90% of the cost of doing the job, the probability of winning goes down to 99% [i.e. 100% – 1% (*being the probability of them bidding at 80% of the cost*)].

If we bid at 110% of the estimated cost of the job, the probability of winning goes down to 92% [*i.e. 100% minus 8% (1% from 0.8 bid, plus 2% from the 0.9 bid plus 3% from the 1.0 bid*)] etc. etc.

We can plot these probabilities of winning as shown below.

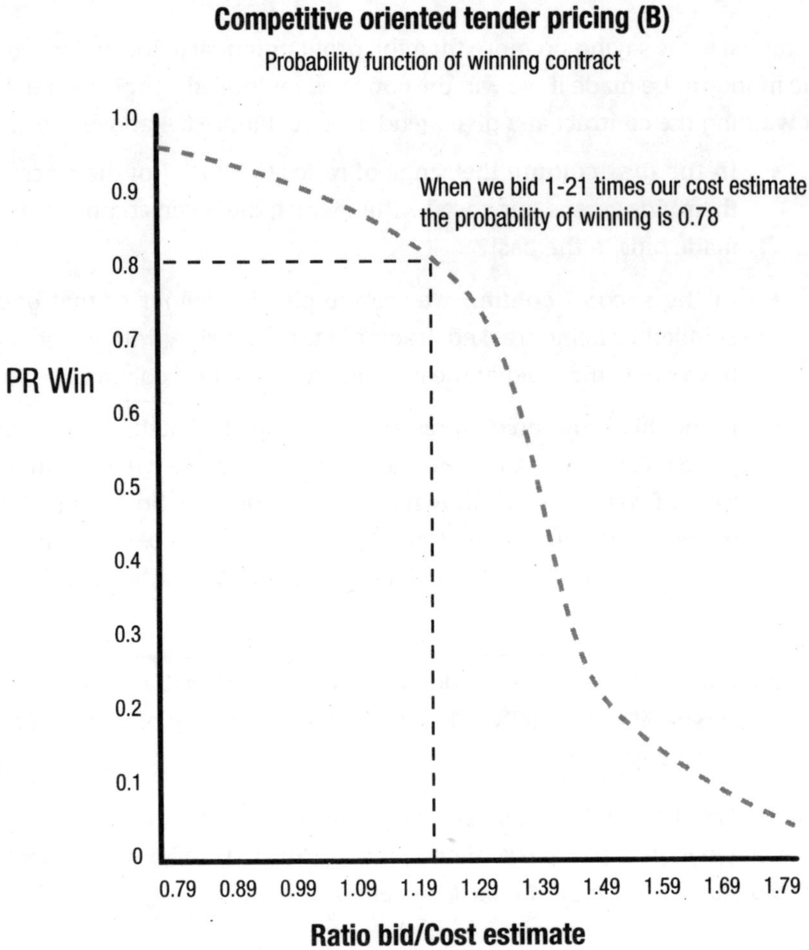

FIGURE 6.5: COMPETITOR BID HISTORY

So, if we were to plot these probabilities, the picture would look something like Figure 6.5 above. The probability of winning the bid is shown on the 'Y' axis, and the ratio of price to our cost estimate is shown on the 'X' axis. The reader must have already seen that the value of this situation shown is the area of the table enclosed by the horizontal and vertical lines, i.e. 0.9438, which means that if we consistently bid at this ratio against this competitor, over the longer run, we will average a loss of 0.0562 of the costs of doing the work. (*In percentage terms this means that in the long run, using this ratio of bid price to estimated cost, we will expect to make a loss of c.5.6%; plainly unacceptable.*)

So what should be our optimum pricing strategy, all else being equal? In Figure 6.6 we see, using the algorithm set out in Figure 6.4, the computation for every possibility in our range of probabilities.

We see that with the exception of the range between 1.19 times our cost and 1.49 times our costs we will be on a losing streak against this competitor – going by their past behaviour. The best situation for us will be found when we bid at some 129% of our costs of doing the work. When we win the bid we will be making 29% margin, and we will do this some 67% of the time. 33% of the time we will lose against this competitor, but will not incur any cost other than that of preparing the bid. (*Mind you in some industries this can be a very substantial cost indeed, but that is a different model.*)

Competitive oriented tender pricing (C)

By using the formula E(B) = [B-C] [Pr (win)]

We can calculate expected pay-offs
E.g. E(1.09) = (1.09-1.00) (0.92) = 0.0828C
for any point on curve

Thus for the following points

E(0.79c) = -0.21c
E(0.89c) = -0.1089c
E(0.99c) = -0.0097c
} **Loss**

E(1.09c) = 0.0828c
E(1.19c) = 0.1558c
E(1.29c) = 0.1942c
E(1.39c) = 0.1716c
E(1.49c) = 0.1176c
E(1.59c) = 0.0531c
E(1.69c) = 0.0138c
} **Profit**

Implication:

1) We bid at 1.29 (129%) of our cost estimate
2) We make 29% profit, 67% of the times we bid
3) We make no **direct** loss and lose the contract 33% of the times we bid

FIGURE 6.6: COMPUTING THE ODDS

AND for the desperate

So far so good, but there is one more stratagem that firms may use when competing via tender. One can say that in all honesty it is only for the desperate, but it is amazing how many firms tend to exploit this practice, even though they are not desperate. Perhaps they are cynical, but in the right circumstances it can be very profitable, especially, but not exclusively, against national governments.

The main thread of this tactic is to use the customer's weaknesses against them. This is often the case with governments, but not exclusively. On the one hand they are bound to accept the lowest bid, and on the other hand they lack the technical expertise and/or experience in the technology to ensure that all the bases are covered in their specification. In situations like these, the unscrupulous can have a field day.

The practice is to go through the specification provided by the invitation to tender with a fine tooth comb. This is to identify all the areas that have the potential to cause problems in the completion of the work to be commissioned. When all these areas are identified, then the bid is established to deal with only those parts of the work to be done which are clearly and unambiguously specified in the invitation to tender, no more.

The bid will often be at some 40% to 50% below the cost of doing the work – this almost guarantees that the firm so doing will gain the contract. As part of the bid, and as a condition of the proposed contract, comes a menu setting-out the costs of doing any work which is extra to the original specification. This is where the firm so winning the contract will make its money, by cashing-in on the client's naiveté. All the extras will more than make up for the original price cutting, and then make a substantial contribution to the bottom line.

If there weren't the laws of liable in the Author's home country, he could name names and point-out the guilty. But they are so profitable that they can hire many more, and sharper lawyers that the Author ever could.

Presenting your bid

However, let us assume you are not one of the 'sharp' practitioners, so how then should we present our bid, given the freedom to design the physical characteristics of the document.

The quality of the document's physical presentation is critical. It is usually the first impression that the adjudicators will get of your submission. If you seem not to care about the appearance of this package, and everything that surrounds it, then why should they take you seriously? In the Author's book *Marketing Your Service Business*[2] (*very much based on the Author's experiences gained when marketing his market research agency for nearly 16 years*), there is a whole chapter about the importance of the physical evidence which accompanies anything that is intangible like ideas and experience etc.

So tailor make your quotations

Use the following as a checklist:

- **High quality binder, and a well desktop published proposal.** First of all ensure you know your audience, and make sure that the physical presentation is commensurate with the client's culture (*business, corporate and ethnicity etc.*) and behavioural type[3]. Make sure that the final document is of a high quality. The paper, its weight, colour and finish, the typeface, the layout of the text, the use of white space, the use of colour and graphics etc. will all speak for you when you are not there to speak for yourself. Ensure it says what you want it to.
- **Deliver the quotation earlier than promised.** The mantra here is to 'under promise and over deliver'. There are three issues:
  - **Firstly,** the moment you make a promise that will stretch your capacity, you can count on the fact that the gremlins will come out of the woodwork. Anything that can go wrong to prevent you meeting this tight deadline *will go wrong*!
  - **Secondly,** by coming in early (but not too early) you have over delivered and, hopefully, you have impressed your client with your professionalism and eagerness to do this work.
  - **Thirdly,** this stratagem has set the agenda for the future, and this will be the client's expectation next time, "you were able to deliver in eight days, when you said it could take ten". So if you have the work ready to deliver in eight days and you promised ten, then don't make it harder for yourself in the future. Rather wait the extra day, and deliver it on the ninth. The client will still be delighted, and you will not have raised the bar too high.

Plus you have provided yourself with some extra room in which to deal with those pesky gremlins next time.

- **Outline client's problem.** Do this clearly and succinctly, and in your own words – not the clients. The aim here is to demonstrate your understanding of the situation that the client faces, and if relevant, the danger of doing nothing.
- **Show your proposal's objectives.** Be very clear about your thinking here, by these objectives shall ye be judged! So make them as SMART[4] as possible.
- **Show your proposition.** This section should be your interpretation of what you believe should be the best approach to the situation faced by the client. If you can see several, then outline the two or three most attractive ones that the client may not have thought of. This is mandatory if the client is a 'driver'(*see previous end note re behavioural types*), by definition they will be the ones who will make the decision, so give them several possible approaches – all of which should suit you, and let them make the decisions.
- **Show the benefits of your proposed approach(es).** The aim here is to demonstrate how your proposition will address the client's needs in a way that is advantageous from the client's perspective (*other than price/cost of the project*). Perhaps you have ways of doing the work faster, more accurately, with more safety, that will provide (*more*) prestige for the client; the list is endless.
- **Show your cost-analysis versus the savings.** You must assume that your price to do this work will be an issue, the client would usually not have gone out to tender if cost had not been a factor[5]. So address this, **but from the flank**, i.e. don't so much defend your price as sell the value-added reasons for using your business versus the competition.
- **Show your unique qualities.** Stress and sell your competitive differential advantage (*CDA*). Here the aim is to demonstrate your capability to handle this project (or *whatever*). A brief analysis of your and your teams relevant experience, qualifications, and if germane, your clients list. A few relevant case histories (*perhaps as appendices*) will help to bolster your case.

  NB If you don't have a competitive differential then you have no reason for having got this far and all you will have to sell is a price lower than the competition (this often at the expense of quality and/or your bottom line).

- **ONLY THEN show specification, price and terms.** A major handicap of having to produce a tender document which you will not have the chance to personally present, at least at the start of the evaluation process, is that clients can turn to the 'financials pages' without even reading the pages in between. This is a clear justification for the BritFilm strategy (*see above*) of being on the scene before the tender specifications are even drawn-up. However, we can't all be a BritFilm, so at this point in the document, i.e. where the price is central, it is important to be clear and concise.

  If the proposal features several mutually exclusive approaches, announce them all at the start of this section, with the total cost of each option clearly stated. This section should also indicate whereabouts in the tender document each approach is dealt with separately, and in detail, and the form in which each option will be enumerated. Then deal with each approach, completely, in its own unique section – summing-up that section by again showing the sum cost of that option and the trade-offs (*if any*).

- **SUMMARIZE.** The author believes strongly that summaries are wasted if they occur at the end of a proposal document. His experience has convinced him that the summary should be a clear and concise précis of the whole proposal (*except for prices*) – pointing out where in the document each aspect of the proposal can be found. This so that the busy reader can get the overall picture without and/or before reading the entirety. **Therefore the only place for a summary is right at the very start of the document – perhaps even before the table of contents.**

- **PRESENTING YOUR PRICE (if you have the chance to do so).** Sometimes we do get the chance to submit our proposal/price document to the decision-makers personally via a presentation, sometimes even before they have seen it (a situation to be greatly encouraged).

  OR you have submitted a bid and a modus operandi for the work to be done, which has perhaps put you on a short-list and won an invitation to make a presentation to the people who are going to decide who wins this project and who does not. How best should this be done?

Here follows seven clear elements of a checklist of dos and don'ts when presenting price.

The seven guidelines for the price presenter

KEEP YOUR PRICE UNTIL THE END

If there is any golden rule, this is it. You must build up a platform on which you can justify your price, before naming your price.

The author well remembers his lesson in this principle. He had been asked to propose for some market research for RNIB[6]. He had the chance to present his proposal to the relevant committee and at the start of that presentation, as he made his opening remarks, the author could see the Chairman of the relevant committee perusing the back of the document, where the price for the project was outlined. Right in the middle of the Author's opening remarks, up spoke the chairman, said he:

> ***"Thank you for coming Mr Brown, you have obviously put a lot of work into this proposal, for which we thank you, but the price you wish to charge is way beyond your competitors quote for this job, and our budget. We won't waste any more of your time – we are all busy people, I am sure you know the way out."***

And with that he stood-up and left the room, followed by all but one of his committee. A salutary experience.

From that day to this the Author's golden rule in such situations is:

DON'T INCLUDE THE PRICE PAGES IN THE DOCUMENT HANDED OUT AT THE START OF SUCH A PRESENTATION!!

Bring these pages to the meeting separately and resist the client's urging to hand them out until you have made the case for your proposal, and have been able to show the extra value you bring to the table. It is never just a question of price unless you are in a real commodity market (see Chapter 2). It is always a matter of value for money, i.e. what price for what value?

MAKE THEM OPEN FIRST

Try never to be the first person to open the bidding. Let the other person open – then you have a benchmark from which you can work. After all, if you come in at a price lower than the customer would have paid, then that is the point from which the negotiations will start. If your price is said to be too high then that is the point from which they have to start. Rather than you trying to get the price up, they now have to try to get the price down – and you will have the initiative (*unless, that is they have the freedom and incentive to walk away*).

MAKE THEM DO THE WORK

As we say in the point above, you must keep the initiative – and this is best done if the other side are doing all or most of the work. Only ever make concessions in return for something from the other side that justifies doing so. You may have to lead them, look for things that are of little value or cost to them but are of relatively high value to you and, if you need to lead, offer this as a trade.

SANDWICH YOUR PRICE BETWEEN BENEFITS (*MAXIMIZE THE BENEFITS – MINIMIZE THE PRICE*)

Price is never absolute, it is judged in the context of what you can get for that money elsewhere, versus what you have to offer for it at that point in time. For example, the price of an artificial hip to replace an arthritic one is not the cost of the hip joint plus the surgeon's time to do the operation, but what the patient is willing to forego to be free of the pain. But there can also be other benefits, the Author knows this only too well; having had a hip replacement a few years ago (*the conception of the form of this book took place in the post-operative ward*). Almost a year to the day after the operation, the patient may be able to ski again! How much more will s/he be willing to pay for the joy of rediscovered youth?

So, do your homework, discover what benefits you can offer, and categorize these in terms of cost to you, and value to the customer. Trade the high value to them, low cost to you first. Strongly resist any attempt to trade high cost to you items.

PRICE SHOULD BE NON-NEGOTIABLE

At least in the opening stages. The moment the smart client hears a price stated in the following sort of terms, "Our price per day is $ 2,400.00 for this kind of work, negotiable depending on volumes" is the moment they no longer believe your price as stated. They will now get more active in pursuing a price discount, than they would have, had this statement not been made. The key principle, as stated above, is always to let the other side open first.

SHOW THE CLIENT THE PENALTIES OF NOT BUYING

In the profession of life insurance sales there used to be a saying that to get the best deal from a prospective customer one had to 'back the hearse up to their front door, and let the client smell the flowers' – in other words frighten them with what could happen if they were not to buy. If it is possible to enumerate these penalties in your market, don't hesitate to do so. It also helps if you have real life chapter-and-verse examples of what happened to another client who did not buy – and how now they wished they had.

Finally:

DON'T SQUEEZE TOO HARD AGAINST WEAKNESS

The pricer's job description does not include deliberately making enemies. Be tough , but also be sensitive – it is better to build-up obligations toward you, than to create resentments and risk a vendetta.

Paradigms putting up the price

- **Put up the price when everyone else does:** There are occasions when, for any person in charge of the firm's pricing, it serves us well to emulate the browsing beasts of the Serengeti. When price is being raised by the main body of your competition you must move too, whether you need to or not.

  On the Plains of Africa, the beasts who live the longest amongst any of the prey species, springbuck, wildebeest, zebra etc. are the ones who stay within the herd. Those who either move ahead of the herd, because (lets say) they are greedy and are looking for the best grazing, or those that lag behind because they are tired, old or lazy, make the predator's job easy and thus don't tend to live very long. The same principle applies to pricing.

  So, whether you need it or not, whether you have planned it or not, when the herd moves by putting-up the price, you too move. If you don't move with the herd, when eventually you do have to put-up your prices you will be 'picked off' by customers who will conveniently forget that you were not one of the herd when the 'market price' was previously raised!

- **Not too much at any one time.** Prices can be raised via small increases, occasionally done, a sort of 'creeping inflation'. (*See 'The ways to raise price without appearing to' following.*)

- **Talk it well up beforehand.** Some years ago, just after the fall of the Berlin Wall, and just before the total collapse of the old Soviet Government, one bright May day a letter appeared in the *Financial Times* complaining of an imminent rise in the price of a basic commodity, known as Titanium Trioxide (or was it Dioxide?) which is an essential for the paint trade. This particular oxide of titanium is apparently a vital ingredient of nearly all paints because it improves coverage, i.e. it is very effective at ensuring that the paint containing it hides what lies beneath. Thus the paints which contain this substance require fewer coats to be applied and so save cost. Russia is the major supplier of this commodity to the world, they almost have a monopoly.

  It appears that the person who had written this letter to the FT had learned that the Russian Government were intending to raise the price of this commodity by 25% as of the first of October that year. Questions were raised in the Houses of Parliament and their equivalent in most of the capitals of Europe. The theme of most of the protesting speeches was 'How dare the Russians hold the world to ransom this way!' A heated debate was opened in the letters pages of most of the business sections of the European press. By August several trade delegations had gone to Moscow to protest.

  To cut a long and interesting story short, early in September an advertorial from the relevant department of the Russian Government appeared in the business sections of many of the up-market European newspapers. The theme of which was that the Russians had listened to their customers in the West and wished fervently to maintain good relationships with them – thus they had decided that in October they would only raise the price of this commodity by 10%. This news was greeted by a reaction from all of the Titanium Trioxide users (plus others) in Europe along the lines of 'There, you see, protesting does work'.

  However this Author believes that the Russians had very successfully 'talked-up the price'. He believes that they only wanted an increase of 10% in the first place, but like many who have been through hard times, they had learned that you never ask for what you need, you always ask for at least twice that and negotiate.

  The industry wisdom is that the supplier must not do this too often or they will make the market wise to their ways – and true to form, the Russians desisted thereafter. That is until the winter of 2005/2006 when once again they 'hiked' the price of an essential commodity to Europe, this time it was petroleum gas which is mainly used for domestic heating and electricity generation. Note, they waited until the winter, when demand is high, and options limited.

- **Do not do the above too often.** Dramatic ways of raising the price require subtlety and cunning. If ever these ways are repeated too often, the seller will create an unwelcome reputation for themselves. Thus the market will get wise and be henceforth suspicious of their every move. Not a comfortable situation to be in.

- **Move something down at the same time.** Be generous (or at least seem to be), a good way to ease the pain of a price rise for the customer is to lower the price of some other product that they buy from you at the same time. If it is possible to lower your costs, say by raising the minimum order quantity, some of this saving can be passed-on to the client. (*See following: The ways to put-up price without appearing to.*)

- **Look after your key/major accounts.** These are the equivalent in commerce, of the military's lines of supply in wartime. Lose them and you lose the battle. Therefore they must be husbanded with great care and skill. However, you must still put up the price! What if the rest of the market were to hear that the price rise was only for them, and that your favourites did not have to pay it? The moment that this became public knowledge, your business will be in deep trouble.

  But how to do this without putting their custom at risk? The answer is simple – if you adhere to the follow rules of thumb (*i.e. it is the principle that counts in this strategy, not the actual figures which are purely for illustration*).

The tactics are in two parts:

i Warn the key/major account of the intended price rise beforehand. Just enough notice to get-in a timely order at the old price, but not enough time for the word to spread far and wide, and;

ii Phase-in the price rise over a given period – using the following method:

  – For all orders after the given date for the rise, the invoices will be at the new price (*that must be firm and non-negotiable*).

However, over the six months following (*say*) these invoices will come with a credit note attached. Such that the credit note for:

- the first post price-rise month, will be for five-sixths of the price increase, and for:
- the second price-rise month will be for four-sixths of the price increase,
- the third price-rise month will be for three sixths of the price increase,

and so on until the price to the key/major account is finally in line with the price everyone else is paying (*not withstanding any volume etc discount policy there may be*).

The reason for discounting the price rise this way is because if the extra discount is printed on the invoice it can easily become fact. Such that either:

- the buyer develops a conveniently short memory and will insist that this discount is the firm's normal discount, or
- the original buyer leaves for pastures new, and his/her replacement will select an invoice from this series and claim the same total, though temporary, discount as the norm for the future.

By the use of a clear attached credit note the probability of any ambiguity should be substantially reduced.

- **BE FIRM – The rise is non-negotiable.** It is critical that the price rise be enforced across the board – much easier to do if it is the whole market moving as per the Serengeti herd (*mentioned above*). This is often difficult to do, especially when times are tough for everybody in your value chain; but sentiment must be resisted as firmly as possible – your business must also survive.
- **Provide sound and true explanations.** Don't lie – *you **will** be found-out*, and if this is via your competition, they will delight in using this to damage and even destroy your good reputation. Therefore, whatever you say MUST be the truth, however, it does not necessarily need to be ALL THE TRUTH!

Raising price without appearing to

- **Revise your discount structure.** As we have seen at the beginning of this chapter, good management practice in the control of discounting is vital for the firm's long-term survival. One of the approaches to (*surreptitiously*) putting-up prices is therefore to revise the discount policies of the firm which may mean reducing:
  - the range of occasions where a discount is given,
  - the extent of any discount being given,
  - the range of conditions that warrant a discount in the first place,
  - the number of people who have the authority to give (*certain levels*) of discount.

All plus increasing the levels of management accountability for the discounts given by their teams compared to the benefits gained in return.

- **Increase the minimum order size.** Transport is always a cost – (*unless the business is in what was once known as 'cash-and-carry'*[7]). The cost of making two or more deliveries must be more than the cost of delivering just one. So reduce your costs by making fewer deliveries but which amount to the same overall total volume. This will also help cash flow – another cost reducing ploy.
- **Charge for deliveries and special services.** Many years ago when the author ran his own market research company, amongst his collection of clients was one run by a gentleman also named Brown. Tom was his first name. Over the first few years the MR company worked very closely with the client's business. However, gradually over these years Tom took to commissioning research closer and closer to the deadline for him to have the research results. For example, what he could have briefed us about on the Monday of any given week was often left until late the following Friday afternoon. Several times he caught us just as we were about to disappear for the weekend.

  The work was important as was the client, often the project would cause the MR team to have to work over the weekend in order to meet Tom's deadline for the results – all at an extra cost to our business. But we did not complain until we realized that this had become Tom's regular habit, and if his work was to remain profitable to us we could not continue to carry the extra cost of overtime wages thus incurred (*for those who had to give-up their weekend*).

The next time Tom phoned with a project on a Friday afternoon, it was our good fortune that this project was time-critical to Tom's business. During this initial telephone conversation it was pointed out to Tom that he could have told us of this work on the previous Monday. We confirmed that we were happy to do this work, but that he had to pay the weekend overtime consequently incurred by our staff. Of course there was much bluster from Tom, but he eventually agreed on that occasion, and thereafter was much more careful to brief us as soon as he knew about the need to hire us. Thus from that day forward his work was more profitable than it would otherwise have been.

- **Invoice for any repairs to equipment bought** (*not covered by warranty*). It is not unknown for firms to repair damage done by the customer to the equipment they have purchased; damaging the product by misuse rather than fair wear and tear. We are often very concerned not to upset and thus lose these customers so we agree to repair that which is not our obligation so to do, just to keep them, by keeping them happy.

  This is a cost to the business, and should be minimized, but it does depend on just how much risk of losing the customer you are prepared to take, as to how much you stand-up to them should they make such spurious claims.

- **Charge for engineering, installation, supervision etc.** In reality you can't normally get away with doing this with customers with whom you have been dealing over time, and/or where, traditionally, you have provided these services free of charge.

  However, if your business is such that there is normally a high turnover of customers, such as, for example, tourists coming and going from year to year, then doing this will not meet much resistance.

- **Make customers pay for the extra cost of rush orders.** Very similar to the bullet above, 'Making the customer pay for deliveries and special services.'
- **Collect interest on overdue accounts.** Great if you can do it without losing customers! However much this may be written into law in many European countries, the evidence shows that when the customer is a large company this rarely ever happens. There are many stories of the large customer bringing disproportionate pressure to

bear, and even using their considerable legal staff to lock the supplier into a legal battle from which they are lucky to get away without going bankrupt.

A very large international business machine manufacturer did the same to this Author's business in 1998. They did not pay him the c.£50,000 owed by them for some six months – just to set an example to the others in the faculty who dared to ask that the client should keep their side of the bargain.

And again, one of the largest silicon chip manufacturers, entered into a contract with the author to pay his firm 30 days after the invoice date, and yet for the year and a half when that contract was running they took an average of 90 days to pay.

The moral of these stories? Stay away from the big customers as much as you can, it is better to have a large collection of small to medium customers, each of whom you can afford to walk away from, than to have a small collection of the so called 'Blue Chip' firms where, if you are not careful, you too can end up subsidizing their business.

- **Slightly reduce content in the packet.** Many years ago, a major UK chocolate manufacturer's leading brand was a milk chocolate bar that sold for two shillings (*c.10p in current UK money, or c.147c in Euro's*). They believed that this was an important price point, and so, when the price of cocoa began to rise instead of putting up the price of the chocolate bar, they just put less chocolate into the pack. They kept the 'plan-form' size and shape constant, but made the bar thinner and thinner with every rise in the price of cocoa.

  This practice became ridiculous when the chocolate became so thin that the manufacturer had to insert a cardboard tray under the chocolate bar just to stop the bar from cracking.

  Eventually a competitor grasped the nettle and launched a chunky narrow bar of chocolate, at the original weight of the competitor's original bar, but at a realistic price. The advertising that supported the launch featured a rather clean-cut 'Chippendale'ish' lorry driver eating the new bar and it out-sold the former brand leader by many multiples.

  The moral of this story is that there is a limit to the amount by which you can reduce the content of the product so as to maintain the contribution margin, before it becomes so ridiculously obvious that your customers feel that you are insulting their intelligence and complain and/or leave in droves.

- **Produce less lower margin models.** If your products (*goods and/or services*[8]) have few (*direct*) substitutes in the market you may be able to get away with this ploy. The fewer lower specification models the firm produces the quicker they will sell-out. Then unsatisfied customers will have to buy the more expensive items in the range or go without.
- **Use currency fluctuation and escalator clauses.** Some businesses, such as consultancy and training, are carried-out world-wide. International exchange rates vary sometimes dramatically, and frequently without warning. Therefore it is important to ensure that, if your business is like this, you write clauses in your contract to counterbalance any unfavourable changes in the exchange rates. Similarly, with any other commodity the price of which could effect your profitability should it change during the lifetime of the contract.

  Even so, it is often wise to write escalator clauses into long-term contracts. It is frustrating to be paid the same rate per diem (for example) as some three or four years ago, especially when general prices have risen. This means that in real value your prices are being eroded. Thus consider including in your contracts an escalator clause that will tie your fees into some indicator commodity such as the price of petrol or the Retail Price Index.

- **Change the physical characteristics of the product.** Perhaps the most obvious example of this is the motor industry, and also the market for laptop computers.

  Every few years motor manufacturers like Ford, Volkswagen et. al. launch a new model to a given range. Take the VW Golf. First the Mk. 1 and then the Mk. 2, followed by the more rounded shapes of the Mark's 3, 4 and 5. Each of these last three being bigger overall and having more features than the ones before. The current VW Golf is a much larger car than the original Golf, and much more expensive, not just in the amount of money paid, but also in the buying power of that money (*i.e. even adjusting for inflation and currency exchange rates, today's VW Golf is more expensive than the Mk.1*).

It is interesting to note that the VW Polo is now about the same size, internal capacity etc. as the original golf, if not also the Mk3 Golf.

As for laptop computers, at the time of writing, whilst many manufacturers such as Dell were churning-out the standard 12 inch by 11 inch model, other manufacturers such as Toshiba, Sony and LG (for example) were segmenting the market furiously. Some laptops being super large with screens designed so that the machine could easily replace the PC in a small office, home office environment. Some were highly portable, getting smaller and smaller therefore (*one hoped*) more portable for the over-laden traveller/businessperson on the move etc.

New features were being added, like including fingerprint readers to ensure laptop security and hopefully discouraging thieves.

At the time of writing Dell was in deep financial trouble, whilst Toshiba and Sony were doing very nicely thank-you!

- **Change the way you calculate the price.** Consider a major financial institution in the UK who boasted the lowest interest rates on their credit cards, we will call them Leedsgate. Rather than being seen to be putting-up their interest rate they just changed the way it was calculated, i.e. from a monthly basis on the monies outstanding at the end of that month, to a daily basis.

  This does not seem much to write home about, but it has very substantially improved their bottom line. Consider, under the former method the customer has the interest on their debt compounded[1] some 12 to 13 times in any one year. Under the new rules the customer now has their debt calculated on a compounding of 365 times per year.

  At a published rate of 17.5% this equates to an effective interest rate of 18.97% for the monthly situation, and 19.12% for the daily interest charge. The amount of extra interest earned is only 15 pence per hundred pounds[12] per year, but the average credit card debt is said to be some £15,000 and there are said to be some half million credit card holding members of Leedsgate. Thus, on average, their bottom line is improved by £22.50 pa. per member which equates to a total improvement to the company's profits of some £11,250,000.00 (*less the expenses of doing this exercise*).

References

1 A major British Airline once admitted that this 'overbooking' could be in the order of 36%.

2 See *'Consumer Behaviour'* by L.G. Shiffman & L.L. Kanuk Prentice Hall 1978.

3 Ian Ruskin-Brown, Thorogood, 2006.

4 Published by Thorogood 2006.

5 See Susan Dellinger's book, *'Phycogeometrics'* and/or her video published by CareerTrack/TimeWarner.

6 i.e. **S**pecific, **M**easurable, **A**ctionable, **R**ealistic, **T**ime based and **T**rack-able.

7 There are often additional reasons for a client to go out to tender, such as the search for new thinking, novel approaches, and keeping their current supplier on their toes.

8 Royal National Institute for the Blind.

9 So called 'Cash-and-Carry' was a system whereby the smaller business could reduce its costs by paying cash to the wholesaler before physically taking the goods back to their facilities.

10 A product is a so called 'bundle of benefits'. This can be provided by a 'good' (e.g. a saloon car), or by a 'service' (servicing that car), or some combination of the two (e.g. car comes with 5 year warranty: parts and labour).

11 'Compounding' = charging the customer interest on the still unpaid interest.

12 See J.F.Weston & E.F.Brigham, *'Managerial Finance'*, Holt Dryden 1975, also see the compound interest calculator at www.1728.com/compint.htm

i This graphic tool was originally used on *'Profitable Product Management'* by Richard Collier who has kindly allowed it to be used in this book and on many Pricing courses the Author has run over the last twelve years.

ii *'Trains Grands Vitess'*.

iii Business Process Outsourcing is the process whereby the firm out-sources/hires-in the non-critical functions of the business to firms who are expert in these functions, and thus pays for them only as and when used.

iv *'According to Kotler'* published by AMACOM, in which the mix is said to be 5 p's. The first which he calls P1 'positioning' is about segmentation, targeting and positioning the 'product' see Chapter 4 in this book *'The Strategic Principles Prior to Pricing'*.

v After *'Pricing For Results'* John Winkler.

SEVEN

PRICE WARS – ANTICIPATING/ PREVENTING/FIGHTING THEM

(but only if you have to)

PRICE WARS – ANTICIPATING/ PREVENTING/FIGHTING THEM
(but only if you have to)

"Most price wars are started by customers not the competition." **John Winkler**

"In modern times everyone involved in a price war loses out." **Anon**

Synopsis

This chapter describes the conditions that can bring about a price war, how to recognize these conditions early, how to analyze from which direction/ competitors could come, with what level of aggression, with what sort of strategy and how best to prevent price wars happening, if at all possible. It proceeds to describe the principles of how to fight a price war, if fight you must.

An example price war

Some time ago, when the *Independent*, the *Times* and the *Telegraph* newspapers were all in broadsheet format, the latter two ganged-up against the first one, trying to put it out of business. At that time the *Independent* was a relative newcomer to the British newspaper scene and was becoming quite successful with a steadily increasing readership. The history of the price war that followed is long and interesting, but we will just look at the essentials.

The advent of the *Independent* had increased competition for advertising revenue. The *Times* and the *Telegraph* perceived that the *Independent* was going after their readers. The advertising agencies who placed advertisements in newspapers targeting these readers reached the same conclusion.

So, unless they did something to change this situation the *Times* and the *Telegraph* had to share the revenue from these advertisements between three papers where there had formally been just two. If it were not possible for these three publications to grow the number of the types of readers they were targeting, then one of the papers had to go.

The *Times* and *Telegraph*, probably did not conspire to work together, although this could be an interpretation of their actions. Almost simultaneously they dropped the prices of their newspapers dramatically. The *Times* even differentiated their price by the day of the week, 25 pence on Mondays (later dropping to 10 pence on Mondays) and half price during the rest of the week. The *Telegraph* did something similar. The *Independent* had to join in the fight, but because the *Times* and the *Telegraph* belonged to large international media groups, each with huge resources, and the *Independent* did not, it looked initially that it would only be a matter of time before the *Independent* went out of business.

The battle was long and hard, but at the end the *Independent* still survived thanks to the support of a consortium of European news groups who saw that if the *Independent* were defeated, they may well be next in the firing line. Even so the war lasted a good twelve months or more.

After the price war was over, it took years for any of these three to get their cover price back to where it was before.

In the meantime they had lost a great deal of reader confidence due to the degradation of each paper's content caused by the inevitable cost cutting that each had been forced to adopt during the war.

Finally, it is worth noting that the winners emerging from this conflict were not any of the combatants but the *FT* and the *Guardian*, both of whom had abstained from the war, had maintained the quality of their content <u>and</u> their cover price, and to whom many readers of the main combatants had migrated in disgust during the price war.

LESSON?

In commercial war, as in modern shooting wars, no one wins – with the possible exception of those who remain neutral!

Therefore, do everything you can reasonably do to prevent a war breaking-out. Even then try to stay neutral as long as you can.

The best way to prevent a war, is to be seen to be capable of winning one, or at least being able to cause considerable damage to the other side should war ever break-out. And that means, expect the best by all means, but always be prepared for the worst, hence this chapter.

Dealing with extreme competition

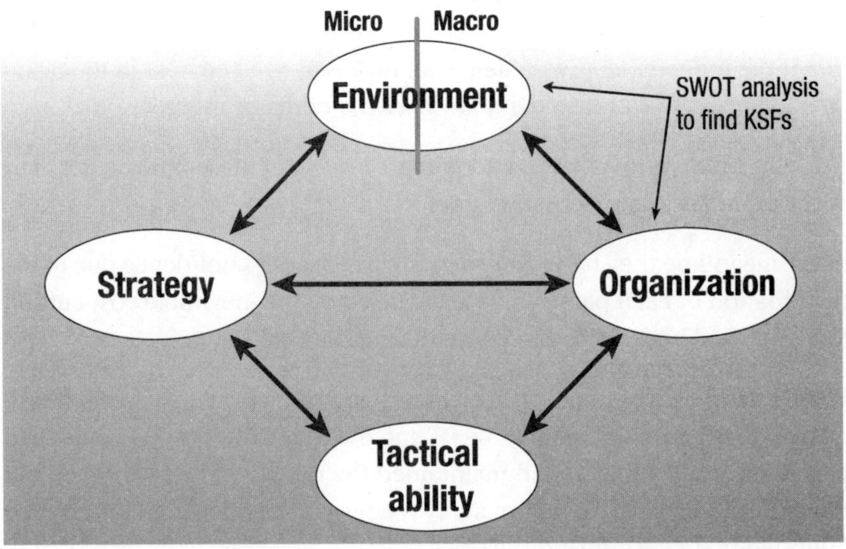

FIGURE 7.1: THE STRATEGIC DIAMOND

It is conventional in most books on marketing strategy to talk about the strategic triangle, with the top three items as in Figure 7.1 above, being linked. But just as we have quoted General von Molke at the start of Chapter 6, so it applies in this chapter also. In short, the success or otherwise of any given strategy depends very much on the presence of the tactical skills required to deliver it.

This chapter therefore will deal with the aspects of extreme competition (war!), both from the strategic and the tactical perspectives.

Lets start with an hypothetical scenario – say the market for a major, profitable product of yours is in decline. Price-wise what are the:

a) Considerations to bear in mind

and the

b) Things NOT to do ?

If your market IS in decline

You have to be certain that this IS the situation, and that you are not under attack. And if it is a declining market, know (or at least ask) what is causing this situation. It could well be that the general economy is suffering, or that the part of the economy which drives demand for your product is suffering (*e.g. if you are in the travel business, an unfavourable change in the exchange rate of your currency versus that of the holiday destination's, could cause a drop in custom. In this case it would be good to look for different destinations*). Alternatively, your product could be approaching the decline stage of its product life cycle. If so, in crude terms, look for alternative products and/or different markets (*i.e. refer to the Ansoff grid as examined in Mastering Marketing*[i]).

The things to remember, when you are witnessing a decline in your business are:

a. **Low price will not compensate for product deficiencies or poor service.** Maybe you service has not kept-up with that of the competition. It may well be that lowering your price will not compensate those customers you have lost, for the extra value they perceive they are getting from your competitors 'bundle of benefits'. Indeed, lowering your price when faced with this situation can frequently confirm the customer's opinion that your offering is inferior to the one they patronize.

b. **In business to business (B2B), low price only works if it is passed on to the end customers/consumers.** So called 'middle-men' (be they OEM's[1] or dealers/distributors) have a great tendency to boost their own profit and loss account via 'pocketing' your discounts (bonuses, special offers et.al.) rather than, preferably, passing these extras on to their customers, and by so doing benefiting you both.

There is only one distribution/value chain that does not end with the consumer – the defence industry. It is often worth considering how possible it may be to reach the consumer from wherever you are in the chain. Nearly all of us are aware of Intel being inside many computers – yet they are far up the chain. So it is possible to influence the consumer even from so far back in the chain. What we have to do is to add value for the consumer in such a way that the middle men cannot benefit other than by increased sales. For example, the beer brewers often use bigger sizes of cans when on promotion to boost sales, so the consumer gets (say) 13% more beer for the same price per can, and the distributor cannot drain-off this 13% extra beer and sell it seperately – their only benefit is via a legitimate growth in trade. [**NB** *This price tactic also ensures that the promotional price is the normal price plus extra beer and this does not contaminate the price point per can.*]

c. **Full pipelines will clear themselves.** Sometimes, for many reasons, distribution channels/value chains get so full of the goods being carried, that it can seem that trade has stopped. It is like the so called Mexican wave often experienced on motorways or auto routes at peak traffic times. One moment vehicles are bowling along, then, for no apparent reason, they all come to a crawl at best, a stop at worst. Then, after a while, again for no apparent reason it all starts moving, and no cause for the recent sudden halt can be seen. If you were to witness this phenomenon from the air, you would see standing waves of stopped traffic moving back against the direction of that traffic. This phenomenon, the so-called Mexican wave occurs when the conduit – in this case the motorway, is at full capacity. So it is with distribution channels and value chains. Suddenly they slow-down or even stop which is a natural phenomena that must not cause panic.

   To throw money at this situation is a waste of time and money. The short-term action is to be patient, the longer term is to encourage more capacity in the chain or see if there are ways that you can go direct (e.*g. to build wider motorways/channels of distribution – so to speak*).

d. **Low price will NOT cause an upturn in a declining product life cycle.** Many things can cause a hiatus in demand in any given market, we have discussed one of them, the Mexican wave above. Most, but not all of these situations will clear themselves, the important exception being a down-turn in the product life cycle.

It is a real down-turn, not a response to capacity constraints, or trading conditions, *IF* it is the customer migrating to new (*and perceived better*) ways of satisfying the needs they previously satisfied via your type of products[ii] then, no amount of effort, or expenditure will reverse this trend. Either go with the flow, and get on this new band-wagon or change, and/or get out of your current business.

In a declining market there are seven things NOT to do

These are:

e. **Don't confuse rumours with reality, beware price wars started by customers.** As we will see later in this chapter, via some reliable but casual research, we know of at least ten or twelve consistent lies that customers (*mainly the 'procurement departments'*) admit to telling suppliers as part of the (*what they see as legitimate*) way they do business. Always remember that it is in the (*at least short-term*) interest of buyers to pit one supplier against another, that way they can drive down the prices they have to pay.

f. **Don't confuse sales decreases with market share decreases.** From time to time the size of a market can fluctuate because of a whole collection of reasons. There can be seasonal fluctuations, fluctuations in the economy, or for whatever reason fluctuations in the driving markets at the base of the value chain et.al. If the market even temporarily goes into decline, then so will your business, assuming that you have not seen it coming and have taken no remedial action.

   One of the big advantages of being further-up the value chain, i.e. far from the consumers, is that you will get plenty of warning of the potential down-turn to come. At the consumer end – the down-turns can come as a complete surprise, for example, to the retail end. So whether it's the PLC down-turning or the economy, even though you can experience a slowing of business, you may not be losing market share. The emphasis is on the term 'may not', it does no harm to check nonetheless.

g. **Don't blame price alone for a decline in sales.** As mentioned in the two points above, there are many reasons that sales can fluctuate so don't automatically blame price alone, although your sales force will often be spooked by this and tell you that your products are too expensive, and they could sell even more than their targets if only it were just 5% cheaper. That's their customers speaking – not them. Never forget that any fool can drop their prices, but it takes experience, skill and courage to be able to put them up afterwards (see Chapter 6).

h. **Don't concentrate on some prices to the exclusion of others.** As per line pricing discussed in Chapter 4, your customers may view your product range as being in some continuum, high to low: quality, ease of use, nutritional value, whatever. In that case whether you have designed it that way or not, they will perceive you're pricing to reflect where in this continuum each product is positioned. If so, then to change one price and not the others will cause confusion. Move them all in the same direction (and lose even more money) or move none at all (and only lose money on the one that is under pressure).

i. **Don't wait for the crisis to resolve itself.** Although patience is a virtue, sloth is not. Act when you are ready – but do act. Get information and ensure you act sensibly, stay in charge of your own destiny, don't let others decide it for you because of your inaction. If you have a problem, time will not make it go away.

j. **Don't drop prices before it is necessary.** Remember, in this section we are discussing actions and re-actions when the market may be in decline. In this case timing can give you a great advantage. Too early and you will lose money unnecessarily, and perhaps even start the panic which could (at worst) turn into a price war; too late, and you could lose business to your competition that you may not recover without much effort – timing is everything in pricing as in many other areas where people compete.

k. **Don't believe that you offer the right price for all time.** Over time prices change for a whole stack of reasons. In the short-term they can rise because of increasing demand and not enough supply (i.e. the capacity to produce does not rise a pace). They can rise because the prices of basic commodities are rising, such as the price of oil for example. If this rises so does the cost of almost everything that directly depends (such as motoring) or indirectly depends (such as the resin for fibreglass articles from boats to baths) on it. In the short-term they can decline because the above goes into reverse.

In the long-term, in all but commodity markets, price declines naturally, and the values of the products increase, i.e. values are added. That is the natural way of markets for manufactured goods and performed services. Don't believe it? Then consider laptop computers – a great example of this long-term trend in manufactures.

Key issues, re price wars etc.

- **The best pricers avoid price competition.** Why go to war when you don't have to? War damages everyone who takes part as we have seen on the case of the newspaper wars, in the early part of this chapter.
- **The effects of aggressive price competition ARE ALWAYS NEGATIVE and last much longer than most expect.** It took the three warring newspaper titles some five to six years before they could get their prices (in actual monetary terms) back to the levels they were before the war, and to the day of writing this they have still not been able to re-coup their prices in value terms, to where they were before. As to the prices charged for their advertising space, one only has to look at the ratio of the relatively small space given to the news content versus that given to advertising, to see that they have adopted a strategy of 'pile it high – sell it cheap' (compared to the *FT* and the *Guardian*).
- **The majority of price wars ARE NOT the result of intentional downward pricing – THEY ARE mostly due to overreaction on the part of others.** The real life situation recorded above is more the exception than the rule.

  Most price conflicts are the result of a poor reading of what is actually going on in the market. The cause of this being the absence of a good 'quality' market information system (MIS) which can provide the decision-makers with reliable market intelligence. (*It is a good job that NATO had a quality intelligence system during the cold war. If it had been as poor as most firms still use, the western powers could well have suffered a 3rd World War.*)

- **There is no substitute for good, fast, market intelligence.** There are things you can do to prevent/deter a price war (*niche, add value etc.*) As well as being in possession of a professional market intelligence system, the best way to deter a price war is to niche the market and defend those niches with enthusiasm. Remember that by definition a niche is just big enough to supply good business for that one incumbent (see the pie chart on page 256).

  As well as niche-ing, the incumbent can add much value. Adding unique values (*by type and quality*), that your competition cannot offer, is another good way of protecting your customers from being poached.

  A good example of this, with which the author is familiar, is a butchers business in deepest rural mid Wales. The business is based in a fairly large English town close to the Welsh borders (lets call it Wrexbury). In Wrexbury there are many direct competitors – mainly in the form of the butchery departments of international, national and local supermarkets. Our heroes are the only independent butchers in that area. Our heroes add value in several ways which the local competition cannot match.

  Firstly: three days a week the business takes the butchery to their customers who live in the plethora of small villages and hamlets of rural mid Wales. This 'tour'is done by a small fleet of well-equipped and attractively presented travelling butcher's vans.

  Not only do these vans sell meat from the van, but they also take orders to be collected by the customer the next time they visit Wrexbury, e.g. when they do their monthly shopping or on market day.

  Secondly: All the travelling butcher/drivers speak the Welsh language (as do many of their assistants), which although not strictly required, proves to be a strong link with the rural communities they serve. The competition in Wrexbury hires their staff from those who can accept the minimum wage (or close to it). The result is that many so hired are 'Welsh-less', i.e. they were not taught the Welsh language at school and thus can't speak it.

  Thirdly: This business makes a point of buying Welsh-grown lamb, pork and beef, and wherever possible, as much as it can, from the Welsh farms in the areas served.

Result: Higher than average local prices, and higher than average revenue per employee, i.e. both volume *and* value are very healthy.

Why price wars must be avoided

- **Profitability is highly impacted by the low price levels.** Assuming that a business was 'competitive' prior to war breaking-out, so the margins, although healthy, were not dramatically above (or below) the market average. War, with its intrinsic extra costs, and its lower prices, could well bankrupt the firm.
- **Industry rationalizations rarely occur over the long-term.** The aim at the start may well be to 'kill' some of the competition and, although rare, this sometimes does happen. But even then – the hole left in the market by the competitor's demise may well be filled by a newcomer to the business. Better the devil you know, than the devil you don't!
- **Low prices set market expectations and undermine the value of the product.** Both B2B and B2C[2] customers have a tendency to forget what prices were like before the war, especially if they have come down dramatically. Thus they treat the low prices enjoyed and the extra values added during the war, as being the current norm and will strongly resist any rise in prices or loss of value (wouldn't you?).
- **Price advantages are rarely sustained.** In the long run price cutting (as apposed to promotional pricing) undermines any customer loyalty. Price is so often perceived by customers as being the largest single indicator of quality – that any reduction in price will be perceived as a reduction in the values previously obtained (see Pricing strategies Chapter 4).

BEWARE GOSSIP

Buyer's unverified 'information' is not the solution. It may, however, be the PROBLEM!

after John Winkler

Know from where to expect the threat

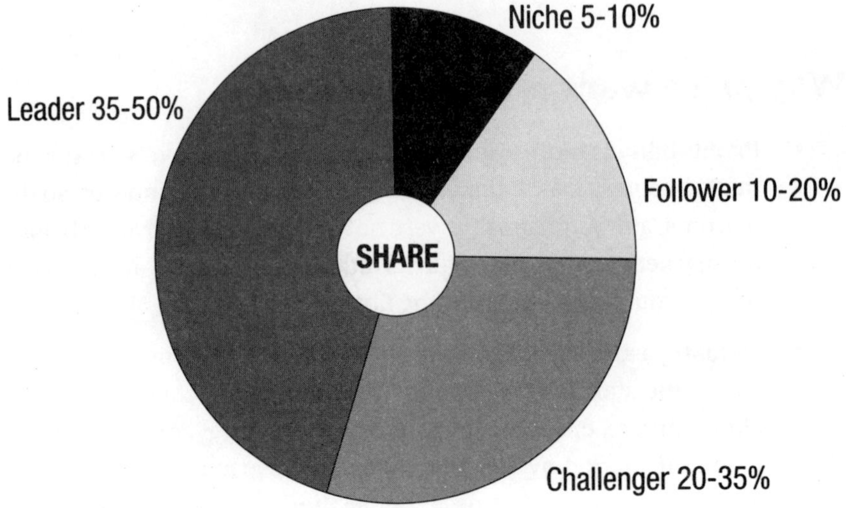

FIGURE 7.2: RELATIVE COMPETITIVE POSITIONS BASED ON MARKET SHARES

We see in Figure 7.2 above, a fictional situation which illustrates the different types of players that may simultaneously be competing in a market, or a substantial segment of that market. This helps us to identify where the threats could come from.

Taken in the order of size (*i.e. mainly their market share by revenue*):

The leader

This type of player has the strongest position in their segment; they **may** attack, but only if provoked. They have a lot to lose, so if wise, they will try **not** to provoke a price war. However, in most cases if they see a real threat looming, they will want to 'get their retaliation in first!', so to speak. **IF** they are attacked they **WILL** defend most vigorously – after all, if you are the biggest kid on the block, there is only one way you can go if you are defeated, and that is down! If this describes your business, at all costs you must, on the one hand avoid complacency, and on the other hand have a professional market intelligence system at work, at all times.

The challenger

This is a strong position, yet one with the least security; they could be attacked from both sides, i.e. by both the larger and the smaller firms in their market. So they too require a professional level of market intelligence to hand at all times. Thus if they are attacked, they will defend their position vigorously, if you are the attacker, don't expect a 'walk-over'.

From the larger player's point of view, it would be wise to have good relations with this type of competitor. Although forming cartels is an illegal activity in most markets in the developed and developing world, this does not mean that efforts to create an 'orderly market' cross that line.

As a virtual 'piggy in the middle' the challenger needs to watch their back AND their front. If they perceive a threat to be real they can be expected to attack, and this may often be very aggressive (*a sort of Pearl Harbour of the commercial world*).

The follower

Followers are businesses which, compared to their size, have the most to lose from any conflict. A price war could mean their annihilation. So, along with the leader they have no interest in making waves. But unlike the leader, they don't have the muscle to do so even if they wanted to.

Thus followers are often passive by nature. They frequently cannot afford the cost of a professional MIS and will rely on watching the bigger players and, by trying to read their motives in the light of past experience, guess what is going on in their market conflict-wise. If there is some sort of apparent 'orderly market' in their marketplace, they will be keen on keeping the apparent truce. However, if the smaller players in the market do attack, they will want to defend themselves vigorously, and on the basis that 'my enemy's enemy is my friend', will tacitly join forces with the leader and any other big boys on the block.

Niche/micro segment – players

A small player may outgrow their niche, or micro segment (*indeed they may be cherry picking in that they take all the high value micro-segments, and leave the low value segments for other players to pick-up*). If they are very smart they too will not want to provoke the bigger players but so often they are over confident and, believing that their current 'cherries' are safe from potential retaliation, will move aggressively to take the cherries away from the leader and the followers in their market. If this over confidence will one day make them tread on the commercial equivalent of a mine field, then all hell can break loose.

If you are a niche player (*or cherry picker, i.e. market to micro-segment/s*) it is wise to stay parochial.

What implications do the above have for the way we manage the marketing pricing side of our businesses?

Chiefly, it means that we must at all times:

- **Know our market/s.** In short, we must frequently carry out a G-PLeEST analysis (O's and T's)[3], you can never know too much, though it is often the case that the major 80% of what you know of a market will have cost you only 20% of the total you would need to spend to know all there is to know, i.e. information will often obey the law of diminishing returns, so it is wise to manage this process carefully.
- **Know your competitors.** Classify them (as above) and identify the dangerous ones.

> *'Know your enemy as well as you know yourself and you can fight one hundred battles without disaster.'* **Sun Tzu (The Art of War)**

Characteristics of strong vs. weak rivals

Here are some paradigms – which are a self-explanatory list of the things to look out for in your competitors:

The **strong** tend to be:	The **weak** tend to be:
Alert	Slumberous
Aggressive	Docile
Lean	Flabby
Innovative	Complacent
Effectiveness focused	Efficiency focused
Growth focused	Profits focused
Loyal buyers	Sceptical customers
Shares growing	Shares are stagnant

FIGURE 7.3: THE CHARACTERISTICS OF RIVALS, RE THEIR STRENGTH

The above will indicate the ability to fight, but the pricer/marketer will also need to have an idea whether they pose a threat or not, and if so to what extent, so they will need to classify their competition into those who are '**good**'- meaning they are predictable, and they tend to be logical, and those who are '**bad**'- meaning that they seem illogical in their behaviours and thus tend to be unpredictable.

'Good' vs. 'dangerous' competitors

Some more paradigms but these need a little explaining:

Characteristics	Good	Dangerous
Capacity	Realistic	Ambitious
Objectives	Logical	Unpredictable
Strategic	On benefits	On price
Share fighting	Realistic	Optimistic
Targeting	Focused	Broad scope
Offerings	Differential	'Me too'

FIGURE 7.4: THE PREDICTABLE (*I.E. THE GOOD*) VS. THE UNPREDICTABLE (*I.E. DANGEROUS*) COMPETITION

A competitor's **capacity** can be a revealing aspect of their business. None but a fool would go to war without the capacity in troops and material with which to fight. Additionally it is the capitalist way to be as efficient as possible particularly with the shareholders' money. So that that money which cannot be put to productive use is often returned to the shareholders, or if not they will want to know why not!

So oodles of spare capacity could well indicate that there is an un-revealed purpose in mind, which could be that they are preparing for conflict!

Similarly the predictability, or otherwise of a competitor's apparent **objectives** can be a source of re-assurance or alarm. War is best won by surprise[iii]. If you can't read the competition's intentions easily, if their objectives seem unpredictable and illogical, you would be very wrong to leap to the conclusion that they are fools. Many a nation has survived by letting their opponents gain that impression, and when their opponents are off guard they strike hard and effectively (*witness the survival, each in their own way, of the indigenous Irish and the Polish nations, whilst suffering years of foreign occupation*).

Also, what sort of **strategies** do the competition use when gaining business, do they do this on Benefits, i.e. value-based advantages, or do they do this solely on Price. Those who undercut you dramatically, with no obvious cost advantages, will have to reclaim the lost income sometime, and it could be from your own customers if you are not careful.

When pursuing an increase in **market share**, do they try to win customers using logical approaches toward logically selected customers, or are their approaches very optimistic and opportunistic. If the latter, beware, the next target could be YOUR customer base.

Similarly, do your competition choose the customers they **target**, i.e. those they wish to win away from you, with a logical selection process and logical proposals, the spear-gun so to speak, of business, or is this approach more like a wild and widely spread fishing net.

What is it that they offer to their **targeted** prospects (*i.e. those they hope to be future customers*)? Is this a specific bundle of differentials, versus yours, or do they target on a 'me-too' re: product characteristics basis? The more of the above that is in the right-hand column, then the more threat and danger you will have to deal with in the future. 'Keep your eyes peeled and your powder dry!'

Finally, in this list is the way that the competitor/s are competing with their **offerings**. If they choose to fight using a 'me-too' product, i.e. something almost indistinguishable from yours, in terms of the product's features, advantages and benefits, the only advantage that they can have is a lower price, either because they are going to be aggressive and/or they have a dramatically lower cost structure (*e.g. at the time of writing The People's Republic of [Mainland] China had a very low wage basis to their economy and thus were able to compete at very low prices for almost everything they produced. And, at the same time, they were seen to be expert at copying their competitors, additionally the business culture had very little respect for Copyright and Patent Laws*).

The following figures outline the sort of market manoeuvring that can lead to conflict.

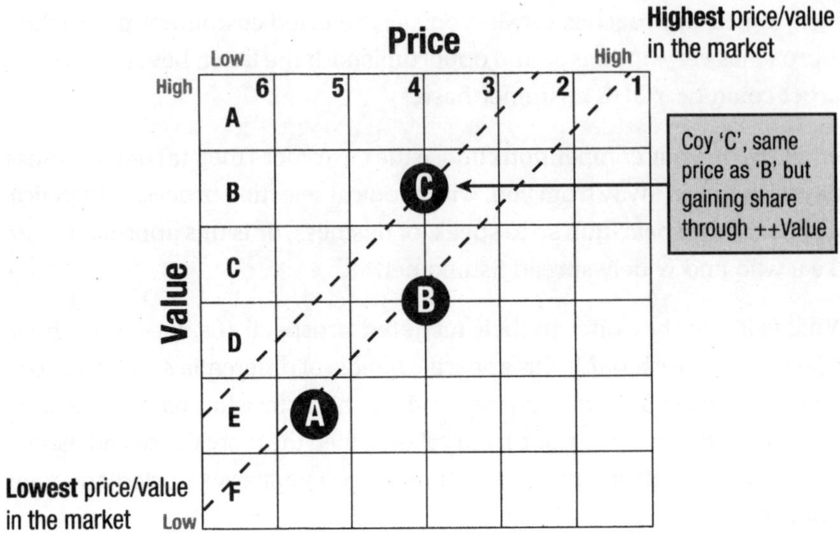

FIGURE 7.5: THE IMPACT OF PRICE WARS ON THE PRICE/VALUE RELATIONSHIP (I)

In the above figure we see three players. (*Remember, if you discover that your business in this market has more than three competitors, then examine your segmentation strategy with a view to identifying a part of the market where you can have sufficient differentiation to reduce the numbers of direct competitors back to a maximum of three* ***including you***)

One of them (here identified as 'C') is competing directly with 'B' and has provided its CDA[4] via adding value. This is taking market share from 'B' and also probably 'A'.

The quickest and easiest way for 'B' to fight back, as shown in Figure 7.6 below, is to reduce price. This will force 'A' to do the same, just to stand still in terms of market share.

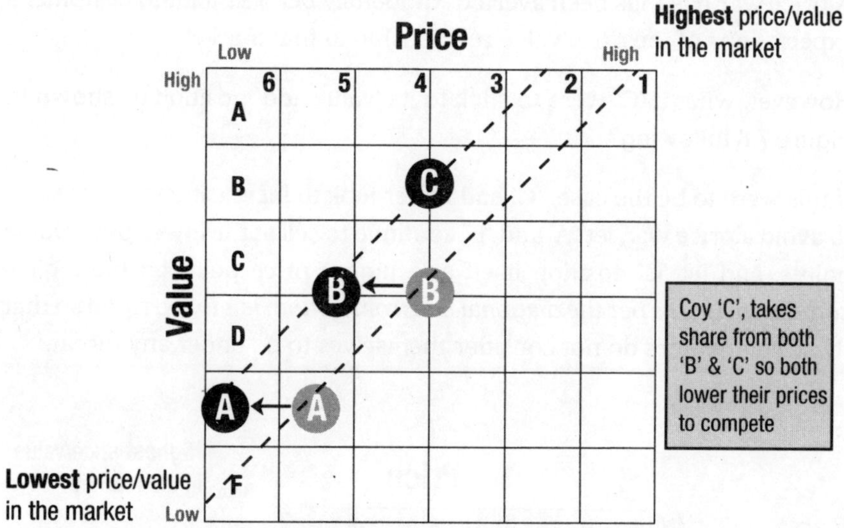

FIGURE 7.6: THE IMPACT OF PRICE WARS ON THE PRICE/VALUE RELATIONSHIP (II)

The question is how should 'C' respond? The quickest and most common sense solution is for 'C' to unbundle these value additions, bring down their costs and thus be more profitable than 'B' whilst staying in the market position in terms of its perceived value for the customer.

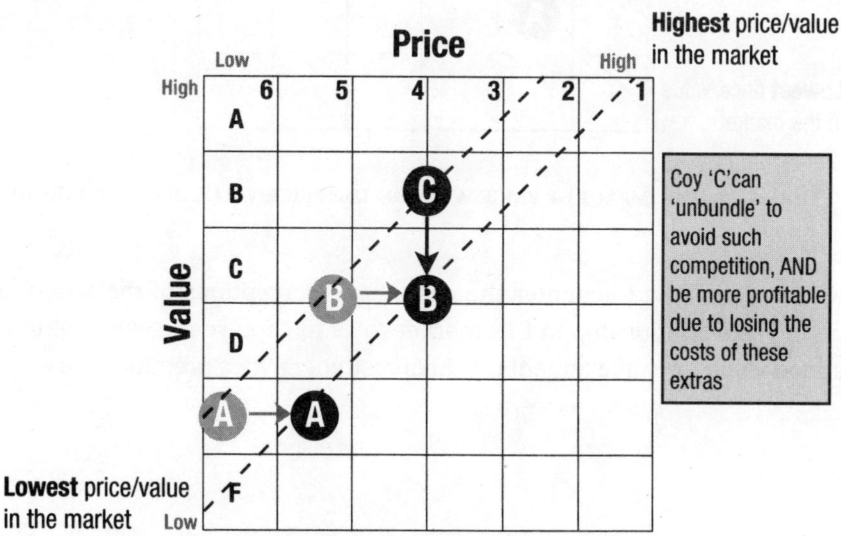

FIGURE 7.7: THE IMPACT OF PRICE WARS ON THE PRICE/VALUE RELATIONSHIP (III)

A price war has thus been averted – hopefully before building customer's expectations of the price value relationship in that market.

However, what if 'C' were to stick to its 'value add' position as shown in Figure 7.8 following?

If this were to be the case, 'C' had better look to increasing its price so as to avoid a price war, let 'A' and 'B' continue to sell at the lower price/value points, and let 'C' position itself at a higher price point on the logical continuum (*i.e. as per the diagonal line from bottom left to top right*) so that these competitors do not consider themselves to be under any threat.

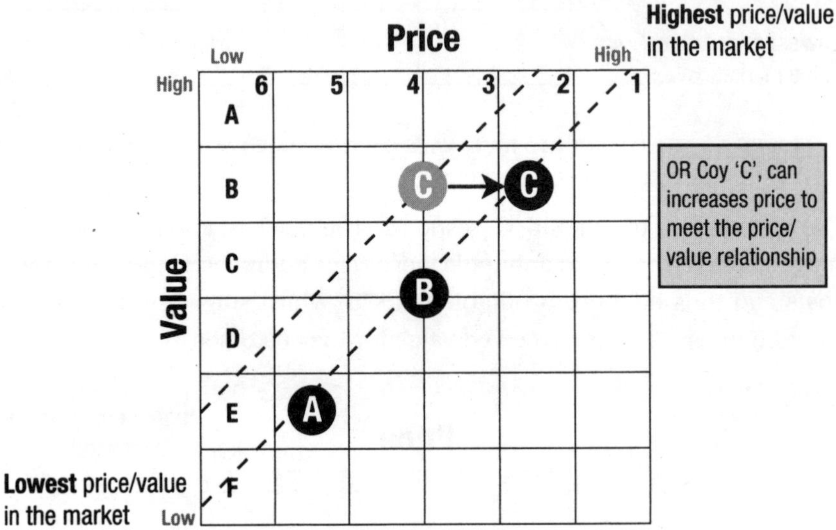

FIGURE 7.8: THE IMPACT OF PRICE WARS ON THE PRICE/VALUE RELATIONSHIP (IV)

'C' has somehow to counter the customers' perceptions of the absolute price/value relationship in this market so as to capture the value, of that added value (or value added) for their customers via a premium price.

Root causes of price wars

Misreading/over-reacting to the competition

- **Comparability misread/lack of price comparability:** It is often easy to believe that we know who the competitors are, and what their competitive offerings are which compete with us, when in reality this may not be the case. Often, when the Author ran a market research company, he was briefed by the client as to who their competitors and the competing products were, only to discover when in contact with the market, that the client was mistaken about this. It could often be a shock to the client to discover via our reports, as to who the competition really were, and with what products. You must do your market research into your customer's perception of who is actually competing with you and with what offerings.

- **Qualifier misread:** This is to say that we often lack current and reliable information about how our competitors' customers have qualified for the very keen prices they have been charged. We often see only the perceived price the customer has paid, where in reality this may have been part of a much bigger deal involving, say, bulk delivery or increased annual quotas, or even reciprocal trade between the two etc.

- **Competitive risk misread:** We could be reacting across-the-board to what is an isolated competitive move and not a real threat to our business.

- **Intention misread:** 'Don't leap, before you have looked'! It is so easy to misread and misunderstand the actual intentions of a competitor when they make an unusual price move.

Symptoms to watch for

INTENTIONAL COMPETITIVE INITIATIVES SUCH AS:

- **Penetration pricing strategy:** The competition are entering your markets, either where they have not been before, and/or taking (or attempting to take) customers away from you. This is an aggressive move that threatens your livelihood and should be discouraged and resisted.

- **Competitor/s gaining market share via aggressive marketing including pricing:** Again your future is coming under threat and the sooner you signal that this could mean conflict which would damage both sides, the sooner the opposition will signal whether they care about stability or not – thus the sooner you will know if this is an intentional aggression and can react accordingly.

MARKET CHANGES, SUCH AS:

- **A decreasing number of competitors in your market:** If this is the case you must discover why. Is the product and/or market at the end of its life cycle? Can the departing competition earn better returns on its efforts elsewhere? What is going on?
- **Rising barriers to entry in the market:** Say it is getting harder for any new competition to gain a foothold in your market, i.e. fresh blood, and fresh ideas are becoming scarce. On the surface this may not seem too much of a threat, the greater the barriers to entry, i.e. the more structured the market is, say the economists, then the more stable that market will be. However, this stability often results in stagnation until there are innovations to the basic industry business model. These innovations can change the rules of the game, as per the advent of low-cost airlines such as South-Western in the USA, easyJet and RyanAir in Europe, and AirAsia in South East Asia etc.
- **Developing cost advantage/s:** The South-Western Airline business model, in comparison with how conventional airlines were run, yields tremendous cost advantages particularly for the short-haul market. Neither Go nor Buzz or any of the other 'fighter brands' have been effective in countering this advantage. If a similar situation applies to your market/s, your decision is simple, if you can't beat them, join them, if you can't join them, leave for markets where you can.

How to avoid a price war

- **Avoid any over-reaction re any competitor's pricing initiative**
  - If you believe that you need to respond, do it with a non-price lever.
  - If price response is required, make that response limited, 'surgical' and reversible if the other side signals that they had no intention of attacking your business.

- **Play the value map correctly**
  - Invest in researching the source of, and the amount of customer benefits that give you any advantage over your competition.
  - To align your price levels with the value advantage that these benefits give you.
- **Communicate price properly**
  - Which means clearly, and linked unambiguously with the benefits inherent in your total 'package' of benefits.
- **Exploit market niches wherever you can**
  - Be these channel niches, or
  - Product niches.

But if all else fails you may have no alternative but to fight – so it is good to know:

The principles of war.

(*It is also good that your competitors' know that you know – this is called deterrence*!)

The offensive battle and fighting the day to day pressures on price.

There is nothing novel in what follows. Some of the principles go back as far as the book *The Art of War* by Sun Tzu. This gentleman (or gentlemen[iv]) was writing well in excess of some two thousand years ago. Sun Tzu's book is a slim volume brimming with good and sensible advice on how to address conflict successfully.

The second author is more familiar in the west, he being of Saxon origin, his name was Karl von Clausewitz – his book *'On War'* is specifically mentioned by Riese and Trout in their book *Marketing Warfare*[v].

You may think this is going over the top but an expression reportedly much used by those Japanese who are in commerce/business is that 'business is war' (i.e. **by other means** – as Karl von Clausewitz would say).

So what are these principles that we would be silly to ignore when contemplating having to fight a price war?

The general principles of any fight

1. First of all, as we have stressed above, try your level best not to get into one – certainly **do not be the one to start a price war**. However, if a price war is forced upon your business then:-
2. **Stay cool at all costs**, don't make this personal, the opponent who gets angry is almost always the one to lose.
3. **Evaluate the situation** – i.e. which event offers the biggest threat, long-term, short-term? Bring as many trustworthy minds to bear on this analysis as you can – the more different points of view the better will be your final decision. However, this is not to say that you abrogate responsibility for the decision, only that you strive to have a wider perspective.
4. **Pick when and where you will fight.** Try your hardest not to fight on ground of the assailant's choosing – the military call this the 'killing-ground'- it is deliberately chosen by your opponents BECAUSE it puts you at a disadvantage!
5. **Fight only one battle at a time** (*ex feints*). Throughout history generals have sought to split their opponent's forces, so as to gain a numerical superiority at the place where they wish to fight the battle. This they do by posing simultaneous threats from several different quarters (*i.e. feints*), aiming to force their opponent to try to fight two or more battles simultaneously.
6. **Obtain and maintain the initiative.** In boxing terms, strike hard, fast and where not expected. The aim is to get your opponent on their 'back foot' (i.e. off balance). And when they are off balance, keep them there. Do everything you can to keep them from regaining control of the situation. So choose when and where you will strike, and how you intend to follow-up and follow-through BEFORE you commence the offensive – you will have little opportunity to plan once committed to battle.
7. **Be ruthless, fight to kill – or forget it.** It is well to remember that your opponent is threatening your livelihood, the ability to feed, clothe, educate and house your family. You would not treat lightly any burglar who was to do that, so why pussyfoot with a commercial opponent – just because they wear a suit when doing it.

8. **Don't dither – speed is of the essence.** This is not to abrogate 2 above, i.e. keep your 'cool', but it is to say that you must be clear eyed, clear headed and decisive.
9. **Ensure one clear war aim,** AND MAINTAIN THAT AIM THROUGHOUT!! If we are to choose an offensive price strategy we need to know what our price war aim is!

   For example here are some basic price war aims:

   - To deter competitors from attacking us in future,
   - To pre-empt/meet, a specific competitor,
   - To 'kill' a **specific** competitor,
   - To achieve the stabilization of price etc.

   War aims should be:

   - Consistent with corporate **objectives and goals,**
   - Consistent with **the resources of the organization,**
   - Address the organization's business environment, **i.e. the S and W and the O and T situation**[vi],
   - Above all they should be **'SMAARTT'** i.e.,
     - **S**pecific,
     - **M**easurable,
     - **A**ctionable / **A**greed,
     - **R**ealistic,
     - **T**ime Based and **T**rackable.
10. **Secure your base areas/lines of supply.** In this context, this means the main sources of your business income – which for many of us are our major customers/key accounts. Ironically these accounts may not actually be the most profitable (*measured by the percentage margin we make from their business*), but when times are tough, it's the volume and flow of cash which is king. If your competitor were to capture these accounts from you, your business could literally be starved to death for lack of revenue. So protect these accounts as though your life depends on it (*your business life certainly does*).
11. **Maintain morale.** When times are tough there is a temptation for good people to look for employment elsewhere. The danger is that

it is always the best people who go first, because they can. Their talents make them attractive to other employers. Your least able people cannot so readily jump-ship. The only way this tendency can be countered is via high quality leadership on your part. Keep your people in the picture, have a good 'stump speech[vii]' tell them what is happening, make sure what you tell them is true (*you will have to trust them not to be indiscrete. However, although what you say* ***must be true****, this does not mean it must be all the truth – as we have said elsewhere in this book*).

12. **Defence in depth.** In a commercial context this means, having a range of different products, different types of customers and these (if possible) all melded within a range of different markets. The chances that your opponent can attack you on all these fronts simultaneously, diminishes as the inverse square of the levels of complexity you can build into your defence. That is to say, two main markets is four times harder to attack than one, three is nine times harder and so forth. And these markets which are beyond your opponent's ability to attack can be feeding your combatants in the main battle with the necessities for survival.

    It happened in the 1939-45 war. The British war effort from September 1939 to the end of 1941 was sustained by the British Commonwealth, without whom the UK could not have survived until late 1941 when the USA entered that conflict courtesy of the Japanese Imperial Navy's attack on Pearl Harbour.

    It happened in the broadsheet war between the three newspaper groups mentioned at the start of this chapter. The *Times* belonged to the Murdoch Group which not only had more uninvolved titles in the UK (e.g. the *Sun*), but also numerous global businesses both in the printed and broadcast media (e.g. Sky Satellite Broadcasting). The other main protagonist, the *Telegraph*, was part of a media group run by Conrad Black, which similarly had resources out of reach of the *Independent* they were attacking.

13. **Take offensive action.** As von Clausewitz has said, the best defence is attack, and as Napoleon once remarked, the army that retires to its fortress has already lost.

So, when you are ready, war aims defined, targets identified, contingencies well thought out and prepared, go on the offensive, grab the initiative, and keep it.

That means ATTACK and Counter Attack!!

Attack what?

Attack where it hurts your opponent most! Attack where it is least expected!

For example their:

- **Base areas that is to say, their home markets**

  If you can reach your opponent's main sources of income then you would do well to at least threaten them. If your opponent is wise they will have arranged to protect them – so any battle could be costly for you. However, if you have the resources to place a threat to these assets within reach of them, a relatively weak force can ensure that the competitor dare not leave these resources unguarded.

  In Chess, and in the right hands, a pawn can threaten a queen, quite effectively keeping this powerful piece out of play for some time.

  In the 1914-18 conflict, a German general[viii] operating within Tanganyika (*now Tanzania*) for four years and without fighting one real battle, successfully tied-down the powerful Kenyan and Ugandan Kings Own Africa Rifles ensuring that they could not go to Flanders (or Gallipoli) for fear of Britain losing East Africa.

- **Key/major accounts**

  As we have already said, protect yours and go for the throat of your opponent's main sources of income.

- **Most profitable brands**

  Income is often skewed, so that a few brands will bring-in a disproportionate amount of profit compared to their market share or the effort committed to them. These are often cash cows in the Boston Matrix[ix] tradition and are therefore frequently taken for granted. They can be quite thinly protected, i.e. they are the opponents' soft underbelly – commercially speaking.

- **Sources of supply, mutual suppliers**

  This is a very delicate area, a minefield even for lawyers. The extent to which we can be seen to 'collude' with mutual suppliers (i.e. those supplying both belligerents) is very limited, and yet it is in everyone's interest that you do so co-operate. Consider, from the supplier's point of view, if your opponent puts you out of business, then there is one less customer for your supplier to deal with. If and when this becomes the case, the opponent will have more negotiating power than previously and the supplier could well get screwed on price etc. So, whilst there is a chance of cooling the conflict, it is in your supplier's interest to support you, and those like you in the market.

- **The weaknesses in their strengths**

  This is a barely understood concept, but one that is important nonetheless. Often we are well aware of our weaknesses, and the wise amongst us guard against these being used against us. But often our strengths are not complete and there are flaws in-built therein. If we can identify where these lie within our opponent's repertoire of strengths, we can often discover an undefended underbelly ripe for attack. In our first book the author discusses one such situation in the case of Agfa v. Kodak competing for the Amateur /Professional photographer's market in Queensland[x].

The basic principles of commercial attack

1. **Use (create) a fighter brand(/s) at their level:** A major danger of any price war is that in the fight we can irreparably damage the brand/s we are trying to protect. In the 'broadsheet' case at the start of this chapter, we see that the three protagonists were not able to regain their price point until many years AFTER the war had finished. This could happen to your brands too if you don't keep them out of the conflict. How do you do this? – Do everything you can to ensure that your brands are not involved in the war! How? Use a fighter brand (or brands) to combat the opponent instead – here's an example of how:

   Many years ago the author was a divisional manager for a major international Tyre company in the UK, lets call that firm GalloChronos (say GC for short). At that time the Communist Block was still extant and one of its foibles was the habit of creating five-year plans for their industrial output. These plans were heavy on volume produced and very light on whether there was a need for the product in the first place, and if so, where and for what industries.

So it was with motor vehicle tyres. Once per year, almost like clockwork they would realize that they had produced too many tyres, and looked to sell these in western European countries. Of necessity these sales would be at knock-down prices, which were designed to at least create some foreign exchange for their respective countries. Lets call their tyre brand DayBands (say DB for short).

GC did not want to give the business to DB tyres, nor did they wish to damage the price point of their leading brand. So, as soon as we heard that DB tyres were once more trying to enter our market – out came the moulds for Rhino tyres.

Now the reader should know that motor vehicle tyres are created by very skilled hands, first the carcass of fabric that gives the tyre its strength and final shape is loaded on to a mandrel (*think of it as a sort of highly shaped rolling pin*), and then strips of raw rubber sheeting, which will eventually bind the whole thing together, are laid on that textile carcass. When complete, the whole thing is enclosed in a metal mould, and vulcanized (i.e. heat treated) for several hours until the raw rubber is cured.

The finished tyres' road-tread pattern, brand name, tyre size and specification details that appear on the tyre walls, are all part of this steel mould. The vulcanization process pushes the raw rubber into these shapes, so when the process is complete, and the rubber is cured, the mould is removed and we have a complete tyre for our vehicle as we know it to be.

GC Tyres Ltd owned a brand called Rhino with the moulds to match. So that when DB tyres entered the UK Rhino tyres were already in the market at the same prices as DB.

Compared to Dunlop, Pirelli, Firestone and Avon, GC, via Rhino, lost hardly any business to DB. Eventually DB would leave the UK for easier markets elsewhere in Europe and, wonder of wonders, suddenly Rhino tyres were no longer available in the UK, but there were plenty of tyres from your friend GalloChronos to be had. Of course at the normal pre-DayBand tyre prices. Whilst for our competitors, their customers remembered well how Avon, Pirelli, et al could reduce their prices when under attack from DayBand and they strongly resisted any subsequent reversion to the old price (i.e. pre DayBand). It took our competition almost a year to get their prices back-up again, by which time DayBands were once more appearing in the UK.

The moral of this story is price wars can damage prices irreversibly, so use a fighter brand to take the heat – and when the war is over, put it back in its cage until next time, and major on your (undamaged) leading brand once more.

However, it is important to realize that if fighter brands are to be effective they cannot be cheap substitutes – if they are, they will fail, as per Go and Buzz. When the so called low-cost airlines, particularly easyJet and RyanAir, started to bite into the profits of the major European carriers, such as British Airways (BA), KLM, Lufthansa, Air France, SAS, Finn Air etc. these carriers hit back by launching their own low cost versions (as fighter brands).

Two examples being called Go, and Buzz. But they were poor imitations of the chief protagonists.

Whereas easyJet and RyanAir used new aircraft, kept them clean and presentable, and fielded well-trained ground staff and cabin crews, Go and Buzz seemed only to use old aircraft, which although airworthy, were otherwise dilapidated and dirty, e.g. the isle carpets were often torn, and so were many of their seats, with little sign of either having met with a vacuum cleaner within the last six months.

In addition, their cabin crews gave every sign of having been recruited from the rag-tag of the employment exchange; poor demeanour, very poor elocution which resulted in many of the non-UK passengers being unable to understand what was being said, and so on.

Needless to say, Go and Buzz failed to stem the tide of the low cost airlines in Europe and were eventually run-down or sold off, a delicious irony being that Go was bought by easyJet, which after absorbing the new routes promptly closed it down.

2. **Use a 'diverter' to keep them on the back foot** (à *la the Scipio Brothers strategy*). The Punic Wars[xi] finally came to an end when

two Roman Generals known as the Scipio Brothers defeated Hannibal in his own country. Up to then, Hannibal had been fighting on the Roman's home ground, mainland Italy, and had consistently defeated any army that Rome could put in the field. At every encounter Hannibal had chosen his ground with great care, and then forced Rome to come to him (*remember, NEVER fight the opponent on the ground of their choosing – they will always have the advantage*). But the Scipio Brothers decided to change all this. Rather than confront Hannibal in Italy, they sailed to North Africa to directly threaten the city of Carthage. The Carthaginian politicians called Hannibal home to save them, and when he came ashore the Scipio Brothers were waiting. This time Hannibal had to fight on ground he had not chosen and was soundly defeated. The point is, 'can you do something similar?' Can you turn the fight to your advantage by diverting your opponent's attention away from attacking you directly, and toward defending something they hold most dear (e.g. some special customers, leading products, and/or key markets)?

These next five issues are at the core of what was known as Blitz Krieg, i.e. lighting war. This was developed by the German army to avoid the horrors of trench warfare experienced by both sides during the 1914-18 conflict. Had the two belligerents of the broad-sheet wars we discussed at the beginning of this chapter, adopted this approach, things could have turned-out very differently.

3. **Concentrate/focus effort.** When you attack – it is very important that this is done with the maximum of focus, speed and vigour. It has more recently been referred to as 'shock and awe' – the effectiveness of this is magnified by surprise –

4. **Use surprise.** Attack where and when you are least expected, catch the other side off guard and off balance as much as you can – and when you have commenced the attack –

5. **Keep the initiative.** Anticipate your opponent's moves (*a bit of pre-war study of your potential opponents will never go amiss – remember "Time spent on reconnaissance is rarely wasted" – Napoleon*) and keep them off balance and on the defensive – and when they do something unexpected –

6. **Flexibility.** Stay flexible enough to change your plans to meet the unexpected – so that you can always -

7. **Maintain your momentum and follow through.** The point is to keep your opponents off balance (re item 5 above) so that they will have difficulty launching a counter attack and turning the tables on you. However, never underestimate your opponents – expecting the unexpected means that you must –

8. **Prepare for the counter-attack.** If they are successful at launching a counter attack you will be the one on the back-foot and at a disadvantage. These considerations should be well thought through BEFORE you launch the first assault – once battle commences there will be little time to think tactically let alone strategically -

9. **Ascertain if they are able to follow up.** If so don't stand back, **block their next moves,** i.e. keep thinking two or three steps ahead at all times –

10. **Economy of effort.** Whether this price war was your initiative, or your opponent's, in the early stages you never can tell how long it will last. It is like a heavyweight boxing match. 'Will the bout go the full 15 rounds, or will you be able to deliver a knock-out blow well before then?' As much as you think you can knock-down your opponent – you must be prepared for the long-haul – so pace yourself.

However, what if the attack on your market appeared to be the commercial equivalent of Pearl Harbour and you were the USA's sixth fleet? What then?

First of all, keep your cool: You may **not** be the one under attack and your segment bunker could protect you (*e.g. Guardian's and FT's respective market segments protected them during the Times' and Telegraph's attack on the Independent in the early 1990s*).

But if you are the one being attacked, then:

- **Actively engage your antagonist/s:** (*tit-for-tat)* for example, if they attack a key account with a special promotion, attack an equivalent size key account of theirs with a similar promotion.

- **React in kind** (*not disproportionately*) **to every competitive price volley**: This will require a cool head, and rational decisions. If you are getting 'hot-under-the-collar' then it will be best to delegate the tactical control of the fight to one of your Lieutenants.

- **Communicate your tit-for-tat intentions** (*so your opponent knows they cannot win*): One of the best ways to do this is to openly brief your sales force on how you plan to proceed, and how you would like them to keep a vigilant look-out for your opponent's moves, letting you know straight away of anything new so that you can organize a riposte. One or more of the team will then undoubtedly tell one or more of your customers and, in due course that will inevitably be communicated by these customers to your opponent.
- **Immediately and openly support/reciprocate any return to rational pricing by your opponent:** Just as escalation should be commensurate with the threat, each step being measured so as not to be 'explosive', so should the steps for any de-escalation.

Exercise

Using the ideas as per Figures 7.2 and 7.5, analyze where you stand in your market and which competitors occupy the other places. Take the three most 'muscular' of these (remember, if there are more than three protagonists in your market you need to do more serious segmentation). Analyze these as per the Figures 7.3 and 7.4 (and the explanatory text). Now you know which ones you need to watch most carefully.

Finally, examine their position to your price as per the price landscapes (Figures 7.5 and 7.6) and their product portfolios. Then start putting together what you believe could be their moves against you should they want to, and putting together your deterrence and, should deterrence fail, your counter-strategies to fight the war that you envisage coming from that direction.

References

1 Other Equipment Manufacturers – that's what they do – but some like to interpret this as 'Original Equipment Manufacturers'.

2 'Business to Business' and 'Business to Consumer'.

3 See page 230 et.seq. of *'Mastering Marketing'*, 2nd edition, by this author, Thorogood 2006.

4 Competitive Differential Advantage.

i *'Mastering Marketing'* (2nd edition), Ian Ruskin-Brown, Thorogood 2006.

ii For a more full discussion of the PLC, see *'Mastering Marketing'* as cited above.

iii See *'On War'* by Karl Von Clausewitz.

iv There is some debate as to whether this was just one man or a collection of Sages who, in concert, acted in the role of Hereditary Military Consultants to several Chinese Emperors at the time.

v Al Ries and Jack Trout, *'Marketing Warfare'* McGrawHill, 1995.

vi Re the GPLeEST analysis as per *'Mastering Marketing'* pp242 et seq.

vii A concept from *'Thriving in Chaos'* by Tom Peters (Macmillan, 1988) Tom tells of the exceptional leaders he has encountered in the businesses with which he has worked. They always have a rousing stump speech to encourage the troops, much in the same mould as Henry the Fifth's speech to his troops before Agincourt (according to Shakespeare), or General Montgomery's speeches to the Allied troops prior to the Battle of the Alamein.

viii General Paul von Lettow-Verbeck re "The war in the Colonies 1914-1918", the *'Encyclopaedia of World History 2001'*.

ix The Boston Consulting Group Matrix (aka BCGM) – the 'Cash Cow' type of product has a large market share but is in a Static or Declining Market – which is often not a contested area. Therefore can, and should be a very profitable product. See David Jobber, McGraw Hill, 1992 p45, 268 et seq. Hugh Davidson, Penguin, 1997, p254, 402 et seq.

x Fuji vs Kodak my book *'Mastering Marketing'* 2nd edition Chapter 5, p211.

xi Rome fighting Carthage over who was to control the trade in the Mediterranean Sea.

EIGHT

THE ART OF PRICE NEGOTIATION

THE ART OF PRICE NEGOTIATION

Price negotiation Truism:

"Buyers can be real miseries when they try hard to get a lower price from you... Their mothers should have kissed them more." **'A Provocative Thought' by John Winkler**

Synopsis

This chapter should be read in conjunction with Chapter 6 Pricing Tactics. It summarizes the essentials of the final stage of pricing, i.e. the act of negotiation.

Bargaining is not negotiation, but negotiation has bargaining at its core.

At the heart of negotiation is the following process:

- **Prepare,**
- **Discuss,**
- **Propose,**
- **Bargain** and
- **Agree.**

This is the sequence in which we will take this overview of the process of negotiating price.

Co-operative versus adverserial negotiation

Some people see negotiation as 'A process for removing conflict between parties...' This definition clearly assumes that conflict, or the threat of it is a pre-condition to negotiation.

Historical experience of class wars, have reinforced the notion that negotiation/bargaining must be a series of 'zero-sum' games; where some win and some lose. This is not necessarily the case. Co-operative negotiation/ bargaining allows both parties to reach mutually advantageous, win-win outcomes.

Essential conditions for co-operation in negotiations are:

- Genuine trust between the two parties and/or that
- Both are aware that co-operation is more 'profitable' than confrontation and conflict.

The conditions for successful co-operative bargaining are:

- Trust
- Acceptance of implicit 'rules',
- A clear, communicable strategy,
- 'Nice' does not mean 'soft',
- Willingness to reach mutually acceptable solutions,
- Willingness to make concessions,
- Participants with the authority and ability to make and 'trade' concessions,
- A win-win stance.

"The objective of negotiation is not a dead opponent."

Napoleon.

Price negotiation

In its commercial sense, negotiation is a means of reaching agreements acceptable to all parties. Thus sales negotiation at its most co-operative promotes the exchange of concessions to provide the optimum profit to buyer and seller, i.e. a win/win outcome.

It differs from other methods of reaching an agreement such as:

- Persuasion (i.e. selling)

- Accommodation
- Compromise
- Confrontation
- Conflict

As we shall see below:

- **Persuasion/selling** implies that one party knows best and will subtly impose their will on the other. It may succeed at the time but runs the risk of creating tension or distrust in future relationships.
- **Accommodation** is a one-winner strategy, one party simply gives in, yet the winners derive dubious satisfaction from this: they are often left with the feeling that they could have obtained even more.
- **Compromise** is a no winner strategy. It may result in each side giving up something it does not want to and it often involves splitting the difference. In sales negotiations this usually favours the buyer, who can pitch their starting offer anywhere.
- **Confrontation** describes a situation where both sides initially refuse to budge. This results in either surrender or no deal.
- **Conflict** describes a situation where one or both sides believe (and act on this belief) that they can acquire what they want by threat of force, e.g. a strike, a war, a verbal or physical assault etc. to cow the other party into submission.

The golden rules of buying

- *First find out the market conditions (re. supply and demand)*
- *Find out what's on offer elsewhere (and in the immediate vicinity)*
- *Find out how much discretion the sales person has and get it from them (if not enough – go for their boss)*
- *Go for an overall price without specifying detail – Salami-slice the extras until the seller 'squeaks'*

after John Winkler

Prepare (to negotiate)

OBJECTIVES FOR THE PRICE NEGOTIATION

When negotiating you should set minimum and maximum volume and profit objectives. The minimum objectives will approximate to the fallback position. The maximum objectives may be expressed in the initial stance taken by either side.

During the negotiation process, each party should keep a running score of the value of each concession given and received. This process of keeping the whole package in mind is essential to controlling the later stages of the negotiations process called 'bargaining', which determines the final result.

IDENTIFY THE VARIABLES (POTENTIAL TRADING CHIPS/CONCESSIONS)

Available to us	Available to them

FIGURE 8.1: A NOTES FORMAT FOR ANALYSIS OF POSSIBLE/PROBABLE TRADING CHIPS

As a negotiator you will try to work out what trading chips your side can reasonably use (*i.e. they may be able to give a discount but they can't usually give it away*). Similarly you should try to derive which trading chips the other side can reasonably be expected to have within their power to trade.

Once these chips have been identified it is important to classify both sets of 'chips' along the following lines:

Classifying the chips

The first stage of this process is to place them on a two by two matrix consisting on one axis of 'the value of the chip to the other side' versus, on the other axis, 'the costs of the chip to us'. Like so:

VALUE TO THE OTHER SIDE

COST TO US	LO	HI
LO	STARTERS	GOLD DUST
HI	PHONY CONCESSIONS	DEFER

FIGURE 8.2: CLASSIFYING THE POTENTIAL TRADING CHIPS.

As can be seen from Figure 8.2 the chips that fall into the top right quadrant should be traded with a great deal of care – only if we get something of high value to us in return.

Other things that we trade with care are those that cost us a great deal, we must ensure that we get full value in return, these are the very last things we trade and then with caution.

The second stage is to analyze those chips that we believe are available for the other side to trade with us. At this point, and not before, we can start to create a dealing strategy.

We will decide what concessions we want from the other side and what we will be prepared to trade in return:

- Hopefully
- Reluctantly
- Only under duress

Then we try to work out in what order these chips will be used. This can't be a rigid schedule, but it does help us to prioritize what we must do and to identify which chips we keep up our sleeve.

Issues when preparing to negotiate

What is the strategy?

Initially the price negotiators must decide on a strategy, which will be based on the following considerations:

- How much he/she needs the business.
- How much their customer needs them (*i.e. where are they on the buyer's matrix? See Chapter 6*).
- Their strengths and weaknesses in relation to the competition or any alternatives facing the client.
- Where are they on the supply and demand cycle?

What are the tactics to use?

In choosing suitable tactics, they must take into account:

- The customer's wants and priorities.
- Which perceptions will need to be changed.
- The advantages their product or service has over any alternative solutions.
- The time and place of the negotiation.
- The behavioural style of the negotiators.
- The history of the relationship.
- **The cost of each concession**, which might be at issue and its perceived value to the receiver.

Analysis of potential trading chips/concessions

FROM SUPPLIER e.g:	COST OR VALUE TO SUPPLIER e.g:
Discount	Actual
Retrospective discount	Actual less 6%
Credit	1.5% per month
Free products	List less 10%
Extra deliveries	60c. per mile
Operator training	$200 per day
Promotional allowance	Actual less 25%
Extra level of service	Actual less 25%
Help with design, installation	Labour cost + 50%
Holding stock against future orders	2% per month
FROM CUSTOMER e.g:	
Payment in advance	1.5% per month
Extra volume	Allow percentage of value off existing volumes and lines
Orders for other lines	
Collection/reduced number of deliveries	60c. per mile
Help with installation	Actual labour cost, plus 10%
Promise of future business	Nil, unless it is an actual order percentage of value off current order

FIGURE 8.3: POTENTIAL TRADING CHIPS

What will be your/their initial stances and fallback positions

Experienced negotiators do not start by making their best offer. They test the other side by various tactics. During these overtures, each side may take its initial stance.

During the bargaining which follows, each side moves towards its fallback position. The relative skills of the negotiators will often determine the resting place. When the skills are equal, it will be at the point of need balance.

Checklist for assessing buyers likely needs, strategies and tactics

THE CUSTOMER'S COMPANY

- How well or badly is the company doing?
- What are their main problems and opportunities which could affect their negotiating policy?
- What are their competitive strengths and weaknesses?
- Who are their main competitors?
- Are they growing, declining or stable?
- In what ways are they changing?

THEIR BUYING/NEGOTIATING TEAM

- What are their functional problems and opportunities?
- What are their personal motivations?
- What are their levels of negotiating skill?
- What are their likely behaviour styles?
- What do we know about their tactics and techniques?
- On what criteria are their successes judged?

THE COMPETITIVE SITUATION

- Who are our competitors?
- What are their strengths and weaknesses?
- How do they compare with us?
- How do our customers perceive them?
- How do they perceive us?
- How much do we need the business?

- Which concession will they value that will cost us little?
- What will they want which will cost us dearly?

Discuss

Co-operation and buyer roles

According to game theory there are four possible outcomes to any two party conflict, win/win; win/lose; lose/win; and lose/lose; the real negotiating tragedies occur when the parties are playing lose-lose tactics in a position where there is the potential for mutually beneficial results. It is far more profitable for both parties to focus on **collaboration** rather than **competition.**

Second only to this terrible waste of resources is the situation where sub-optimal performance occurs when one party cannot resist its primal urge to harm the other (*as often happens in divorce*).

Lack of trust, caused by a perception that the other side is withholding information, is a major determinant of negotiation style.

The basic negotiating stances can be characterized as either a hard-line position (*competitive*) or a more soft-line position (*co-operative*). During the negotiation we must know our natural position and that of the other party, so as to consciously adjust our behaviour as appropriate.

Effective negotiators make a conscious style choice and do not just behave reactively. Generally, the choice of either a competitive or a co-operative style depends on the level of concern we have with the goals of the other party.

The five negotiating styles are shown in Figure 8.4 below.

Negotiation roles

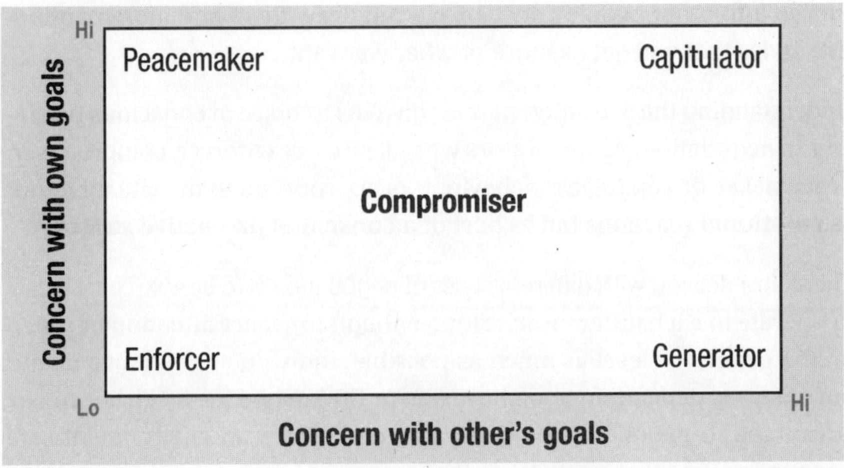

FIGURE 8.4: THE FIVE POSSIBLE NEGOTIATION STYLES

- **Enforcers:** self centred, use force, threats, demands and intimidation to get what they need from others; win/lose orientated; often they will withdraw if they cannot win.
- **Compromisers**: (or scorekeepers) are suspicious of the other party's motives and measure each concession, demanding reciprocal movement, issue by issue; afraid of not getting their fair share.
- **Peacemakers:** fear trouble and/or confrontation and neither clarify their own concerns nor probe the concerns of the other party. Nothing is ever finalized and withdrawal may result, without notice or explanation.
- **Capitulators:** are so anxious to please they lose sight of their original objectives and fail to appreciate their own strengths; they often become 'the customer's friend' and rarely thrive as negotiators in the longer term.
- **Generators** are less defensive and more trusting and therefore invite others to be less defensive and more trusting too. Thus both parties find it easier to be pro-active and effective. Generators assume there are more than enough advantages in a good business relationship to satisfy everybody so they negotiate to find solutions to the needs of all parties. What the other party needs is as much our problem as it is their's, IF we want their co-operation.

To be effective is to negotiate as much as possible in the generator style. People often match the behaviours used by the other party. We can get sucked into other people's style **or** we can draw them into more **productive** styles that will get us more of what we want.

Understanding the five different roles gives us a choice of **conscious** behaviour in negotiation. As generators we will practice enforcer, compromiser, peacemaker or capitulator behaviour as appropriate to the situation, not as **emotional** reactions but as part of a **conscious pro-active** strategy.

The skill of dealing with different styles of negotiation is to be able consciously to operate in each different style long enough to secure attention but keep on the generator level as much as possible. Individuals will move in and out of styles, depending upon how safe or threatened they feel. It is to our advantage to negotiate as a generator and create an environment safe enough for the other party to do the same.

Decision-makers who make good partners

There are six types of decision-maker who have high partnering potential. Below are summaries of their principal characteristics and frequent negotiating modes:

- **The bureaucrat:** it is generally not difficult to partner a bureaucrat, they have rational and systemized policies, procedures and rules governing them, and the selling climate is impersonal. Things get done systematically but not speedily. Selling to a bureaucracy depends on understanding its traditional nature and cultivating its key decision-makers. It is almost always a long-term process.
- **The zealot:** these are loners and are usually competent. Zealots have an apostolic fervour for pet projects, which they always present as being precisely what the organization needs most, they welcome anyone who can help them attain their objectives. Other people's ideas are often ignored. Zealots negotiate by bludgeoning, they divide the world into 'friends' and 'enemies', you must be wary of becoming unduly identified with zealots and their causes.
- **The executive:** these are professional managers, battle-wise, firm-minded and strong-willed. Negotiating with them is a straightforward

matter of providing them with demonstrable benefits, if they cannot be perceived, negotiations will most likely end promptly.

- **The integrator:** is a team-building manager. They are easy to negotiate with; they see their role as managing the decision-making process by consensus and collaboration. The integrator is a catalyst and co-operator by nature. Since most of their decisions are group decisions, you must also partner with their key group members.
- **The gamesman:** are analytic, flexible, fast moving, competitive, sharp, and aggressive. They love playing the game of business. Their preoccupation is with forming and re-forming winning teams, you also must become a team member when negotiating with them. Like the executive, the gamesman relates without being emotionally involved. Since gamesmen respect peers who are shrewd and adroit, they will challenge every negotiation skill that you possess. Yet, gamesmen negotiate within the rules and will be co-operative as long as they believe they can achieve a win/win outcome.
- **The paternalistic autocrat:** they see their role as all-knowing. They can be somewhat patronizing authority figures who demand personal loyalty from subordinates. Friction and conflict are smoothed over. If not antagonized, and if offered personal loyalty, they can be kind and considerate. If 'adopted' by an autocrat, a win-win relationship will often develop.

Decision-makers who make difficult partners

There are six types of decision-makers who have low partnering potential. Below we summarize their principal characteristics and most probable negotiating modes:

Manager type	Characteristics	Negotiation modes
Machiavellian	Self-orientated, shrewd, devious and calculating, insightful into weaknesses of others, opportunistic, suave and Charismatic, can turn in an instant from collaboration to aggression.	An exploiter of people; cooperates only for selfish interests; totally impersonal negotiator, unmoved by human appeals; will win as inexpensively as possible, but will win at all costs.
Missionary	Smoother of conflict, blender of ideas, must be liked, identifies harmony with acceptance, highly subjective and personal.	A seeker of compromise and leveller of ideas to lowest common denominator; negotiates emotionally with personal appeals to agree for his sake.
Exploiter	Arrogant, what's-in-it-for-me attitude, coercive, domineering, rigid, prejudiced, takes advantage of weakness, makes snap judgements unswayed by evidence.	Exerts constrictive personal control over negotiation; makes others vulnerable by using pressure and fear to get own way; demands subservience; sees others as obstacles to be overcome.
Climber	Striving, driving, smooth and polished demeanour that masks aggression, opportunistic, without loyalty to others, goes with the flow.	Excellent politician; uses self-propelling change to call attention to himself; always thinking ahead; self-serving negotiator based on what-will-he-do-for-me?
Conserver	Defends status quo, resists change, favours evolutionary improvement, uses the system skilfully to safeguard personal position and prerogatives.	Imposes own sense of order and non-immediacy on negotiation; slows everything down; preaches traditional values; defensively blocks innovation and undermines agreements before implementation.

Manager type	Characteristics	Negotiation modes
Glad-hander	Superficially friendly to new ideas but essentially a non-doer, effusive, socially skilled and politically skilful, superior survival instincts.	Over-reactive and over stimulated by everything, but impressed by little; promises support but then fades away; endorses only sure things that can do some personal good; never takes risks.

The language of negotiation

The vocabulary of negotiation should be chosen to promote an atmosphere of co-operation. The following words and phrases will help achieve this:

'Perhaps...'

'Could we look at...?'

'What if we...?'

'I wonder if we could consider...?'

'It might be an idea to...'

'May I suggest...?'

'I can see why that's important to you.'

'Let's look at some alternatives.'

'What else is important to you?'

'I'd like your opinion on...'

'I appreciate your point of view.'

Conversely, there are words and phrases which should be avoided whenever possible.

IRRITATORS:

'This is a fair offer.'

'We can afford to be generous.'

Fair and *generous* are value judgments. They also imply that the other party is unfair or ungenerous.

ARGUMENTATIVE WORDS:

'But'

'However'

'I'm afraid'

But can always be avoided by using short sentences, which obviate the need for that dangerous conjunction:

*'I see your point, **but**...'*

Becomes:

*'I see your point. **However**, the effect it would have on us is...'*

WORDS OF REJECTION:

'Can't'

'No way'

'Impossible'

These can be replaced by phrases such as:

'The problems that would create for us are...'

'That's clearly very important to you. The difficulty from our point of view is...'

THE BARGAINING AREA:

In the early stages of every negotiation a prime aim for the savvy negotiator is to decide whether there is room for negotiation between the goals that each side brings to the table.

We can visualize any side's position as follows:

- What that side sees as the best outcome they could wish for; and
- What is the worst outcome they can still deal with... but lower than which they would not dream of going; and
- If they are coerced below this 'worst' situation – at what point would they walk away or fight if cornered!

This can be expressed graphically as follows:

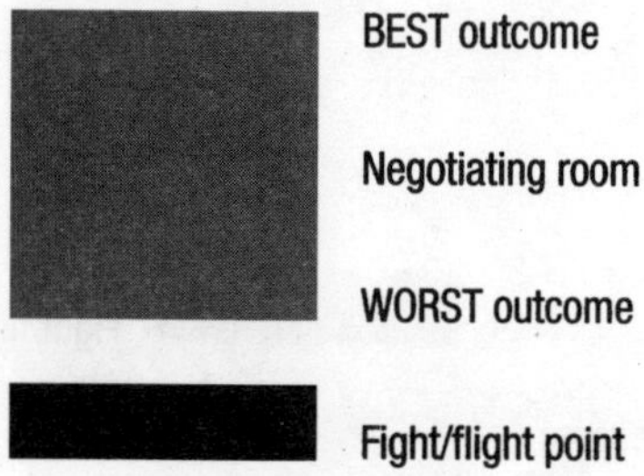

The savvy negotiator sets out to determine whether there is good roon for manoeuvre available to each side.

A best case scenario can be expressed thus:

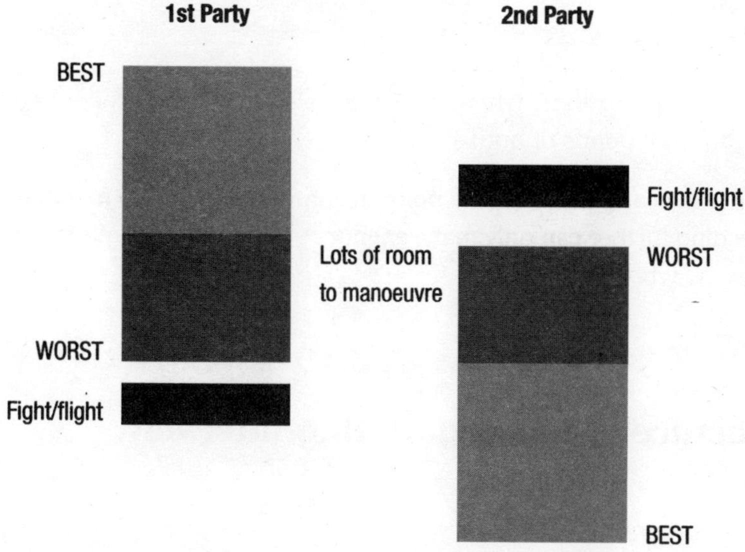

A tough case scenario could look something like this:

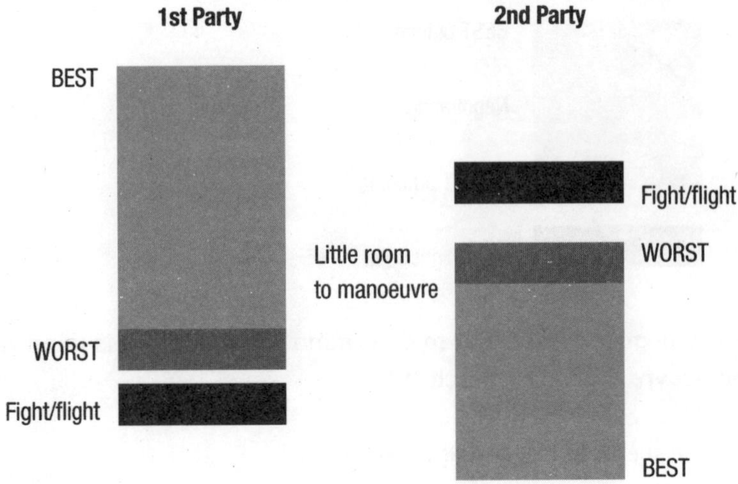

But the worst situation is where there is no overlap except perhaps between the fight/flight points of both sides!

IF this is the case, there is little point in continuing with the negotiation – proceeding further can only make enemies – and in the commercial world at least . . . who needs them!

Structure of the negotiating interview

The 7 stage structure

A cohesive structure should favour both sides. It certainly favours the price negotiator. Chaos, on the other hand, may favour the buyer. The following is a 7-stage structure, developed through long experience by expert negotiators to ensure achieving the maximum progress in the least possible time.

1. OVERVIEW
2. BACKGROUND MUSIC
3. DEFINING THE ISSUES

4. SELECTING ISSUES FOR DISCUSSION
5. REFINING THE ISSUES
6. FALLBACK
7. SETTLEMENT

The early stages

Before the negotiators present their overview, there will be the inevitable 'social' period. The buyers may take control during this phase, either by giving their overview or raising issues which might affect the negotiation. The price negotiators should remain neutral, limiting contributions to the acknowledgements of what the client says:

'I agree that costs are important. That's one of the points on our agenda.'
'Clearly, if mistakes of this kind are happening, we need to identify ways of avoiding them.'

Then, at an appropriate time, they can use the issues which have been mentioned to introduce their overview:

'In fact, that brings us to the purpose of today's meeting, which as we see it is...'

Overview

Aims:

- To agree the purpose of the meeting.
- To agree that the parties have mutual aims.
- To establish the decision-making process.

Scenario of overview (price negotiator to the 'buyer')

"Miss X, as we see it, the purpose of our meeting is to agree your needs over the next twelve months, and make sure that we provide you with the best possible service at the right terms. We'd also like to feel that the relationship will continue to develop to our mutual benefit. To achieve these aims, I'm sure there are several issues to be resolved. If we can do that, do I take it that we can reach a decision today?"

If the response is affirmative, proceed to the next stage. If not, ask why. This may reveal that the customer needs to refer the offer to another party or compare it with an alternative possibility. The price negotiator may have to reconsider their strategy, possibly delaying the negotiation or proceeding but holding something back for a subsequent meeting.

When the customer responds to the price negotiator's overview they must be careful not to be lured into a premature discussion of any specific issue. This will destroy their carefully planned structure and thwart the objectives of each stage. As in the opening, social phase, remain calm and neutral, acknowledging and reflecting, but never over-reacting.

Background music

Aims:

- To create the best climate for a co-operative negotiation.
- To establish (and for the other side to eventually acknowledge) our **advantages and benefits.**
- To assess the other party's **strengths, weaknesses, needs and likely strategy** and tactics.

Some of these aims might have been partially achieved during the social phase. However, the reason for putting this section after the overview is that this session can lead to an in-depth discussion of several matters and if this occurred earlier it could well deter the customer from agreeing that the occasion is a decision-making meeting.

The reason for establishing advantages and benefits early on is that if we use them later to rebut a client's demand for a particular concession, we may create confrontation.

Negotiation should never be a contest, and if we can get the customers to agree our benefits from the outset, they may never make extravagant demands only to suffer loss of face when they are rejected.

Prepared questions

To assess the other party's position at this stage, ask open questions, such as the following:

- *'Before we draw up our agenda, has anything changed since we last spoke?'*
- *'Tell me, Mr. X, before we discuss the reasons for dealing with our company, what do you feel are the main benefits?'*
- *'You've had our proposal for several days, could you tell me how your colleagues reacted to it?'*
- *'We feel that our proposal meets all the needs we identified when we last met. Are there any other requirements or concerns which have occurred to you since then?'*

Scenario of introducing benefits

- *'I'd like to draw up a list of topics you'd like to discuss today. But before we do this, I think it makes sense to establish the benefits of dealing with us because they may affect the other issues. As we see it...'*

Handling requests and complaints

During this phase, as in the earlier stages, the customer may raise demands, requests, concerns or complaints. In that event ask questions to ensure understanding but don't encourage detailed discussion. Even a complaint can be turned into a negotiating issue.

So cultivate phrases such as:

- *'Thanks for bringing up this point. It's something we should put on our agenda.'*
- *'That's an important subject. When we discuss terms and conditions, we have some ideas which we feel will answer your needs in this area.'*

Moving to the next stage

In the same way as we moved from the early discussion phase into our Overview, we can proceed to the stage of defining issues:

- *'Let's put this on our agenda. I think this is a good time to make a list of the other points you'd like to discuss…'*

Price negotiation truism

Q: 'How much is that:

- Basket?
- Spice?
- Gold bracelet?
- Carpet? etc'

A: 'How much were you expecting to pay?'

Lesson: Never be the first to open the bidding!

Defining the issues

Aims:

- To get the client's complete shopping list.
- To avoid reacting while doing so.
- To avoid revealing our own agenda.

As previously mentioned, we need to evaluate whether there is room to negotiate and, if so, how much overlap there could be, and if not how can we 'walk away' – now or later?

Negotiation truism:

'The person / party that can afford to walk away from the deal has the ultimate negotiating leverage!'

Reacting to the buyer's agenda

We should acknowledge every request the customer makes, by re-stating rather than repeating it. A request for 5% reduction in fees should be re-stated:

'So we need to discuss fees for the period. What other subjects will we be discussing?'

By simply repeating the request, we might seem to be agreeing with it. Asking for other issues immediately after acknowledging the request, helps to prevent discussion until we have the whole shopping list.

Summarizing

When the customer states that there are not other issues, we should summarize and then ask

'Then can we take it that when we've reached agreement on these issues, we can reach an agreement today?'

If the answer is no, we should ask:

'Then what else should we put on the agenda?'

Avoiding giving our own shopping list

There are two reasons for not revealing our own issues at this stage. First, the need to stay flexible, matching the concessions received with those given. Secondly, showing a 'hand' too early might provoke the client to increase their initial demands.

Selecting issues for discussion

Aims:

- To reach early agreements on specific issues.
- To create a spirit of co-operation.

The order in which various issues are discussed can be vital to the success of a negotiation. The other party's aim might be the converse. Often they may wish to get the most controversial issue/s out of the way. The sales negotiator should counter this by introducing 'bridging issues' which can readily be agreed by both parties. Their introduction requires impeccable timing, immediately after the clients agree that they have given us their whole shopping list and that it is a decision-making meeting:

Seller: *'Do I take it that if we can agree these items, we can settle the contract today?'*

Buyer: *'Yes, if we agree those issues to my satisfaction.'*

Seller: *'Fine. I suggest we should begin with...'*

If the client insists on beginning with a difficult issue, the other party must 'stick to their guns'. The best argument is that the contentious issue cannot be resolved until the client's other issues are clearer.

Refining the issues

Aim:

- To promote mutually profitable trade-offs.

Principles

The best concessions are those which cost the giver less than their value to the receiver. This is why accommodation is not a sound method for reaching any price agreement. Weak negotiators give in too easily and miss the chance of exploring alternatives, which have a more attractive cost/benefit ratio. Refining the issues is often known as the pre-bargaining stage, in which each side tests the other.

Techniques:

- Trial balloons
- Deferring the issue
- Summarizing
- Bleeding
- Offering alternatives
- Appealing for help
- Recording, calculating, note-taking

Fallback

Aims:

- To protect net profit objectives.
- To obtain compensations by last minute trade-offs.

This is a stage which may be simply a part of refining issues. However, if the refinement process has included some tough bargaining, either side might find itself uncomfortably close to its fallback position. If there are still issues to be decided, the threatened party will take stock and effect a tactical change to make sure of achieving a good deal.

Techniques:

- Trial balloons
- Summarizing
- Bleeding
- Appealing for help
- Standing firm
- Re-examine previous agreements
- Delaying tactics
- Adjourning

Settlement

Aims:

- To confirm all decisions
- To prevent misunderstandings
- To counter any last minute requests from the other party
- To leave the customer feeling he has achieved a good deal
- To agree any future actions

This is the stage of confirming all agreements and decisions, checking each side's understanding of each agreement and establishing that final agreement has indeed been reached.

Propose

Co-operative negotiating techniques

THE TRIAL BALLOON

This is a device for producing trade offs. The principle is to put the proposal in the form of a suggestion or discussion point. The proposer does not necessarily expect the other side to agree, merely to begin a discussion on the idea of discussing two issues in conjunction. In other words:

- *'What if we...?'* from the seller leads to
- 'How can we...?' from the buyer

The 4-stage trial balloon

It is possible to change the order, but this sequence is usually effective:

- Agree in principle the other side's request
- Introduce the concept of a trade-off
- Make a specific offer, often less than was originally requested

This:

- puts the client at ease by showing that the other party is prepared to consider the request
- breaks the news gently, because it is non-specific
- is the first danger point. The client is being asked to give something. But they suspend disbelief until they hear stage 4
- may produce any number of reactions; for example:
  - complete acceptance,
  - haggling, or refining the trade-off,
  - complete refusal.

In the second case, we can refine the proposal and retreat step by step to a prepared position. In the third case, we can launch an alternative trial balloon, perhaps based on an entirely different return concession.

SCENARIO OF A 4-STAGE BALLOON

- 'I can appreciate that the question of quick response is important to you. I wonder if we can look at this point in conjunction with...'
- 'If you could help us by agreeing to give us...we would be prepared to grant you...' (See 'signalling' below.)

The 3-stage balloon

- Agree in principle,
- Introduce the concept of a trade off,
- Ask the client to suggest a concession in return.

This has the effect of getting the other side to take the first step and leaves the option of suggesting further steps.

SCENARIO OF A 3-STAGE BALLOON

- *'I realize that payment terms are a key factor and we would like to explore ways of helping.'*
- *'Could we look at linking extra credit to finding ways of reducing our delivery costs?'*
- *'What suggestions could you make to help us in that area?'*

Signalling that there is a trade-off to be made at this point:

- *"If you could guarantee more work...then we could possibly reduce our price."*

Deferring the issue

When a trial balloon or balloons have failed to lead to a trade off, there is a risk of confrontation. The aim should always be to delay potential arguments until the 'Fallback' stage.

SCENARIO OF DEFERRING THE ISSUE

- *'I can see that this is a problem for you and we'd like to help. Could I make a suggestion? Suppose we left this until later in the meeting. Then when we've agreed some of the other items, we might find a way of getting around this one. Could we move on to...?'*

If this succeeds it may provide two psychological advantages. The other party, anxious to get agreement to the request, might be more co-operative about the next few issues. Secondly, when the contentious issues are revived, expectations might have been reduced by the delay.

Summarizing

When an issue has been agreed, either side might choose to summarize what has been achieved so far. The sales negotiator should endeavour to be the summarizer because it will give several advantages:

- Summaries can be used to remind the other party that they have achieved a good deal so far.
- They can motivate the other parties by reminding them of the excellent progress that has been made.
- A summary can be used to terminate fruitless discussion or cool down tempers.
- The summarizer is in control and can use this fact to introduce the next issue.
- A summary is an effective technique for achieving agenda control.

Bargaining

Following on from the above (in a live negotiation this should be seamless).

Bleeding

It is bad business (*AND poor psychology*) to agree to give a concession which costs more than the other party think. If we are wounded, we should let them know it. 'Bleeding' should begin with a phrase such as:

'I realize that this is important to you. Could I tell you what granting that request would mean to my company?'

Bleeding may be used to preface stage two on the trial balloon. This will strengthen our hand when we ask for a concession in return.

Offering alternatives

Some customers like to feel that they are in charge.

When making the proposals, perhaps at stage four of the trial balloon, we should have at least two alternatives to choose from.

Appealing for help

When all else fails, an appeal for help often appeals to the other person's sense of justice!

> *'Jim, this creates a problem for us. I can only justify such a concession to my Board if it's linked with an increase in the business you place with us. Have you any suggestions which might help me?'*

Even if it does not succeed, we can always revert to a concrete proposal in the form of a trial balloon. But it is worth trying; sometimes the customer will make a suggestion which exceeds our expectations.

Recording, calculating, note-taking

Good negotiators have to be good secretaries and will realize the importance of taking accurate notes and calculating the cost of every concession given. They should also realize that these operations have other values. They give thinking time. They help absorb an attack. Above all, they create a professional atmosphere.

Defensive negotiating techniques

STANDING FIRM

Sometimes we have to refuse a request, possibly because to grant it would be against company policy, OR perhaps because we have already conceded enough.

There are several ways of denying a request, for example:

POLICY, PRECEDENT, ETHICS

'Mr X, to grant that request could be contrary to my company's policy. I realize that policies can sometimes be altered, but I have never known us to deviate on this issue. And even if we were to find a way around the problem, it would mean that we'd be letting down all our clients to whom we have refused similar requests in the past. Can you see the difficult position this puts me in?'

THREE STAGE REFUSAL

This is a valuable three part technique as follows:

Stage 1: Show empathy

Stage 2: Put forward your viewpoint

Stage 3: Pose a question, inviting sympathy with that viewpoint.

For example:

'I appreciate that this is something you feel strongly about. The situation with my company is... Can you see the problem that this would create for me?'

Re-examining previous agreement

There are two issues here to examine:

- It is sometimes overlooked by price negotiators that no agreement on an individual issue is legally or morally binding until settlement is achieved. Have they kept to the terms, for example, did they pay their bills on time for the last deal?
- Re-examine earlier agreements. It should be made clear that giving way on a contentious issue can only be by reducing concessions previously granted.

[The Author once did a deal with a major French firm, which stipulated that in return for a guaranteed 100 days work in that year and payment within 30 days (they said they normally paid in 60, but in practice this often became 90 days) the Author's daily rate that year, would be reduced to half the normal. The first, and most subsequent payments took more that 60 days to arrive = NO Deal – and the client could not understand why the Author eventually walked away from doing any more business with them.]

Delaying tactics

Delaying tactics may be used to provide thinking time. We might telephone a colleague, or ask for an adjournment for any number of reasons.

The buyer's strategies and tactics

Strategy has been defined as 'the art of moving or disposing forces so as to impose upon the enemy the time, place and conditions of conflict.' Many professional buyers would applaud this definition.

It is the job of professional pricers/salespeople to forge a partnership with our customers, so that the final negotiations are a natural extension of the process of focusing on mutual needs. But it is remarkable how difficult customers can be when selling is over and the negotiation / bargaining begins.

Not all buyers or their managers are accomplished strategists but most have some measure of tactical skill. Tactics are present oriented and are used in order to meet strategic objectives (see Chapter 6).

To become truly professional price negotiators we should know and understand the full range of buying techniques which may be used at each stage of the negotiation. Then we must master a variety of skills to counter them.

Stratagems used by those negotiating

Stratagems used by negotiators		
Overall	**The buyer seeks to:** Maintain competition for his/her business for as long as possible	**The seller seeks to:** Use the uniqueness of his/her proposition and its appositeness to support his/her price
When to raise issue of price	As soon as he/she can – in writing prior if possible	As late as possible only when buyer aroused by 'product benefits'
Extras	Get as many included in price as possible	Unbundle and price each extra separately
Other requirements	Leave open until after signing. Get included at no cost	Leave some part of the agreement open-ended so as to add extras to an increased price

"The way the first deal is set up conditions the mood and behaviour of subsequent deals."

In addition to the above there is the issue of whether to bunch or break:

Bunch versus Break – 1

BUNCH = Package all# you/they want from the other side – or put up-front when presenting the deal.

BREAK-UP = Dissemble into individual chips

Secure agreement on each trade before moving on

Recap what has been agreed at each stage

"If you will … then we will etc."

The best deals provide profit for both sides

= *You don't have to use it all – it helps to keep some back so as to be able to tip the scales if and when needed.*

= *You can only bunch if the buyer understands each of the components – if generally ignorant then break.*

Hopefully, most of our customers will be tough but fair, demanding but open to reason, occasionally devious, but basically honest. Others may be tough, unfair, demanding, unreasonable, devious and dishonest.

The following summary of stratagems and counters should equip us to deal effectively with both types.

Bunch versus Break – 2

The principle is that if the other side bunches then you break!

The reason for this is quite simply you may not know why the other side decided to bunch but you can be fairly certain that they believe it is in their interest so to do. So, as a matter of principle you do the opposite and see how hard they fight. The extent of their aggression in defence of their position indicates fairly reliably, the magnitude of the value they saw in that stance for their own interest.

So, you cost each item separately which means that the total of these costs WILL be higher than the original price offered. In which case the buyer will be forced to either:

- Pay more,
- Take less, or
- Arrive at some compromise between these two.

Conversely if the other side breaks then you bunch!

It is quite a common buyer strategy to get a commitment from you on price then to go for concessions one 'chip' at a time.

(*This strategy is sometimes encapsulated with the following rubric, 'First of all you get the price – after that you salami-slice.'*)

It is therefore important for the sales person not to agree price until they know everything the other side wants. Then, menu style, they can price the whole deal.

Whichever is the case, bunch or break, it must never be forgotten that:

'The best deals provide profit for both sides!'

Stratagems

<table>
<tr><th>BUYING STRATAGEM</th><th>POSSIBLE COUNTERS</th></tr>
<tr><td>Optimize rank of participants
This grandiosely described principle was featured in an American book, Negotiating DP Contracts. Buyers were advised to get the vendor's top ranking people to the negotiating table. The possible advantages were:<ul><li>They had authority to concede more</li><li>They often conceded more to avoid losing the order – and losing face – in front of their juniors</li><li>Often, their negotiating skills had atrophied through lack of practice</li><li>The seller might not achieve a high degree of teamwork</li><li>The buyers had ways of disrupting what teamwork there was</li></ul></td><td>Authority should be delegated – completely:<ul><li>The manager should position himself to the buyers as the salesperson's subordinate</li><li>Managers must plan and rehearse for major negotiations</li><li>Roles should be assigned for each stage of the negotiation and signals should be agreed</li></ul></td></tr>
<tr><td>Creating an uncomfortable climate
Apart from normal, tough negotiating tactics, some buyers use planned interruptions and other discourtesies to put off the sales team.</td><td>As a general rule, sales negotiators should not put up with rudeness and should politely request different lighting, seating, privacy or anything they would reasonably require to negotiate comfortably and effectively.</td></tr>
<tr><td>The hit list
A stratagem which is used by some retail buyers, and is now being adopted by other buyers, is to say that due to a rationalization programme they are reducing their product lines and the vendor's product is under threat.</td><td>The seller's initial response must be to welcome the concept with enthusiasm. This is not a problem, but an opportunity. If the seller manages his tension, the rest of the negotiation will proceed as if no threat were made.</td></tr>
</table>

BUYING STRATAGEM	POSSIBLE COUNTERS
The list of grievances The buying team begins by summarizing the vendor's recent mistakes and shortcomings. This is intended to weaken their morale and bargaining position. Clearly, the sales team should know their weaknesses, but some buyers have been known to 'save up' complaints for the negotiation.	The sellers should listen, reflect and make notes. They should express regrets. After that they should give their prepared overview which in practice will change very little. It is also important to remember that most complaints are opportunities to add a negotiating variable. Late deliveries could be avoided by forward ordering or increased stock levels. Servicing could be improved by staff training. Prices could be reduced in return for long-term commitments.
If it wasn't for them Buyers may begin the negotiation by disclosing that although they are willing to negotiate co-operatively, higher authority has insisted that they obtain swinging reductions in cost or dramatic increases in services. When the vendor suggests a meeting with those in authority, he is told that it is impossible. This can be a very effective stratagem, forcing the seller to deal with an amiable here, controlled by an unseen villain.	The only initial response is to call the bluff – if it is one. The seller should use the same tactics: he too is controlled by a higher authority, equally adamant. Since he and the buyer are powerless, should he ask his director to contact the buyer's supervisor? The buyers response, particularly his non-verbal communication, will give more that a clue about the real situation. Often, the buyer will back down and offer to negotiate, subject of course to subsequent approval from his colleagues. The interview should now proceed smoothly.

BUYING STRATAGEM	POSSIBLE COUNTERS
Good news and bad news This ploy is extremely effective when the vendor is in a difficult competitive situation and particularly when he has not been the favoured supplier. The buyer welcomes him with the good news that after a battle with his colleagues, all of whom favoured a competitor, he is now in a position to give him the order. Before the salesman recovers from this relief and joy, the buyer now says that the salesman would make 'one or two little concessions' that they have always had from the other supplier. This leads to a score of demands known as 'salesmen tactics'.	The counter is quite simple. The salesperson should respond politely, gratefully but without committing his company to any concession. He should then begin a formal, structured negotiation interview: overview, background, music, agreeing the issues, etc. etc. A perusal of notes on interview structure will show that nothing need be changed. All we have to do is refuse to be thrown by the stratagem.
Take it or leave it The buyer may state his requirements and announce that they are not negotiable. If they are really astute, their demand will coincide exactly with your fallback position.	Your best hope of closing the deal with a reasonable level of profit is to persuade the buyer that it is in their interest to negotiate. It may be that if they give a little they could end up with an even better deal. You will need to have done a great deal of preparation on your analysis of concessions and their relative importance to each side, so that you can show examples of why negotiation could be to his advantage. The advantage of this approach is that it can do no harm: you can always give in to their initial demands as a last resort. But if you are tenacious enough you will not have to do so.

BUYING STRATAGEM	POSSIBLE COUNTERS
Price first When you are trying to get the customer's full shopping list, they might decline to give it unless you first agree to a specific demand – often price, or the waiving of a price increase, sometimes another difficult concession.	You must not discuss the central issue, but say that you cannot decide it until you have at least an indication of the other items on his agenda. If this doesn't work, you must tell them firmly that if they insist on agreeing price at the outset he will inspire you with caution. If he lets you have his full agenda, he might inspire you with generosity.
Good guy/bad guy This is the famous double act in which one buyer makes excessive demands and the other (unsuccessfully) tries to argue on your behalf. This need not affect you at the time: it is no more difficult than dealing with a single, tough bargainer. But wait for the switch. The bad guy passes the ball to the good guy who asks for your help on a particular succession. Because he has become your friend, you often drop your guard and give him more that you would have given his colleague.	You must respond to the offer, not the person, and if you recognize the technique for what it is, this will not be difficult. If necessary, you should defer the issue. An alternative is to suggest a very advantageous trade off.
The honest broker The buyer, posing as a reasonable person who has your interests at heart, uses phrases like: *'Fairer to both sides.'* *'I think you'll agree that this is a very reasonable suggestion.'* *'I want you to make a profit.'* *'All we're asking you to do is…'*	All you have to do is distinguish the factual from the persuasive elements of this communication. Remember that it is not part of their job description to increase your profit. Before you respond with a trial balloon, you might try to 'bleed' convincingly.

BUYING STRATAGEM	POSSIBLE COUNTERS
The deliberate misunderstanding If you make any offer or promise which can be misinterpreted, a really clever buyer will not ask for clarification. They will let you know their interpretation after you have struck a deal. Then, when you explain what you really meant, they will say that they agreed every subsequent concession on a false assumption. This is difficult to counter, because you must accept at least part of the blame for the misunderstanding	This can be avoided if you ask open questions to clarify each demand, and state your precise offers as you are writing them down. You can make doubly sure by reiterating your interpretation during one of your periodic summaries.
Columbo As its title suggests, this is the *'just one more thing'* ploy. At the end of the bargaining the buyer remembers something they want that was somehow not included on his original agenda.	They will be easy to handle if you have executed the two trial closes recommended in these notes. If you have done this it is perfectly natural to say that you did not know about the new requirement when you agreed the other issues. You will now have to re-examine all the concessions you have agreed to compensate for this latest erosion of your profits.
Storm and sunshine Another technique pioneered by US computer buyers, 'storm and sunshine' describes the behaviour of the buyer whose mood changes continually from friendly and co-operative to aggressive and dictatorial. It can have an affect similar to that of the 'good/bad guy' strategy, in that salespeople are so relieved that a buyer's manners have improved that they give away a little more than they intended to.	As with the good/bad guy defence, you must focus on the issues, not the personality. Reflection, summary, note taking and calculating will all help you to control your tension and your own behaviour.

BUYING STRATAGEM	POSSIBLE COUNTERS
Guess who that was on the phone? This is the most dramatic version of the end game technique of saying that the competition has reduced their price drastically.	If you have achieved all your overview and background music objectives, this should not be difficult to manage. Any competitor who reduces his price when he feels he is going to lose the order is suspect. You can afford, within the limits of your style and relationship, to be dismissive. If necessary you can even be quite scornful. Ask the buyer to agree that his company is successful because it offers quality rather than low price. When he agrees ask him how his competitors retaliate.
Would you like time to think? At the end of a satisfactory negotiation the buyer asks if there is any way you can improve your offer. You decline, politely, but confidently. He says he has to go to see a colleague about another matter but will be back in ten minutes. He asks you to think about it, as he needs a little more to keep his boss happy. His expectations are that during your ten minutes of solitude you will come up with something. Many professional buyers claim this technique.	One response could be to tell the buyer on his return that you cannot agree to any further concession. A better response, if it is available, is to seek another trade-off, seeking a concession which is valuable to you but costs the customer very little, and offering something that will please him without costing you a great deal.
I'm only one of the committee members After you have agreed all the issues, the buyer tells you he has to refer the deal for approval by a higher authority.	This could not happen if you have remembered the two trial closes.

Agree

Please refer back to the section on 'Settlement'.

This is the point in the process where it all comes together. Your note-taking will, at this point, prove vital. Although you have been diligently summarizing step by step, at this stage everything should fall into place.

Thus it is vital to agree what you have agreed – to ensure no subsequent breakdown in the expedition of the deal between you.

It is quite common at this stage for the other party to make a final demand in the form of casual comments. DON'T let these go unanswered or unchallenged or they will become part of the other side's position.

It is good practice to try to put this in writing as soon as possible, if this is a really important agreement, then a tactic that can be used is to have the minutes of the meeting written by hand, and photocopied for both parties before the meeting breaks-up.

Team negotiation

Occasionally, an Account Manager, Sales Manager etc. might require assistance from a colleague. In some major negotiations the team could be quite large. In either case the team should examine the roles of negotiation and allocate duties to each member.

As follows.

ROLE	POSSIBLE RESPONSIBILITIES
SPOKESPERSON:	Refining issues Achieving volume and profit objectives
CHAIRPERSON:	Overview Background music Summarizing to resolve conflict 'Appeal Court' during Fallback stage 'Good guy/Bad guy' tactics
SECRETARY:	Recording decisions Summarizing, when invited
OBSERVER:	Calculating costs Observing non-verbal communication and change of mood and tactics
EXPERT:	Giving advice on certain issues Help in 'standing firm' and 'bleeding'

Defining roles can improve the teamwork of two people as well as four or five. Clearly, the larger the team the greater the need for a system for exchanging as well as dividing control and signalling to each other. Similarly for pre-meeting rehearsals. It is also clear that any member of the team may occupy more than one role. A final point to bear in mind is that we should always avoid out-numbering the buying team.

Summary

The 11 golden rules of negotiation

1. Aim high.
2. Get the other person's shopping list before you start negotiating (try very hard never to be the person who opens first).
3. Know the cost and value of all concessions before you start negotiating.
4. Never give anything for nothing in return: never **give** a concession, trade it, reluctantly.
5. Keep searching for variables.
6. Keep the whole package in mind.
7. Create and maintain a climate for mutual co-operation.
8. Aim for a win-win outcome.
9. Leave the other party feeling they have done a great deal.
10. Don't ever forget that the negotiation is NOT OVER until you have agreed what you have agreed – and in writing if possible.
11. Prepare and rehearse your negotiations.

Exercise: 8.1

The characteristics of a successful negotiator

This scale is based on personal characteristics necessary to successful negotiation. It can help you to decide on the potential you already possess and also identify areas where improvement is needed. Enter a number between 1 and 10 in the boxes that best reflects where you fall on the scale. The higher the number the more the characteristic describes you. When you have finished, total the numbers circled in the space provided.

EXERCISE 1 – *SCORE 1-10*

I am sensitive to the needs of others ☐

I will compromise to solve problems when necessary ☐

I am committed to a win/win philosophy ☐

I have a high tolerance for conflict ☐

I am willing to research and analyze issues fully ☐

Patience is one of my strong points ☐

My tolerance for stress is high ☐

I am a good listener ☐

Personal attack and ridicule do not bother me unduly ☐

I can identify bottom-line issues quickly ☐

TOTAL ☐

EXERCISE 2 – *SCORE 1-10*

It doesn't bother me to question a price or seek a more favourable exchange than offered ☐

I have nothing to lose in seeking a better deal if I approach it in a reasonable way ☐

Conflict is a fact of life and I work hard to resolve it ☐

Conflict is positive because it makes me examine my ideas carefully ☐

In resolving conflict, I try to consider the needs of the other person ☐

Conflict often produces better solutions to problems ☐

Conflict stimulates my thinking and sharpens my judgement	☐
Working with conflict has taught me that compromise is not a sign of weakness	☐
Satisfactorily resolved, conflict often strengthens relationships	☐
Conflict is a way to test one's own point of view	☐
TOTAL	☐

Now turn to the Appendix for the diagnostics for Exercise 8.1.

APPENDIX ONE

ANSWERS AND DISCUSSIONS FOR THE EXERCISES

ANSWERS AND DISCUSSIONS FOR THE EXERCISES

Exercise 1.1

Secrets of the right price – commentary

These eleven points usually prove to be fallacies in typical open markets:

1. THE LOW PRICE WINS THE ORDER

Where products are undifferentiated in the eyes of the buyer this may be true: typical marketing strategy seeks to differentiate the product.

Where a market is a luxury/high quality segment a low price could be interpreted as indicating a cheap and nasty product.

2. BUYERS ARE RATIONAL WHEN BUYING

Most buyers are human: they may be under pressures, which militate against rational decisions (e.g. delivery is required to a deadline, a well-known trade name will protect from criticism...)

3. CUSTOMERS KNOW WHAT THE PRICE SHOULD BE

They may know what is too high or too low. Rarely will they be more specific. They may be influenced within a wide range by product features such as presentation, image, immediate availability, etc.

4. QUALITY DETERMINES PRICE

Price is often seen as a measure of quality: the price may be chosen to reflect a quality level. Actual quality need not be a major factor in price (or cost for that matter).

5. MATCH THE COMPETITION PRICE TO SUCCEED

It is always advantageous to know the competition's price but it should be one factor of many in your own choice of price. A price positioned below the competition may be taken as an indication of lower quality.

6. IN A RECESSION THE LOW PRICED PRODUCT SELLS BEST

Price is certainly important when economies are being sought by the buyers but, again, quality can be sold as a better basis for economy – less down time or less waste with a high quality product, i.e. then is the time to adopt value-based pricing!

7. START WITH A LOW PRICE TO WIN THE FIRST ORDER – INCREASE THE PRICE ON REPEATS

This practice can lock the seller into low prices from the start. It is difficult to negotiate higher prices when the relationship has been initiated on a low price basis and the competition may be aware of the situation.

8. PRICE IS A POLICY – COSTS ARE A FACT

Price may well be a policy, based on opinions. Costs are usually an opinion based on a series of policies.

Within the figure presented as 'costs' there will be elements of fact – the price paid for some of the components of the product for example.

9. THERE IS A SET OF RULES, WHICH PROVIDES THE BEST PRICING STRATEGY

And some people believe in Father Christmas. Others say they have seen hundreds of Father Christmases.

10. ONLY LARGE COMPANIES CAN CONTROL PRICES

Large companies may be market leaders and imprint their price in the minds of buyers but this does not prevent others from adopting prices above or below them which can be acceptable to buyers.

Smaller companies may have a customer loyalty, which transcends market leader prices.

11. MANUFACTURERS CONTROL THE PRICE CONSUMER CUSTOMERS PAY

Where they sell directly to consumers this may be true or where they control all the stages of distribution. In many industries the intermediaries have the power.

The above Exercise by Ian Ruskin Brown has been adapted from an original by, and with the consent of © 1992 Roy H. Hill, OBE FCMA FCIS FInstAM(DIP) MCIM FIMC FITD

Exercise 2.2

The effect of 1% improvement all round on the profit and loss:

	A	B Effect of 1% reduction in cost of Materials	C Effect of 1% improvement all round	D Where the improvement came from
Volume Required	4 hrs	4 hrs	4.04hrs	
Price per Hour	$25.00	$25.00	$25.25	
Revenue	$100.00	$100.00	$102.01	$2.01
Labour @ $7.50 Plus Materials @ $7.50	$60.00	$59.70	= $14.85 x 4.04hrs = $59.994	$0.606
Gross Profit = $	$40.00	$40.30	$42.016	
Overhead per day	$30.00	$30.00	$29.70	$0.30
Net Profit on the deal	$10.00	$10.30	$12.316	
% profit ±	–	+3%	+23.16%	

Exercise 2.3

Because we know neither your business or your markets (at least from your experience and perspective) do this exercise from your point of view. Discuss this concept with your colleagues and try to reach a consensus as to where your business, your markets and indeed your products are on their life cycles. When this is reached, consider what effect this will now have on your pricing policy (*don't forget that within the PLC there are harmonics of the law of supply and demand also at work*).

Exercise 2.4

Price Per Unit	Forecast Sales	Sales Revenue	Variable Costs	Fixed Costs	Net Profit
$12	517	6,204	2,068	1,000	3,136
$11	600	6,600	2,400	1,000	3,200
$10	740	7,400	2,960	1,000	3,440
$9	910	8,190	3,640	1,000	3,550
$8	1,120	8,960	4,480	1,000	3,480
$7	1,410	9,870	5,640	1,000	3,230
$6	1,800	10,800	7,200	2,000	1,600
$5	2,500	12,500	10,000	2,000	500

The above table sets out the model answer.

So you can check that your calculations were correct. The optimum price is $9.00 per sqm. This is the price that makes the most contribution.

Leaving the penultimate question for last: The last question asks 'What are the factors that could lead to the price being either higher or lower than $9.00 per sqm'. A competitive market could force the price down, and shortages of raw materials could mean that sales to the market may have to be rationed via price.

But what is happening here is the effects of the so called elasticity of demand. The curve displayed in the two left hand columns looks something like this:

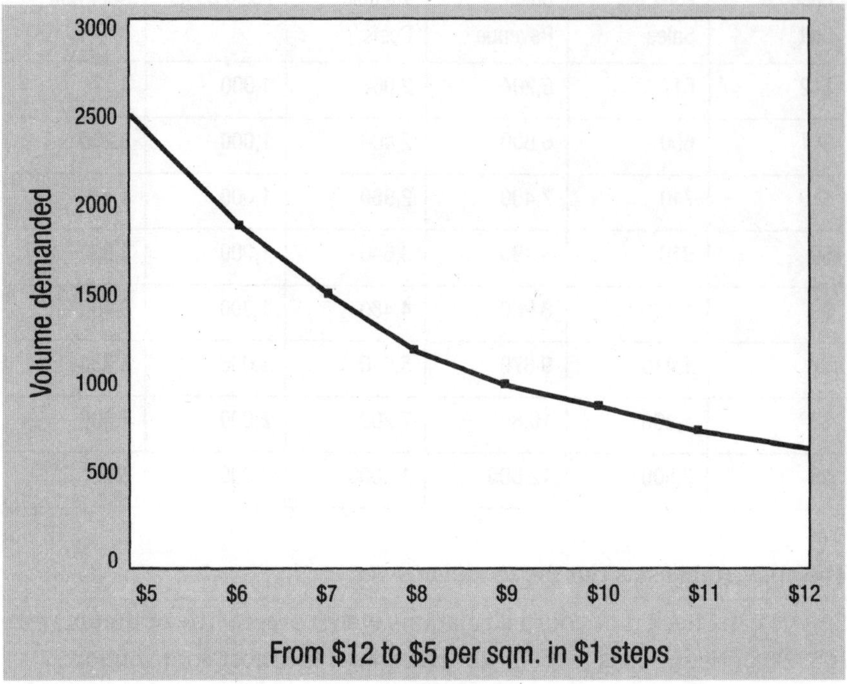

Exercise 2.5

Imagine another case where a drop of $5 in the price of another product, again normally sold for $50, this time produces an increase in sales of say 300, where normally some 700 are sold at the original price – what then is the elasticity of price?

$$\text{ANS} = \frac{300 \div 700}{-5 \div 50} = \frac{42.9\%}{-10\%} = -4.29$$

However, the extent of this elasticity is very unusual; we normally question anything greater than '4'. In addition it is not really a 'forecast' more a 'guesstimate' based on historical data. This data may have been gathered when there were aberrations in the market, lets say the competition had recently raised their price, and/or had suffered stock shortages etc.

Exercise 3.1: 'What price peanuts?'

If I were an investor, I'd put my money with Joe, not the so called efficiency expert. There are many fallacies in his argument, amongst which is that you have to spread the overhead of the business, over all aspects of the business. As Joe says, up to this moment he has been making money – so we must assume that all the overhead has been covered, and then some. What extra overhead will the rack of peanuts bring to the business – just the one time cost of the rack, all else is variable. The only possibility of attributing any overhead to the peanuts venture is if the space on the bar counter has an opportunity cost. That is to say, is the space used for generating income in any way, that now disappears if the rack of peanuts is sited there? There is no way that the total overhead should be shared on such a basis and that now the peanuts will have to carry a load.

The bar serves food, hence the kitchens. If the low priced peanuts are used as substitutes for the cooked meals – then the peanuts should go – but how likely is that!

Buy the peanut stand Joe, and you will not only be contributing extra marginal income with every bag sold, but if they are salted peanuts perhaps they will cause the sale of more thirst quenching beer – gosh, Joe could even justify giving the peanuts away!!

This story, whose origin is unknown, is reproduced by courtesy of the New York Certified Public Accountant and Frank P Smith, Director of Education and Personnel, Lybrand, Ross Bros. & Montgomery, New York. It has been used on my pricing courses and those that I ran with Roy Hill OBE FCMA FCIS FinstAM(DIP) MCIM, FIMC FITD in the mid 1900s.

Exercise 3.2: 'What is the cost?'

The main thing in the above solution is that they can't all be right, indeed what is 'right' in this context. Perhaps the only 'right' solution is the one that suits the department of the firm in which 'you' work, or the product for which 'you' are responsible. So, if you are a member of the product management team for product 'A' you would tend to favour 'formula 5' as a way of apportioning overhead costs, and the reverse is true if you were a member of the 'B' team.

	Product A		Product B
Using Formula 1 or 2			
First what is the rate (R) = ________%			
Per labour hour			
Materials	$3.00		$3.00
Labour	$2.40		$1.20
R x Labour =	$5.04		$2.52
Therefore Full Cost =	$10.44		$6.72
Using Formula 3 (O/H per unit)			
Now what is R? as $________			
Materials	$3.00		$3.00
Labour	$2.40		$1.20
$ R =	$4.20		$4.20
Therefore Full Cost =	$9.60		$8.40
Using Formula 4 (% of 'Prime' cost)			
(i.e. [M+L] +O = R%)			
Prime Cost	$5.40		$4.20
x R =	$4.53		$3.53
Therefore Full Cost =	$9.93		$7.73
Using Formula 5 (rate per machine hour = O + ? = $R)			
Labour	$5.40		$4.20
R x 1½ hrs =	$3.15	2¼hrs	$4.73
Therefore Full Cost =	$8.55		$8.93

Exercise 3.3

Where overhead allocation = Admin ÷ Labour @ % = 150%

Contribution therefore =	50	120	270	440
Central overheads #	15	195	150	360
Thus Profit/Loss =	35	**(75)**	120	80

Where overhead allocation = Admin ÷ Prime @ % = 50%

Contribution therefore =	50	120	270	440
Central overheads #	60	100	200	360
Thus Profit/Loss =	**(10)**	20	70	80

The Initial result – case one (top) vs. case two bottom

Where overhead allocation = Admin ÷ Labour @ % = 150%

Contribution therefore =	50	120	270	440
Central overheads #	15	195	150	360
Thus Profit/Loss =	35	**(75)**	120	80
Result if 'B' is dropped				**(40)**

Where overhead allocation = Admin ÷ Prime @ % = 50%

Contribution therefore =	50	120	270	440
Central overheads #	60	100	200	360
Thus Profit/Loss =	**(10)**	20	70	80
Result if 'A' is dropped				**40**

As can be see from the above, neither method produces a situation where all products are profitable. So, what would be the outcome if supporters of the Case i. method got product 'A' dropped, or 'Case ii' supporters got product 'B' dropped?

As we can see it would be disastrous if product 'B' were dropped, to do so would turn a healthy quarterly profit into a very unhealthy loss. If product 'A' were dropped however, it would not be a disaster for the firm, but would reduce their profitability by some £50,000.00 each quarter, i.e. £200,000.00 per year – that would reduce the CEO's bonus somewhat dramatically. Flippancy aside, all three products are making a healthy contribution to the bottom-line (i.e. 'A' = £50K, 'B'= £120K, 'C' = £270K) **and that is what really matters**.

Exercise 3.4

	Original budget		Including additional sales
Unit sales in units	2,000		2,700
Sales income @ $60	$120,000		$162,000
Variable costs @ $25	$50,000		$67,500
Therefore contribution	$70,000		$94,500
Less fixed costs of	$40,000		$60,000
Gives a trading profit of	$30,000		$34,500
Thus return on sales	25%		21.3%
Break even point in units is =	1,143		1,714
Calculated as	K$40/$35		K$60/$35
BE as % of sales =	57%		63%
Margin of safety =	43%		37%

First the original budget, ex-promotion

The sales income is a multiple of volume times the unit price. Less the unit variable costs of $25.00 multiplied by the 2k volume = $50k

The total contribution therefore, is what is left after this $50k is deducted from the total revenue (*here shown as sales income*) of $120k = $70k.

If the $40k fixed cost for that period is deducted from this contribution, then profit for that month is $30k.

This figure as a percentage of the total revenue is shown as 'return on sales' and is thus 25% (*i.e. 30 as a % of 120*).

To calculate the break-even quantity we divide the period fixed costs ($40k) by the contribution margin, i.e. $35.00 for each item sold.

'Break-even' as a percentage to total volume sales is therefore 57% (*i.e. 1,143 as % of 2,000 items*). The margin of safety, ex promotion, is thus 43% (*i.e. 100% minus the 57% at break-even*). This last (i.e. margin of safety) is a really useful product of this type of analysis – which is not forthcoming from the graphical method.

Now, what about the case of the proposed promotion. The first issue is that the fee for this promotion is non-refundable, therefore MUST be treated as a fixed cost. The calculation methods in the right hand column are the same as in the left hand column.

What changes are the vital indices:

- 'Return on sales' is now 21.3% (down from 25%)
- Break-even point – up by 571 units, and therefore -
- The margin of safety is down 6%.

Should you accept this promotions deal, and it goes wrong – try arguing your case with your principal shareholder why these erosions were accepted.

However, this exercise is not meant to provide definitive answers but to set the mind thinking about what could go wrong, and what are the acceptable levels of risk/penalty in your business. Different business people, in different markets will have different risk thresholds – but if they don't do this sort of analysis they are gamblers, not responsible business people.

Personally, if this exercise was set in say FMCG (*Fast Moving Consumer Goods*) markets, the author would be very leery about the possibility of customers buying forward. That is to say, customers can often be expected to buy more when the product is 'on special offer', and not buying as much, if at all, over the next month and subsequent months. If that were the case the business has just paid $20k to mortgage its business forward, and we have not even considered whether the competition will react, and if so, when and how.

Exercise 4.1

There are no comments we can usefully make here not knowing your market, but the more people in your market, whose opinion you seek when showing them the landscape grid as described, the more information and different perspectives you will have and thus the more reliable picture on which to take your competitive pricing decisions.

Exercise 4.2

Please bear in mind that each of these situations are based (sometimes loosely) on real life cases. Often where the pricer made a poor choice, but also sometimes where the choice of pricing strategy was brilliant.

Let's look at each one at a time:

Case 'A': the handbag friendly sampler of a range of classic French perfumes

This was the brainchild of a French multi-millionaire who had made a fortune innovating cheaper more disposable versions of everyday accessories such as razors for men, then for women, disposable pens etc. (he will not be named, we do not wish to be sued).

He piloted his idea in Paris, France, and it flopped badly. Research subsequently showed that he had miss-priced the product. It was perceived by his target audience, the 'sophisticated French Parisian working woman' to be too cheap. A common attitude was that "This can't be a top of the range perfume at that price". And yet he had priced the product pro-rata for the number of shots in the most popular sized bottle, plus a premium (c.+45%) for the convenience – the same way as he had priced his disposable razors, pens etc.

When the test market collapsed and the entrepreneur in question withdrew – he disposed of all the excess sampling kits as a 'job-lot' to a magazine catering for young ladies in their mid to late teens – the 'sampler' was banded with the magazine, whose circulation that month doubled and had to go into a second printing as a result.

The morale of this story is, the wrong market and the wrong price, don't ignore the wisdom of those who know the market better than you do. The rumour was that the marketing gurus' down at Grasse, the centre of the French perfume industry, where our hero sourced the perfumes for the dispensers, had recommended that the best way to enter the perfume users market would be by a promotion which banded the new 'handbag portable' dispenser with the bottle of the brand of the perfume it contained. This way the customer would accept that the sampler was a small convenient applicator containing the real thing. We could go on and on about what he could have done better – but the above will suffice.

Case 'B': the 'laptop look-a-like portable LCD screen TV'

Another case of a lack of imagination, this time on behalf of the marketers, not by the hardware designers. The pricers' test marked this product in areas of high residential density, targeting up-market people living in fairly new and small apartments, in large cities throughout the UK. The chosen pricing strategy was 'line pricing' setting the price pro-rata with the size of the screen. During the trial period of the launch the product left the shelves faster than they could be re-delivered to the stores. The trouble is the test had established the price point of the product with its target audience – what will they do next – a great idea – with tremendous profit potential (both in margin and cash harvested) but launched in haste.

At the time of writing the product had been withdrawn for 'technical reasons' but the author thinks the real reason is for the market to forget the product so it can subsequently be re-launched as a different 'product' at a higher price. The problem is, that within that period of time, the competition could well launch their own versions and capture the market. The producer has taken a gamble that they won't. This once worked for Cadbury's 'Wispa' chocolate bars, the company is gambling that it could work for them. Let's wait and see.

Case 'C': A new type of data storage 250 times greater than currently available for the home computer

This is not a real situation but a hybrid of what has happened up to the point of writing this book, whenever this type of product is launched.

Not too many years before this book was written, Iomega launched their new disk, physically slightly bigger than the 1.4 mb. 3¼" floppies we were all using then, and able to store 100mb of data. It came with its own read-write disk-drive. The product was seemingly launched at what seems to have been a 'barrier price' designed to keep the competition away – both in terms of the disks and the 'drives'. At that time we had just absorbed the CD disk but it could only be read, there was nothing available for the home or office PC that would also write to the disk. But that state of affairs did not last long. As soon as the first – and difficult to use – CD 'read/writers' became available (max size some 300 to 400mb) Iomega brings out the 250mb disk which can also utilize the previous 'Iomega disk-drive', again at a barrier price.

Since then we have all (or nearly all) acquired systems that both read and write to CD's and DVD's, and some pretty fantastic 'Flash' drives that can carry oodles of data, and are getting physically smaller by the month (it seems). Price now comes down even before the 'pragmatics' in the market appear to have fully adopted it.

The problem seems to have been that the innovators did not act as though they considered that there were other technologies being innovated for data storage that could and would 'leap-frog' them long before a strategy of 'barrier pricing' could re-coup their development costs. The ultimate pricing strategy in such technology driven markets would appear to be a slightly less ambitious (than Sony's Akita Morita's) skimming strategy – 'make hay whilst the sun shines', because sooner or later you WILL be overtaken by another technology.

Case 'D': introducing Bulgarian wine to a new country/market

The pricing strategy can be nothing less than promotional, that is obvious. The country and the wine is not known outside the old communist counties. It will probably need some pretty smart 'positioning' in its target market to succeed and that will involve appropriate pricing.

The key issue to address, re pricing, will be 'how can you use a promotional price at launch **without** establishing the wrong price point for the years to come?'

When this product was introduced to the UK some two years before this book was written, the guiding hand was reputed to be the Saatchi brothers.

Under their guidance the bottle was re-designed to be an unusual shape, the brand name was created to be suggestive of an Australian wine (Blueridge), the variety of grape was chosen as being the one of which the British red-wine drinkers were found to be the most fond (Merlot), and because the name 'Bulgaria' had a poor image with the British at the time (this was before Bulgaria joined the EU) the country of origin was shown as 'Thracia', the name the Romans gave that part of the world.

The product was launched three months before Christmas so there was plenty of time for 'party animals' to stock-up for the festive season. And the wine was only available via an up-market supermarket chain (thus targeting the relatively sophisticated drinker of 'table wine').

The promotional price they used was **'buy two – get one free'**.

The author bought three for the photograph below:

Thus the wine's price-point of c.£8.00 per bottle was not damaged when the promotion finished. The wine is still available via that supermarket chain to the day of writing this.

Case 'E': range of fashionable business shirts and special non-casual social occasions

This was the best example of dual or multiple pricing the Author has ever encountered.

The maker was a Swiss/German firm then called Sachs. On one occasion in the mid 1990's the author received one as a thank you present from the members of a particularly well-received course he had been running at the Chartered Institute of Marketing (CIM). Liking the shirt very much, the Author discovered that the course members had obtained the shirt from a local 'up-market' menswear shop in the village (Cookham, Berkshire) and as a matter of habit, went to buy its twin, in case the first shirt should wear out too soon. To his amazement, in so doing, he discovered that the shirt, top of the Sachs range, had cost c.£135.00. He was impressed and humbled by the amount of cash his participants had contributed to this present and at the same time wondered how the firm had managed to establish such a high price point, which was way above the price charged for a top of the range 'Pinks' shirt from the west end of London. To cut the story short, the Author managed to contact the Marketing Manager for Sachs who gave him the courtesy of explaining his pricing policy. There were three types of outlets they sold through: small up-market men's wear shops in rural UK, such as the one in Cookham, the larger up-market big city stores such as Harrods and Harvey Nichols in London and, surprise, surprise, middle to up-market mail-order catalogues. Not only had Sachs differentially priced each type of outlet but the outlet type with the highest price was the mail-order catalogue. The Sachs marketing manager explained it this way; firstly these outlet types were chosen deliberately as being ones where the customers who used one, would not normally use any of the other two – thus no cross comparison shopping should occur. And the price in the mail-order catalogue, where the purchase was to be a present for someone close to the customer, was not £150 per shirt, but c.£7.00 per month for two years. Beautiful pricing!

Case 'F': a new gold credit/affinity, debit or credit card

In this situation the preferred option would appear to be premium pricing, however, an affinity card is one where, when used, the card accrues points, credits or whatever, which may be donated to some worthy body such as a charity organization. It can also be a card issued by, for example, a motor manufacturer, which, when the owner of the card uses it to make any purchase, will accrue points which can be redeemed to lower the cost of servicing the car, or reducing the purchase price of a General Motors replacement car at some point in the future.

In this case the principal was an energy utility, then supplying domestic gas, electricity and, hoped in the future to also supply telephone services.

Market research showed that their intended gold card did not impress their target group of customers. Gold cards were seen by them as being 'ten-a-penny', i.e. not special. There were many card issuers with 'gold cards' they let anyone have, so it was no longer a symbol of status and a high credit rating. Thus the preferred strategy of premium pricing could not be employed.

Some genius somewhere in the works of the card issuer had the brilliant idea of turning the card into an item of fun, and the card was launched as a 'Gold Fish' credit card. It was promoted by a well known 'out-of-the-box' Scottish comedian acting in the role of a messianic prophet.

Pricing – they had to go for line pricing, i.e. bringing their interest rates in line with their competition. In the long run the card was a flop and at the time of writing has disappeared.

Case 'G': Specialist hotels for people travelling on business

The hotel group's management can either go the Novotel/La Quinta route – which originally had a bait pricing strategy, or the Campanile route.

The first group provided minimalist service all round for a very low price. The hotels had no food service but were located near 'round the clock' sources of meals such as Arbies in the USA or McDonald's, or take-out Dominos Pizzas' etc. The television in the room showed a very small variety of channels, extra channels incurred extra charges. Towels and soaps in the bathrooms were minimal, encouraging you to bring your own; extra people in the room also incurred extra charges etc.

However, the problem with this strategy was that the hotels were more or less empty at weekends, generating little if any income, but still needing to be kept warm, dry and clean, i.e incurring costs with no return.

The Campanile Group in Europe has addressed this issue brilliantly. These hotels offer a basic range of services, all of which are of good quality. They do have a food service on the premises which provides buffet breakfasts and waiter service for evening meals (a limited number of dishes). In many areas their restaurants are also patronized by the local community, the food is so good and so reasonably priced.

Campanile hotels, in the summer, rarely have a problem of being empty at weekends, especially for those hotels located in Italy, France and Spain. The problem in the summer is how far ahead guests need to book to ensure they can get accommodation. However, in the winter this is not the problem – the problem is often empty hotels at weekends, and sometimes less than 60% occupancy during many of the 'low-season' weeks.

At the time of writing, to the knowledge of the author, this had not yet been addressed.

A suggestion is to go for a strategy of dual/multiple pricing. This would have different pricing according to the season (*as is the norm*), but during the winter months there would be different prices according to the day of the week, the length of the stay, and different rates at weekends compared to the weekdays tariff. This would emulate a British hotel chain (*again aimed at people travelling on business*) that, at the time of writing, sells their accommodation over the winter weekends at knock-down rates. The price being just enough to cover the variable costs of the stay plus a small margin. These weekend deals should be promoted on the basis of taking the family away, where the mother does not have to do any of the cooking (*as she would normally be expected to do if they stayed at home*). Thus the chain would keep their staff costs covered and their restaurants full on their normally quiet Friday and Saturday nights.

Further, regular weekday users of the chain could acquire 'points' (*say similar to Air Miles*) which could be redeemed to contribute toward the bill for such away-day weekends.

The point of these exercises is not to lay down any hard and fast paradigm style rules (i.e. if this – then that) but to show that applying the pricing strategy to the situation is very much the 'creative' side of pricing. Pricing is subjective, not objective, in that different pricers faced with the same situation can have different solutions and both can be correct!

The only judge as to whether the pricing strategy employed was a good decision or not is whether or not it achieved the corporate pricing objectives.

Exercise 7.1

Item/issue Sales price per item = $1.00	Basic sale 100 items	With 10% discount No extra volume	With 10% discount & =10% extra volume	Volume at 10% discount to recover profit
Revenue =	$100.00	$90.00	$99.00	**+33% = $119.997**
Material = 0.30	$30.00	$30.00	$33.00	$39.995
Labour = 0.30	$30.00	$30.00	$33.00	$39.995
Gross profit?	$40.00	$30.00	$33.00	$40.00
Overhead = $30.0	-$30.00	-$30.00	-$30.00	$30.00
Net profit therefore?	$10.00	$00.00	$3.00	$10.00
% Profit improvement		-100%	-66%	

We can see in the above that, with these P&L ratios, just giving a 10% discount wipes out all the net profit – assuming that this is the only sale today.

Most uninformed people (sales teams etc.) will assume that a 'quid pro quo' will address the issue of how much volume is required to offset the discount contemplated, in this case 10%. However we see that, again with this P&L ratio, this only puts $3.00 on the bottom-line.

The question is how to calculate the extra volume required just to stand still, i.e. yield a net profit of $10.00 on the deal.

Essentially there are three ways, one illustrated as above.

METHOD ONE

Calculate what net profit is produced with a 10% discount and 10% extra volume (let this be 'Vp'). Divide how many times the product of this last calculation ('Vp') divides into the target net profit, in this case $10.00 (let this be 'R'). Then 'R' times the 10% volume = the volume required for the net profit to return to $10.00.

METHOD TWO

Using the 'lines of constant profit' graphic or the table as described back in Chapter 6.

METHOD THREE

Refer to the table at Figure 6.2, also in Chapter 6.

Negotiation exercises

Answers to exercise one

If you scored 80 or above, you have characteristics of a good negotiator. You recognize what negotiating requires and seem willing to apply yourself accordingly. If you scored between 60 and 79, you should do well as a negotiator but have some characteristics that need further development.

If your evaluation is below 60, you should go over the items again carefully. You may have been hard on yourself, or you may have identified some key areas on which to concentrate as you negotiate.

Answers to exercise two

If you scored 80 or above you have a realistic attitude towards conflict, and seem willing to work to resolve it. If you scored between 50 and 79 you appear to be dealing fairly well with conflict, but need to work towards a more positive approach.

If your score was below 50, you need first to understand why, and then work hard to learn techniques of conflict resolution.

APPENDIX TWO

THE CALCULATIONS FOR PRICING

THE CALCULATIONS FOR PRICING

Profit and loss account

Sale volume **times** Price achieved = Revenue

Revenue **less** variable costs = Gross profit (or Contribution)

Gross profit **less** Fixed costs = Net profit (before tax)

Break-Even (B/E)

This occurs at the point where gross profit exactly equals fixed costs. So the basic formulae is:

$$\text{Break-even} = \frac{\text{Period Fixed Costs}}{\text{Price minus Variable Costs}} = \frac{FC}{P\text{-}VC}$$

Applying the data at a $10 price level:

$$\text{Break-even quantity} = \frac{\$10{,}000}{\$10\text{-}\$8} = 5{,}000 \text{ units}$$

Break-Even Analysis: Sales Revenue

Here we can use the concept of the Profit Volume Ratio – which is particularly useful when we need to calculate break-even for a product range which we know will sell in approximately the same fixed proportions in any given sales period.

Where: BER = Break-Even Sales Revenue

PV = Profit/Volume Ratio

FC = Period Fixed Costs

P = Selling Price

VC = Direct Variable Costs

$$PV = \frac{P - VC}{P}$$

Applying the data at a $10 price level

$$PV = \frac{\$10 - \$8}{\$10} = 0.20$$

$$\text{Therefore BER} = \frac{\$10{,}000}{0.20} = \$50{,}000$$

The formulae for calculating B/E for a given price change is:

In general, for a price **decrease**, the necessary volume **increase** before profitability is enhanced is given by the following formula:

$$\text{Volume increase (\%)} = \frac{X}{PV\text{-}X} \times 100$$

Where X is the percent price decrease expressed as a decimal.

Assume the PV is 30% expressed as a decimal of 0.3 and the price decrease is 9%.

Then the volume increase required (%)

$$\text{The volume increase required (\%)} = \frac{0.09}{0.3-0.09} \times 100 = 42.86\%$$

SO if we cut the price by 9%, we will have to sell c.43% more volume just to stand still.

Similarly, for a price **increase**, the permissible volume **decrease** before profitability is harmed is given by the following formula:

$$\text{Volume decrease (\%)} = \frac{X}{PV+X} \times 100$$

Note the sign on the bottom-line has changed.

Re-doing the above calculation for a price increase

$$\text{Volume decrease allowable (\%)} = \frac{0.09}{0.3+0.09} \times 100 = 23.08\%$$

SO if we **increase** the price by 9%, we can support a loss in volume of up to 23% BEFORE profitability is effected.

Compounding PV's for a product range:

Product	PV	Proportion of total Volume of sales	Weighted PV
(1)	(2)	(3)	i.e. 2 x 3
A	0.40	0.40	0.16
B	0.20	0.30	0.06
C	0.10	0.30	0.03
Composite Profit/Volume for range =			0.25

The price elasticity formula

Price Elasticity is calculated thus:

$\frac{\Delta Q/Q}{\Delta P/P}$	i.e	%Change in Quantity demanded divided by the original Quantity ALL DIVIDED BY %Change in the Price Charged divided by the original Price

NB the symbol 'Δ' means 'change in'

Examples:

CASE #1 – a drop of $5 in a product normally sold for $50 produces increase sales of 200, where formerly 700 were sold.

The calculation is:

$$\frac{200 \div 700}{-5 \div 50} = \frac{28.6\%}{10\%} = -2.86$$

i.e. the market is elastic in that for every 1% drop in price, volume increases by 2.86%

CASE #2 – a drop of $5 in another product normally sold for $50 produces an increase sales of 300, where formerly 700 were sold.

$$\frac{300 \div 700}{-5 \div 50} = \frac{42.9\%}{10\%} = -4.29$$

i.e. the market is elastic in that for every 1% drop in price, volume increases by 4.29%

Please Note: any elasticity greater than 4 should be questioned, it is unusually large bearing in mind this is a forecast, i.e. a 'guesstimate' based on historical data.

Justifying the investment value of your price premium

When supporting your price with added value – a way to communicate the value of the investment (i.e. your price premium) is via one or other of the discounted cash-flow calculations. These come in three 'flavours': net present value, net terminal value and internal rate of return. The principle of all three is to evaluate an investment taking into account the time value of money, i.e. a Euro today is worth more than the same Euro in ten years time, so in order for that Euro to have the same purchasing power in ten years from now, it will have to earn interest – that interest should be no less than the rate of inflation PLUS the cost of that capital, i.e. a 'risk premium'. Anything that enables that original investment to exceed this criterion is a good investment, anything less will make a loss and thus should not be allowed to proceed.

Net present value and net terminal value

These are essentially the same, just looked at from different directions.

The basic calculation can be expressed as: the net the cash flows from a given investment all divided by 1 plus the marginal cost of capital, for each year of the project.

That is to say year one is added to year two, which is all then added to year three etc.

Expressed mathematically each year is:

$$\frac{R}{1 + K}$$

Where **R** = the expected net cash flows for that year and K is the 'marginal' cost of capital.

Over several years the expression is as below:

$$NPV = \left[\frac{R_1}{(1+k)^1} + \frac{R_2}{(1+k)^2} + \ldots\ldots\ldots + \frac{R_N}{(1+k)^N} \right] - C$$

Where 'C' is the initial cost of the project, i.e. the extra premium you are asking the customer to pay, and – 'N' is the numbers of years that the project can be expected to run, i.e. your project to last.

This can be abbreviated by the following expression:

$$\text{i.e. } NPV = \sum_{t=1}^{N} \frac{R_1}{(1+k)^t} - C$$

Here the Sigma ('S') means 'sum of' in this case it is from the start of the project for N numbers of years.

An alternative is **internal rate of return**, here the project is supposed to exceed some internally set 'hurdle' such as the marginal cost of capital in the 'market' plus a premium.

$$\sum_{t=1}^{N} \frac{R_1}{(1+k)^t} - C = 0$$

Everything is known except for 'R' so we solve the equation for 'R' – if 'R' is greater than the internal hurdle, then it is a 'go' project, if not, then it is not progressed. For further exposition of this financial management tool see *Managerial Finance* by J.F. Weston and E.F. Brigham, published by Holt Dryden.

Payback methods

The world is so fast moving these days, and so full of uncertainties that many (if not most) in business would prefer a more simple means of assessing any investment (i.e. paying a higher price for your product in return for a better return on that investment than if they had purchased from your competition).

The favoured method is known as 'payback period'. It aims to assess how long it will take for the investment to pay off its costs. To illustrate this idea the table sets out the cash flows for a fictional investment of $10,000.00.

Year	Project 'A'	Project 'B'
1	$500.00	$100.00
2	400.00	200.00
3	300.00	300.00
4	100.00	400.00
5		500.00
6		600.00

Project 'A' has paid back the initial investment by early year three, and makes a total of $13,000.00 before conclusion, whereas project 'B' doesn't recover its investment until the end of year four, but goes on until the end of year six making by then a total of $21,000.00, i.e. it more than doubles the original money invested.

So which would be preferred? It depends. In tough times the buyer may often opt for project A on the basis that the further into the future one looks the less certain are the outcomes, and at least 'A' gets half of its investment back in the first year. In good times the chances are that they would go for 'B' depending on the amount of confidence that they may have in the stability of the future.

Payback is more simple to understand and hence it is often preferred by the SME – particularly in tough times.

The above calculations are just the basics from which nearly all others can be derived – should you wish to study these further the books to read are:

- *The strategy and tactics of pricing* by Reed, K Holden, and Thomas T Nagler, Prentice Hall.
- *Managerial Finance* by J.F. Weston and E.F. Brigham, published by Holt Dryden.

APPENDIX THREE

MAIN SOURCES AND RECOMMENDED READING LIST

MAIN SOURCES AND RECOMMENDED READING LIST

Pricing for Results, John Winkler, Heinemann: London

Inside the Tornado, Geoffrey A. Moore, Harper Business

Managerial Finance, J.F.Weston & E.F.Brigham, Holt Dryden

Strategy and Tactics of Pricing, Thomas T. Nagler and Reed K. Holden, Prentice Hall

Smarter Pricing, Tony Cram, F.T. Prentice Hall

Power Pricing, Robert J. Dolan and Hermann Simon, Free Press

Value Based Marketing, Peter Doyle, John Wiley & Sons

Value Pricing, T. Fletcher and N.R. Jones, Kogan Page

Competing on Value, M. Hanan and P Karp, Amacom, 1991

Marketing Success through the Differentiation of Anything, Theodore Levitt, Harvard Business Review N.8-107

Marketing Warfare, Al Ries and Jack Trout, McGraw Hill

Clausewitz on War, Karl von Clausewitz, Pelican

The Art of War, Sun Tzu, Delecorte Press

The Price Advantage, M.V. Marn et. al., Wiley Finance

Pricing: Making Profitable Decisions, K.B. Monroe, McGraw Hill

Pricing and Revenue Optimisation, Phillips, Robert L, Stanford Business Books

INDEX

INDEX

C

D

N

O

P

Q